THE YAGYŪ CLAN

Also by William de Lange

A Fool's Journey

Musashi: Fact & Fiction

The Real Musashi, I, II, III

Famous Samurai, I, II, III

A History of Japanese Journalism

A Dictionary of Japanese Onomatopeoia

A Dictionary of Japanese Proverbs

A Dictionary of Japanese Idioms

Japanese Scrolls

Pars Japonica

Iaido

Available in eBooks

A Fool's Journey

The Real Musashi, I, II, III

Through the Eye of the Needle (Pars Japonica)

Famous Samurai: Kamiizumi Nobutsuna

Famous Samurai: Yagyū Munenori

Famous Samurai: Ono Tadaaki

Available in Apps

A Dictionary of Japanese Proverbs

A Dictionary of Japanese Onomatopoeia

A Dictionary of Japanese Idioms

THE REMARKABLE HISTORY

OF

THE YAGYŪ CLAN

WILLIAM DE LANGE

For more on books by William de Lange visit:
www.williamdelange.com

First edition, 2019
Second edition, 2020

Published by TOYO PRess
Visit us at: **www.toyopress.com**

ISBN 978-94-92722-171

For Ray Furse

CONTENTS

True masters conduct all their affairs in perfect equilibrium.

——Yagyū Munenori

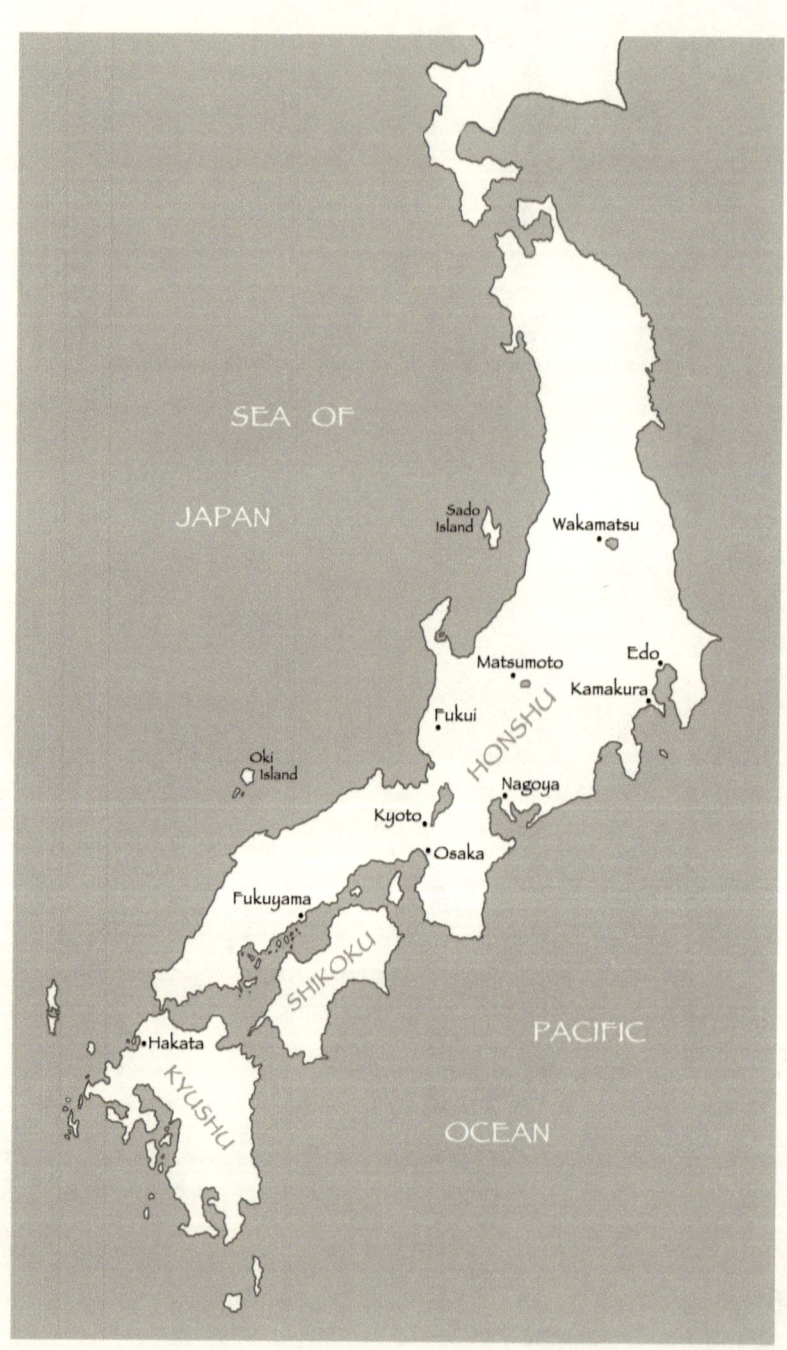

SEA OF

JAPAN

Sado
Island

Wakamatsu

Edo

Matsumoto

Kamakura

Fukui

HONSHU

Oki
Island

Nagoya

Kyoto

Osaka

Fukuyama

SHIKOKU

PACIFIC

Hakata

KYUSHU

OCEAN

PREFACE

It is perhaps no coincidence that the two Chinese characters that make up the name of Yagyū stand for the willow tree and life, or the giving of birth, for both seem to sum up perfectly the particular characteristics that helped propel this ancient clan to such exalted heights. Like the pliable willow tree, their resilience in the face of irresistible forces enabled the Yagyū to outweather the raging storms of fortune and remain standing, alive and well, their spirit intact. In doing so, the Yagyū gave birth to an art of fencing that has survived for more than a half a millennium. Consequently, among the countless schools of swordsmanship brought forth by Japan's feudal era, the Yagyū Shinkage-*ryū* stands out for its sheer continuity.

The epic history of the Yagyū Shinkage-*ryū* hinges on two events, both of them chance encounters. The first was the meeting of Yagyū Muneyoshi and the legendary Kamiizumi Nobutsuna, founder of the Shinkage-*ryū*. The second was his introduction to Tokugawa Ieyasu, founder of the Tokugawa Shōgunate. The first was instrumental in the development of the Yagyū's style of fencing; the second proved pivotal in their success. It was through Tokugawa Ieyasu that Muneyoshi's son,

Munenori, was promoted to the powerful position of Daimyō—the first and only swordsman in Japanese history to do so. Had Muneyoshi not had his two remarkable encounters, it is unlikely that the Yagyū Shinkage-*ryū* would have flourished as it did.

Opportunities lie on everyone's road. Yet that road may be long and hard. So, at least, it was with the Yagyū. During the five centuries before Muneyoshi's encounters, his clan experienced the whole gamut of hardships. They were the kind of hardships only a country at war could create: loss of kinship; loss of honor, loss of hope, loss of life. The low point in the Yagyū's long history came toward the middle of the sixteenth century when in the course of a few decades they first lost their independence, then their castle, then their domains, until finally they were thrown on the mercy of a local temple. Looking back we can now see the obvious—it was the bleak, not the prosperous years that proved seminal. For it was during those years, years in which they were deprived of their worldly possessions, stripped of their rank and status, thrown back on their own devices, that these sturdy men were forced to reach deep within themselves to find their true strength: their ability with the *katana*.

And thus it is not in their eventual success itself that we should seek the true lesson of their history, nor in the opportunities that fate meted out. Rather, it is in the remarkable resilience and the ever-abiding sense of purpose with which this small but indomitable tribe of Japanese clansmen dealt with the cruel reversals of fate, the humbling defeats, the seemingly endless setbacks. Indeed, it may well have been the severity of the raging tempest that made the Yagyū cling to their hard-found refuge with such tenacity. Ultimately, it was their unshaken belief in their ability with the *katana* that sustained them and to which they owed their eventual success. It is from that belief—the belief in one's own talent—that we can still derive true lessons on how to deal with the challenges that life throws at all of us.

Though dramatized in its settings and descriptions, all names, characters, places, dates, and historic incidents mentioned in this work are based on real-life persons, places, and events. Similarly, all block quotations are taken from their original sources.

CHAPTER 1

The name of Yagyū first appears in the historical annals during the Heian period. At that time the Japanese realm was governed by the Fujiwara, an influential clan who derived their power from the imperial court. In name, the realm was ruled by the emperor, whose seat of government was Heian-kyō. Real power, however, lay with the kanpaku, the imperial regent, whose office was a hereditary right of the Fujiwara patriarch. The wealth of the Fujiwara derived from the vast estates they owned in the fertile belt of provinces surrounding the capital. It was in 885 AD, that, according to the Gyokuei shūi, the ancient records of the Yagyū clan, the estates of Ōyagyū and Koyagū in the province of Yamato were granted to the kanpaku Fujiwara Mototsune (836–91).

For the next one-and-a-half century the Yagyū estates remained in the possession of the Fujiwara. Then, in 1038, they were donated to the Kasuga Taisha,[1] an ancient shrine on Nara's eastern outskirts patronized by the Fujiwara since the early eighth century. Government of the estates was put in the hands of shrine officials. The smaller Yagyū estate of Koyagyū was left in the care of a court official by the name of Sugawara Daizen Nagaie, the founding father of the Yagyū clan.

With the decline of the Fujiwara and the rise of the military class in the wake of the Hōgen Insurrection in the middle of the twelfth century Nagaie's descendants were faced with a stark choice: remain

1

loyal to their former masters and perish, or choose the way of the warrior and survive. They chose to fight. Abandoning the name of Sugawara, they assumed the name of Yagyū, after the estate they had managed over many generations and now considered their own. Henceforth it was the beautiful hills and valleys of the Kasagi Mountains from which the Yagyū derived their identity and sense of belonging. Noble blood still coursed through their veins, yet it was Kasagi's mountain waters that nourished and purified their spirits.

With military life came military responsibilities, and in a feudal world the chief responsibility of landed warriors was the protection of their domains. The Yagyū were a small clan, and to ensure their tenuous hold over what was theirs they were forced to submit to the authority of the Minamoto, an eastern clan that emerged victorious from their five-year-long power struggle with the Taira. [2]

Sensitized by heritage to the tastes and sensibilities of the court the Yagyū abhorred the crude and uncivilized ways of the Minamoto and their allies, who hailed from the Kantō and had little affinity for what went on in the Home Provinces—the provinces around the capital. Things did not improve on Yoritomo's death, when the Bakufu became increasingly torn by internal strife and de facto power was seized by members of the Hōjō clan. Copying the Fujiwara regents they ruled by proxy in the capacity of shikken or regent to the infant Shōgun. As a result, the Yagyū were often at loggerheads with the new military regime, which had their headquarters in far-away Kamakura and seemed to know and care little about things that preoccupied warrior clans back in Yamato Province. Being of aristocratic descent the Yagyū loathed the way in which the Kamakura Bakufu had forced the court to cow-tow to its whims and wishes.

During the Jōkyū Rebellion of 1221, the first attempt of the court to reassert its authority, the Yagyū remained neutral. It was a shrewd move, which ensured the clan's survival, for the rebellion was crushed within a month. Emperor Go-Toba was exiled to Oki Island, where he died in obscurity. For more than a century the Yagyū persevered in their neutral stance, until Emperor Go-Daigo (1288–1339) made another bid to restore power to the throne.

As early as 1324 Go-Daigo had begun to entertain contacts with elements within the Bakufu sympathetic to the throne. Within months his plans were exposed. The Hōjō response was unequivocal. They put to death all the warriors who had answered to the emperor's call to arms. Afraid to touch Go-Daigo himself, they had all his counselors arrested, though most were released within the year.

Go-Daigo did not give up on his plan. In spite of the danger, he continued to plot against the Bakufu, visiting the religious centers of power that could help him in his bid to restore power to his throne— Kyoto's Hiei Enryaku temple and Nara's Tōdai temple, both of which had large standing armies of warrior monks, the so-called sōhei.

The Yagyū at this time were led by Yagyū Nagayoshi, eleventh descendant of their founding father, Sugawara Daizen Nagaie. Having gone from court officials to feudal warriors, the Yagyū had never forgotten where their true allegiance lay. Nor had they forgotten the brutal and unforgiving way in which the loyal warriors who had chosen the side of Emperor Go-Toba had been destroyed, their relatives persecuted or driven mad in exile. Determined that Go-Daigo would not share Go-Toba's fate, the Yagyū chose to act. And it is here—in using their talent with the sword to achieve political change—that the history of the Yagyū as a clan of warriors truly begins.

Go-Daigo

Yagyū Nagayoshi was irked. For months now he had been petitioning the officials of the imperial court for an audience with His Highness. Yet from day one his requests had fallen on deaf ears. He knew the reason. Though of noble stock, the Yagyū were just a minor clan. In the eyes of the lofty court officials, he was just another warrior, too lowly to be in the presence of His Imperial Highness. Now the inevitable had happened: the emperor had fled the capital.

Thinking about it angered Nagayoshi even more. Only seven years had passed since Emperor Go-Daigo had tried to overthrow the powerful Hōjō. Within months the Hōjō had uncovered the plot. They had arrested the ringleaders and put to death all the warriors who had risen in arms.

Only one reason could have forced the emperor to forsake the imperial palace: the Hōjō had again got wind of something. Nagayoshi knew what it was—he had known for more than a year now. Only the previous year Go-Daigo had visited the Kasuga Taisha. Officially it had been just another visit, one in a long succession of ceremonies that filled the days of His Imperial Highness. As always, it had been a grand affair. The Yagyū had been among the dozens of patrons who had gathered on the shrine's wide forecourt. It had been a splendid sight indeed. They had been dressed in their white ceremonial garb and had bowed in reverence as Go-Daigo burned incense at the shrine's altar and clapped his hands three times to send his prayers to the heavens. All knew the content of those prayers: to restore imperial powers. He still wanted to topple the Hōjō, and he still hoped to unite the warrior clans behind his cause.

Dark forces threatened Go-Daigo. There was nothing the Hōjō wouldn't do to hang on to power. They had already arrested the emperor's counselor Hino Toshimoto. He had been seized in clear daylight, in the grounds of the imperial palace. Only the heavens knew what they would do to him. The last time around, they had exiled Toshimoto's brother to Sado Island. This time they wouldn't be so lenient. It was only a matter of time, too, before they would turn on the emperor himself.

Nagayoshi cursed; he couldn't believe the stupidity of it all. Not that he was against a restoration of imperial powers. Far from it; it was a noble cause indeed. But to attempt it from within the imperial palace had been pure folly. The time was gone that the emperor could count on the *kuge*, the realm's ancient nobility. Their power had long gone. This was the age of the warriors. Many of them were loyal to the throne. But they would never risk defending the imperial palace. The Hōjō were far too powerful for that. This needed time, careful planning, decisive attacks on the Bakufu's centers of power, followed by quick retreats. They might feel like bee stings at first, but once they covered the whole body, its occupant was bound to die.

What Go-Daigo needed now—what he had needed all along—was a safe base from which to operate, like the ancient emperor of Song China, when the northern tribes had raided Kaifeng. And what better place than the impenetrable mountains around the ancient capital of Nara? There he could rely on the many local warrior clans loyal to the court, as well as the ancient monasteries with their large standing armies of *sōhei*. It might not suit His Highness' dignity, yet it was the only way.

Mount Kasagi

It was on a windswept Saturday, September 28, 1331, two days after Nagayoshi learned of the emperor's escape, that his younger brother, Gensen, a monk attached to the Tōdai temple, came storming into the Yagyū manor at the head of the Yagyū Valley, and shouted: '*Tennō Heika Nara ni araserareru!*' (His Highness the Emperor is in Nara!)

Gensen could hardly contain himself as he revealed the stunning news. Tense with excitement, his usual stutter, which could be bad at the best of times, reasserted itself with a vengeance as he began to stumble over his own words: 'His Highness is at the Tōdai-*ji*. He arrived l-last n-night at the temple's Southeast Cloister, under the c-cover of darkness. And c-can you b-believe it? He was dressed as a w-woman, for fear of being d-discovered! He has been forced to leave the palace in a hurry, without even the time to call his servants! Even his palanquin was c-carried by court officials!'

Nagayoshi frowned. 'Who else was with him?'

'Just a handful of n-nobles—the Great Counselor, Kintoshi, the Middle Counselor, Madenokōji Fujifusa, and the Rokujo Lesser Marshal, Minamoto no Tadaaki. And they t-too were all in p-plain clothes!'

'What happened next?'

'His Highness spent the whole n-night in frantic talks with the temple's abbot, Shōjin, discussing a safe place to go into hiding. He c-cannot stay in Nara. Too many monks there are on the hand of the Hōjō. Indeed, even some of the cloisters of the Tōdai temple are in c-cahoots with the Bakufu. If their *sōhei* get wind of his presence, they will not hesitate to hand him over. He has to get away and he has to get away quick! Somewhere d-down south, among the Yoshino Mountains, is safest. But once there he will be very remote from his supporters: the chieftains from the Home Provinces; the m-monasteries of Nara and Kyoto with their vast garrisons of *sōhei*. The mountains should only be a last resort—if everything else f-fails...'

Gensen gasped for air as he tried to fill in his brother on all the details. He had run all the way from Nara, some eight miles along the narrow Yagyū Kaidō, the old road that connected Nara to Kasagi and the high road from Kizu to Ueno. No one knew this path like the Yagyū. They, after all, had given the path its name when way back they had commissioned its construction.

Winding its way through beautiful countryside northeast of Nara, the cobbled path was often chosen by pilgrims on their way to the temple town. At almost every turn was some statue of Kannon, some engraving of Jizō, carved out of large rocks along the roadside or hewn deep into the rock face of the mountains. Though hallowed, the Yagyū Kaidō could also be treacherous, especially in the current rainy season, when devastating typhoons swept inland from the Pacific. Then torrential rains turned the sloping sections into dangerous rapids that lent the road its second name: Takisaka Michi, or Waterfall Slope Path. If the rain persisted its slopes turned into mudslides that carried everything and anything before it. Many had set out along the path never to arrive at the other end, and every spring large groups of laborers spent long weeks repairing the damaged sections.

For a while Nagayoshi pondered the enormity of the situation. Then he spoke, deliberately, as always: 'We will escort his Highness along the Yagyū Kaidō to Kasagi-*dera*.'

Nagayoshi tried to sound upbeat, but inside he felt numb. For months he had been trying to get through to some court official to warn them. None of them had listened. Now his worst fears had materialized. Kasagi temple was the best choice under the circumstances. Crowning the crest of Mount Kasagi, the old Shingon temple was a branch temple of the Tōdai-*ji*. It was only a few miles north of the Yagyū domain and well situated, with lots of natural protection. Yet without reinforcements, even Mount Kasagi could not save Go-Daigo in the long run. The Bakufu would not tarry in sending down troops, most of them from the Kantō. They had a week—perhaps two—to dig themselves in and prepare for the inevitable.

Nagayoshi poured his brother and himself some hot *sake* as he reflected on this sudden change of events. How odd were the tricks that the gods played on mortal men. It seemed almost ironic that, all of a sudden, the fate of His Highness should now come to rest on the shoulders of men like him.

To Safety

It was late Sunday evening as the small group escorting the imperial palanquin reached the foot of Mount Kasagi. All in all there were some two dozen men. Among them were a number of monks who had joined the emperor's entourage at the Tōdai temple. To Nagayoshi's regret they were not the kind of warrior monks used to mountain life like his brother, but frail men, their thin wrists only trained to wield the writing brush. Yet all except the aged abbot and nobles took their turn in carrying the imperial palanquin, proudly bearing their precious cargo until the skin on their shoulders had all but gone.

By now they had reached the end of their tether. The whole day had been an uphill battle. Leaving Nara before dawn they had run into trouble as soon as they hit the mountains. Earlier typhoons had washed away whole tracts where the path followed and crossed the Nōto River, including the small bridge, forcing them to make a detour of several hours through dense forest. In summer it would have taken them less than two hours to reach Kasagi; now it had taken them almost twenty.

There was still a steep climb ahead, up to the temple. From where they stood a narrow path wound itself up the mountain for two miles to a height of six hundred feet. As children, Nagayoshi and Gensen had often competed who got to the temple gate first. They felt no competition now, just an urgent sense to reach the summit. Never had the ascent been so taxing; it felt as if they gained a pound with every step.

All felt a sense of deep relief when, close to midnight, they finally passed under the temple's imposing gate. There was no grandeur to the procession; all were covered in mud up to their waist, their shoulders bleeding, their clothes stained and torn. Yet at the same time, there was a profound dignity in the motley crew as they lowered the palanquin in front of the temple's forecourt and deeply bowed in reverence as the emperor alighted from his palanquin and expressed his gratitude. Then they slowly raised their heads and watched in silence as he entered the temple's octagonal Hall of Wisdom, followed by the abbot Shōjin and the two court officials carrying the realm's three sacred treasures: the sword Kusanagi, the mirror Yata no Kagami, and the jewel Yasakani no Magatama. Since time immemorial, only the true line of the imperial house had possessed these regalia, and only the true imperial house had embodied their three primary virtues: valor, wisdom, and benevolence.

A loud cheer went up among the men as Gensen raised the brocade imperial banner over the temple's gate, where it defiantly fluttered in the gathering storm. So far the gods had been on their side. For no sooner had the emperor entered the Main Hall than the heavens opened and a torrential rain soaked the men to their skins. Had it struck that morning they would never have reached their goal. Now, the emperor was safe. Yet for how long? Another, far fiercer storm was brewing—one that would last a lifetime and ravage the realm.

Sōhei

From ancient times the Yagyū had been closely connected to Kasagi-*dera*. At least one son out of every generation had been singled out to serve at the ancient temple, which was as old as the Yagyū clan itself. There were only two brothers in this

generation, and thus it fell to Gensen to serve at the temple—
and not just as a monk. Kasagi temple was one of the Shingon
sect's chief bastions.[3] The reasons were obvious. Situated atop
Mount Kasagi, close by the Kizu River, the temple was a
fortress with formidable natural defenses. It had long been the
training grounds of the sect's many *sōhei*, and never before had
a besieging army been able to capture the stronghold.

Gensen had entered the temple at the age of four, spending
his youth in studying the Buddhist scriptures and practicing
with the *yari*. He had grown into a formidable warrior, as skilled
with the *yari* as his brother with the *katana*. A tall and imposing
man, he had made it to the temple's Teacher of Discipline.

Now it was his task to serve and protect the man his brother
had tried in vain to reach. Never before had he been in the
presence of such an exalted being. At first, he dared hardly look
when, on some errand, he entered the Hall of Wisdom. As
Teacher of Discipline it was his task to see to the emperor's
needs, but with absolute discretion. Yet every now and then he
got a glimpse of this god-like figure, steeped deep in thought
over some text or dictating to one of his courtiers. He reminded
Gensen of a Chinese sage he had once seen on an old mainland
scroll at the Tōdai temple. His long, raven-black hair was tied
back from his high forehead, and from his round chin, a long
beard tapered into a pointed tuft that danced comically up and
down before a heavy chest on the few occasions he spoke.

And that voice! It had a high, effeminate pitch, wholly out of
keeping with his stout physique. He seemed to talk in riddles,
for his convoluted sentences were so full of Chinese expression,
that it seemed he was indeed a Chinese sage. It was only because
Gensen had spent his youth pouring over Buddhist scriptures,
all written in *kanbun*, an annotated form of Chinese, that the
warrior-monk could make some sense of the emperor's words.

Gensen could not get his head around the idea that he was in the emperor's presence. Suddenly the barriers that once separated this divine being from the common man had fallen away: no longer was he hidden from their gaze by thin bamboo blinds; no longer did they have to speak through court interpreters. Yet within a few days, Gensen knew enough to understand that the emperor shared a number of human traits with those around him—for one, he was clearly a man in despair.

Honjōbō

Go-Daigo had good reason to worry. The Bakufu had sent word to all its allies to suppress the rebellion. In the province of Ōmi, only a day's travel by foot from Kasagi, governor Sasaki Tokinobu was raising a large army. Farther afield, in Musashi and Sagami, others were doing likewise. Already the Bakufu had moved against Mount Hiei, where Go-Daigo's son, Prince Morinaga, was leading the Tendai monks in revolt. He had gained their support by a ruse. On his flight from the capital, Go-Daigo had sent one of his counselors, Lord Kazan'in Morokata, up the mountain in the imperial carriage wearing his personal dragon robes to trick the monks into joining his cause.

The gravity of his predicament was reinforced when Nagayoshi, on guard at the temple's main gate, spotted a small band of men climbing up toward them. They were dressed in monks' clothes and some of them were clearly wounded and had to be supported by their companions. They were led by a towering man with the physique of a *kongōrikishi*, the huge wooden statues standing guard at Nara's Tōdai temple. Having reached the gate, he spoke with a deep bellowing voice, as he called up to Nagayoshi, 'I am Honjōbō and I have come from Nara's Hannya temple. The others have come from Mount Hiei. Nara is already swarming with Bakufu troops. They are clearly preparing for a large-scale military operation, undoubtedly against you here at Mount Kasagi.'

The news from the monks from Mount Hiei was hardly more encouraging. Joining forces with other Buddhist sects, they had fought hard against the Bakufu troops, dealing them a hard blow at Karasaki, on the shores of Lake Biwa. They had celebrated the event at the Hiei's main monastery. The mood turned ecstatic on the arrival of the imperial palanquin. All had hailed what they thought was the emperor, when suddenly a strong wind had blown up the imperial blinds, exposing the ruse: seated inside was not His Imperial Highness, but merely a counselor. The mood had instantly turned sour, and one by one the gathered *sōhei* had returned to their cloisters. Only Honjōbō and his companions had refused to give up, making their way to Kasagi to join the emperor's cause.

Honjōbō and his men were a welcome asset, but many of them were badly wounded: the emperor urgently needed more reinforcements. What they really needed was a warrior of renown, a man with the experience and strategic insight to outwit the Hōjō Bakufu in Kamakura. There were several such men in the region, some even closely connected to the imperial court, but so far none had declared themselves for the emperor.

The Dream

Early next morning, Go-Daigo called Gensen to his side and addressed him directly. 'Gensen-*bō*, I want to tell you about a dream I had last night.'

Gensen was stunned: had he gone from being a mere monk to imperial confidant overnight?

12

But the emperor went on: 'In this dream, I found myself in a large courtyard, not unlike that of the Shinshinden, my beloved abode at the imperial palace. At its center stood a mighty evergreen, its branches heavy with dense foliage, casting a benevolent shadow over all who sought refuge from the scorching sun. Beneath the tree sat all the great lords of the realm, each according to his rank. Yet one seat, facing south, had remained empty. What can it mean?'

Gensen racked his brain as he looked for an explanation for His Highness's dream. Then it struck him—a name, that of warlord Kusunoki Masashige! Masashige hailed from the neighboring province of Kawachi, where his ancestors had long held domains near the village of Akasaka, some fifty miles southwest from Kasagi. Though Gensen had never met him, he knew he was known as a brilliant strategist, as well as a great diplomat. Masashige descended from the great Tachibana Moroe, who was, in turn, a descendant in the fourth generation of Emperor Bidatsu and thus bound to choose Go-Daigo's side. He was the master of Akasaka castle, built on the slopes of Mount Kongō. The most powerful warlord in the region, he commanded a vast army of highly trained warriors, including a large contingent of mounted warriors. That meant he could bring reinforcements within a day.

'Your Highness,' Gensen said as he reverently lowered his head until it touched the *tatami* mats on which they were sitting, 'It is an omen! And it p-points to Kusunoki Masashige. His clan name is written with the Chinese characters for "south" and "tree." Together they spell the words "Camphor tree," the same tree as in Your Majesty's dream.'

Go-Daigo did not have to think long about Gensen's words. Turning to his Middle Counselor he commanded, 'Call this Masashige-*dono* at once!'

13

Masashige

For a whole day, the few men holding out on Mount Kasagi were held in suspense. Then their hearts lifted when, around Wednesday noon, the valley below filled with the clatter of hoofs. Looking down from above the gate, Nagayoshi counted at least several hundred mounted warriors. Shortly, Kusunoki Masashige and his senior generals rode into the Kasagi stronghold. They were in full armor, one carrying a banner with the Kusunoki crest: a chrysanthemum floating on water.

A loud cheer went up among the gathered men. For them, the crest had a deep, almost religious significance. All knew the deeper meaning of the flower: it was the symbol of nobility and purity, the undisputed emblem of the imperial house. It told of the legend of the ancient *yamabushi*, the enigmatic mountain warrior hermits, surviving on a diet of the flower, which was said to make them immortal. So rampant had the flowers grown on the mountain slopes that in spring their blossoms formed a thick carpet on the mountain streams, causing those who drank from them to outlive their enemies.

That evening, all assembled on the temple's inner court, sitting down in their armor in rows according to their rank. Winter was fast approaching and the temple's monks had lit a large fire at the center of the yard. The guests had been a day in the saddle and their hot breath hitting the cold air made it look as if another fire smoldered in their chests, a sense reinforced by the metal plates woven into their armor, which shimmered ominously in the flames' hot glare. Then a reverent silence descended on the gathering as the emperor appeared from the Hall of Wisdom and took his seat on the building's wide veranda.

Speaking through his Middle Counselor, the emperor welcomed Masashige.

Masashige bowed deeply before the emperor and spoke: 'Recently, the transgressions of the Hōjō have incurred the wrath of the heavens, and it is only fitting that we should inflict on them divine retribution.' He paused for a while to let his words sink in. 'Yet to pacify the realm we need shrewd military tactics, as well as wise counsel. For if we rely on military strength alone and do battle with them head on, we will not be able to defeat the Musashi and Sagami armies, even if we were to assemble all the warriors in the realm. But if we fight with cunning we can easily deceive these Kantō warriors, as their military power merely derives from brute force.'

The Charge

The next few days the small army of rebels prepared themselves for battle. Fall had arrived, the season in which thick veils of mist descended on the surrounding valleys and lingered there till late in the morning, waiting for the sun to gather strength. On cold days the clouds refused to lift, but lay heavily on the landscape, drowning everything in a hushed silence, the terraced rice paddies, the thatched farms, the muddy roads. Among the mountains, long, gossamer serpents of vapor ascended the slopes, sifting upward through high pines toward the crests. They seemed to come from nowhere—as if the mountains were sentient, hot-blooded beings, likewise trying to stave off the cold of the approaching winter.

Then, in the early hours of Friday, October 4, the mountains once more resounded with the clatter of hoofs. Nothing could be seen through the thick mist. Yet the men atop the mountain needed no clear skies to know what was coming: enemy soldiers, at least a few thousand.

Despite their great number, the enemy would have a hard time taking Kasagi temple. Generations of Tendai warrior-monks had turned the mountain into a stronghold with all the trappings of a regular castle. A tall stockade lined the mountain's upper western slope, while the main gate was flanked by walled sections with arrow loopholes. It was the mountain's most fortified section, but also the most vulnerable to attack, as the slope leading up to the plateau was shallow and accessible from the river valley below. Not so the other sides of the mountain, where steep rock-faces rose high above the river and the densely wooded landscape below. It seemed as if a huge explosion had once torn through its heart, for even where the mountain gently sloped huge boulders lay shoulder to shoulder, in defense of the hallowed grounds above. In places where the more intrepid might still try to make their ascent, large rocks suspended from thick ropes above could be leveraged to crush them. No mountain in the region was better fortified.

That morning they had gathered once more to drink their last cup of sake with His Highness. It had been a solemn affair with few words spoken. Now they went about their business in silence. Behind the stockade, on a raised boardwalk, Masashige's archers moistened their bowstrings with their mouths as they spread out their arrows according to weight and length. Back in the yard swordsmen planted spare *katana*s and pikes in the ground, while *sōhei* rubbed their *yari* with sand for better grip.

Then, at the hour of the Rabbit, the first hostilities erupted.

It began when a group of mounted warriors led by Takahashi Matashirō charged the stronghold's most forward positions, at the western foot of the mountain, where the Hakusa River joined the Kizu River. These positions, too, were defended by Masashige's men, skilled and seasoned warriors, all of them. Well-fed and confident of a safe retreat, they were in high spirits, taking great risks as they stormed down toward the river to meet their enemy head-on. The gamble paid off. They drove Matashirō and his men into the river, causing many of them to drown. Only those who abandoned their armor and horses made it to the other side and safety.

Matashirō's charge was followed by another. They were Kobayakawa men, fierce warriors from Sagami, whose ancestors had fought with the great Minamoto no Yoritomo. Yet they too were driven back into the river, where many lost their lives in its cold and swirling waters.

That evening, a raucous cheer went up from the mountain when its defenders celebrated their victory. They were only a few hundred, fighting off an army of almost a thousand, but they had nevertheless prevailed.

Nagayoshi could not bring himself to join in the celebrations. This was only the beginning. There would be more assaults, in far greater numbers.

One Shot

Nagayoshi rose early the next morning. It would be a long and hard day—that much was certain. At least the clouds had now lifted; they had drifted away at midnight, revealing a starlit sky. Already the sky toward the east was brightening. Soon the autumn sun would bathe the hills in its soothings rays, turning the leaves of the maple trees into a checkered golden blanket, from the deepest reds to the brightest yellows.

Eager to have a better view of the enemy, Nagayoshi ascended the temple's three-storied pagoda with Asuke Jirō Shigenori, a chieftain from Mikawa and a master archer. Though small in stature, his upper arms were as thick as Nayayoshi's lower legs.

No one else could handle his huge longbow, which took three men to string. Crouching into position, he carefully moistened the string and pulled it to check its tension.[4]

From atop the tower, Nagayoshi had a commanding view of the surrounding area. In the distance, the Kizu River was about to breach its banks from the torrential rains of the previous days. Huge trees were carried downstream or entangled in the debris in the river's shallows. Closer by, on the other side of the Hakusa River, some seven hundred yards away, a large host of warriors had assembled along its bank. Judging by the number of tents there were at least several hundreds. He could clearly make out the crests on their banners: the Nagazawa, the Suyama, the Komiyama, the Arao. On the bridge across the river, he could see men on guard, the spikes of their helmets gleaming red in the hesitant morning light.

Just then he spotted an Arao warrior on a nearby bluff—an enemy scout! Nagayoshi held his breath as he slowly leaned sideways, carefully extending his arm and index finger to point out the threat to the archer beside him.

It was all Jirō needed. Taking an arrow from his quiver, he weighed it carefully in his hand and rubbed it along his flat fat nose, greasing its shaft to make it travel faster. Then he mounted the arrow on his bowstring and pulled it back along the laminated wood until it groaned under the strain. For a moment he took aim, making calculations for wind, distance, and elevation, as he had done a thousand times before. With a fearful twang the arrow leaped from the bow, hurtling toward its target. Echoing dimly across the valley, the sound startled the scout. But it was too late. With a crashing thud, the arrow's metal head pierced the warrior's armor, burying itself deep in his right side. It was a consummate shot. The arrow had found the weak spot in his armor, right on the flap covering his armor-cord.

18

For a moment the man just stood there, the arrow protruding from the side of his chest. Then, without uttering a sound he fell forward, over the edge of the bluff. For a few seconds he fell, silently, hurtling across the rugged cliff face. Then his lifeless body crashed unceremoniously into the undergrowth below.

Though silent, the scout's death hadn't gone unnoticed below. Nagayoshi could see one of the warriors who had stood guard on the bridge run toward the camp. Soon he could hear commanders bellowing orders to their men. Within minutes the opposite bank was crawling with men getting ready for action. They quickly fell into formation, forming tight units, the front row carrying narrow, six-feet tall shields. No sooner had they done so than archers behind them unburdened their bows, launching humming bulb arrows over their heads to direct them toward the second tier of the mountain stronghold, the small plateau on which stood the temple's main gate. It was followed by a deafening roar from the battle formations, which in turn was echoed by those defending the castle—the battle for Mount Kasagi had begun in earnest.

Fire

For three weeks the fighting raged, the stronghold's defenders repelling one assault after the other. As the days wore on the losses on both sides mounted. By the end of the second week, most of the reinforcements brought by Kusunoki Masashige had been either killed or wounded. Yet with each new day, fresh troops arrived in the valley below, sent from Kyoto and Kamakura by a Bakufu determined to suppress this contagious rebellion. No such means were open to the men holding out atop the mountain. Cut off from their allies and thrown back on their own resources, they kept fighting on dwindling rations until there were only a few dozen left.

Only the elements worked in the defenders' favor; the southeastern winds had gained in force, and dense torrents of rain now battered down on the mountain. Atop the mountain, the defenders huddled below the scaffolding along the wall or under the wide eaves of the cluster of buildings. Far more exposed were the armies encamped at the foot of the mountain. Within days the Kizu River burst its banks, sweeping away half of the erected tents and drenching the content of the rest. By the time the typhoon landed, the mountain's slopes had been turned into a slippery slide of mud and gravel, making it hard for the advancing armies to find their footing.

Yet a small group of intrepid enemy warriors set out to do the impossible. They were led by Suyama Yoshitaka and Komiyama Mototada, renowned chieftains from the western province of Bitchū. Both were masters of their own castle, both of which were mountain strongholds like Kasagi. They knew there was one place where the defenders would not expect an attack: from where it was most unlikely.

On the night of October 30, the two men and some fifty of their warriors made ready for a foray from which they realized they would probably not return. It was the last night of the lunar calendar, a cloudless yet pitch-black night, the only thing to stimulate their senses the stars and the howling winds in the treetops. They had discarded their harnesses, only holding on to their *katanas*, with which they now began to cut their way through the thick undergrowth at the foot of the mountain. For half an hour they proceeded in this manner until at length they reached the mountain's northern side facing the Kizu River. There, out of the undergrowth, a steep perpendicular cliff face rose high up to the stars above. All knelt in reverence, for chiseled into the granite surface was a fifty-feet tall image of Buddha. Once, in a distant past, when Nara was still the capital, the awe-inspiring image had drawn pilgrims from all over the realm. A special thirteen-storied pagoda had been built at the foot of the cliff. But it had caught fire and the place had fallen into neglect, the pilgrims had stayed away, nature had taken over. Even now one could see the scars on the smooth surface, whole patches had been blackened by the tar, hiding from sight large swathes of a delicately chiseled image of the Buddha looking down benevolently on two acolytes paying homage.

Having paid their respect, the men stripped down to their waist, rubbed themselves with mud, and bound their *katana* on their backs with a thin piece of cord. Then, toward the far left of the towering granite wall, at a place where cracks ran through the rock face, they began to climb the mountain, slowly but steadily, feet following hands gingerly as they sought to find a foothold on the wet and slippery surface. Several hours they spent in scaling the treacherous mountain. Toward midnight, they reached a bluff that gave way to a shallow slope covered in smooth green moss running up to a low palisade.

Within a few moments, the men had crossed the clearing, climbed the palisade, and killed the few monks on guard at the rear of the compound. No other men were on guard; the only movement came from the shadows cast by the dancing flames of the torches placed around the courtyard.

The intruders exchanged only a few words. Then they spread out, taking the torches and moving toward the cluster of buildings at the center of the court. There they split up, homing in on the scattered structures to do what they had come to do. A tense moment of silence followed as they withdrew into the shadow to do their dastardly work. Then, at first hesitantly, flames began to lick the bamboo blinds, the paper folding screens inside. Soon they reached the latticed ceilings and thick smoke began to bellow through the damp thatched roofs.

By now the buildings had come alive with the shouts and cries from those inside. It was as if a stick had been poked into an ant nest, as court officials and monks poured out in all directions to escape the flames. Some tried to get water from the large trough at the court's center, but were cut down mercilessly by the intruders who had now emerged from the shadows, *katanas* in hand. Some fled back inside to perish in the flames. Others fled toward the stockade, hurling themselves over and ungraciously slithering down the muddy southern slope on their backs toward safety among the forest below.

Flight

Like most of the warriors, Nagayoshi had been resting against the stockade encircling the plateau with the main gate. After another week of intense fighting, they had spent much of the day repairing defenses and preparing food from the meager provisions left. Toward evening he had fallen into a restless slumber. Now he was being prodded awake by his brother, who had been sleeping in the building next to the Hall of Wisdom.

Pointing toward the burning buildings higher up the mountain, Gensen shouted, 'All up there are dead! I saw the c- counselors flee, but not His Highness. He might—'

Gensen had no time to finish his sentence. Even as he spoke the intruders came storming down toward them along the narrow ridge leading down to the plateau on which stood the main gate: they had only moments to act. Turning to his fellow warriors on the stockade Nagayoshi bellowed at the top of his voice, 'Haul up the ladders!'

Chapter 1

Seeing the enemy advance, the great monk Honjōbō stepped forward above the main gate. He had tied back the sleeves of his wide robe with hemp rope, exposing his massive arms. Seemingly inexhaustible, he had spent much of the day hauling huge rocks up the high scaffold above the gate. Now he made the most of them as he cast them down on the enemy below. Unprotected by armor, they veered back as one after the other was being crushed by the shattering weight of the massive rocks. Enraged, the group now fell on the scaffolding below and began to hack away with their *katanas* at the supporting beams below.

Nagayoshi felt his heart sink. In spite of their superhuman efforts, they were fighting a losing battle. The main buildings were lost, they were being fought from within, and soon they would be assailed from without too. Already he could hear the whining sound of humming bulb arrows fill the valley below: they were going for the final crush. Then, with a crash, the scaffolding over the main gate collapsed and Honjōbō, still striking out madly around him, went under in a hail of blows.

Again Nagayoshi felt Gensen tug at his sleeve. He too had heard the bulb arrows. He had clearly come to the same conclusion, for he now beckoned toward the north, farther down along the scaffolding, where the stockade ended in a cluster of huge boulders. 'The Tainai Kuguri!' he shouted.

Nagayoshi knew instantly what he meant: the ten-yard 'cleansing tunnel' hewn out in the granite wall that separated them from the forest below. Meant to purify those who passed through it, it was part of the ancient pilgrim route that led to yet another image of Buddha carved into a massive slab of rock overlooking the plateau. The small tunnel gave access to a hidden path down the mountain, to the charred remains of the thirteen-storied pagoda. It was the only way out.

Raising his voice once more and beckoning to the others, Nagayoshi shouted, 'Come!'

As if on cue the two brothers and the handful of warriors rushed headlong down the scaffolding toward the tunnel. They reached it well before the enemy had satisfied their wrath on the towering monk. Apparently, the collapse of the pagoda had hidden the path from sight, for the heavy door at the end of the tunnel was still intact.

Nagayoshi was the last to enter the tunnel. Just once he looked back up the mountain, only to see the roof of the Hall of Wisdom collapse, sending a blaze of cinders up into the dark sky above—if the emperor was still inside, all was lost. He winced at the thought. Then he ducked and made his way through the narrow tunnel toward safety, but not before he had kicked away a long wedge below a supporting beam at its center he and Gensen had put there during the longs days of preparation. A thin trickle of sand began to pour from the granite ceiling above, a sign that their ingenious timing device had been set in motion—now there was no way back.

They were well into the woods when a massive thud caused the ground below them to shudder. Then all fell silent, as the small band of men began to descend the mountain along the narrow and winding path down the wooded slopes. Above them the morning sky was ablaze with fire—this battle they had lost, but the war was far from over.

CHAPTER 2

Emperor Go-Daigo had not perished in the flames; like many of the others he had been caught and taken to the Byōdo-in in Kyoto, where he was placed under house arrest. In the clampdown that followed, he was sent into exile on Oki Island, while many of his co-conspirators lost their posts and possessions if not their heads. Yagyū Nagayoshi and his brother were spared, though they lost everything. Stripped of their rank and status, their possessions confiscated, they were forced to throw themselves upon the mercy of the Kasuga Taisha.

A bleak future now lay in store for the Yagyū. With Go-Daigo's capture and exile, it seemed that all was lost. The only rays of hope were the heroic exploits of the indomitable Kusunoki Masashige. He had made it back to Akasaka castle, from where he embarked on a type of guerrilla warfare, continually harassing the Bakufu troops stationed in the Home Provinces. When Akasaka castle, too, was finally reduced, he still refused to admit defeat, moving higher up into the mountains. There he built another stronghold, Chihaya castle, to continue his campaign.[1]

Spiritually sustained by these tidings, the Yagyū kept themselves alive on a small plot of land they were allowed to work by the head priest of the Kasuga Taisha. Then, in the spring of 1333, word reached the temple that Go-Daigo had escaped from the island of Oki and had landed on the mainland of Honshū.

Soon it was followed by even more encouraging news. Nitta Yoshisada, a powerful northern warlord had taken up Go-Daigo's cause. He had raised a huge army and marched on the Bakufu's headquarters in Kamakura. By the summer the fate of the Bakufu had been sealed. After four days of frantic fighting with Nitta's superior forces, the Hōjō leaders had withdrawn to the Tōshō monastery and committed suicide en masse. That same year Go-Daigo returned to his palace in Kyoto. With full powers restored to the throne, he set about reverting all the punitive measures the Bakufu had taken against his supporters.

That fall of 1333, the Yagyū brothers were summoned to the capital for an audience with the emperor. Rewarding them for their valiant services Go-Daigo granted Gensen the name of Nakanobō, 'The emperor's monk,' and restored to Nagayoshi and his clan the lands that had belonged to them for so long. From now on they would be known as the Yagyū han (domain), proud possession of the Yagyū clan.

Yet the calm that followed in the wake of Go-Daigo's restoration did not last. Two rivaling factions emerged: one under the command of Ashikaga Takauji, one loyal to the emperor under the command of Nitta Yoshisada. Within months fierce fighting ensued throughout the realm. At length, it centered around the imperial capital. For many months the outcome hung in the balance, but eventually the forces of Ashikaga Takauji emerged victorious. On September 20, 1336, he installed an emperor on the throne from a line different to that of Go-Daigo's and founded the Ashikaga Bakufu. Once again Go-Daigo had to abandon his palace. Again he fled southward, this time to the Yoshino Mountains, deep down in the south of Yamato Province. There he set up a rivaling, Southern Court, from where he continued to coordinate the resistance with the help of local clans like the Yagyū.

Not all of Yamato's clans sided with the Southern Court. From ancient times there had been a sharp division between those who patronized the Kōfuku temple and those who patronized the Kasuga Taisha. The clans who patronized the Kōfuku temple were collectively known as the shuto. *With the rise of warrior houses during the twelfth century, its monks had become increasingly militarized. They had evolved into the so-called* sōhei, *or warrior monks, whose weapon of choice was the lance, or* yari. *Clans who patronized the Kasuga Taisha were known as the* kokumin. *Their ancestors had once been shrine officials who, like the Yagyū, had developed their own martial traditions.*

Most powerful among the shuto *were the Tsutsui, who hailed from the eponymous village at the heart of the Yamato basin. They supported the Northern Court. The most powerful among the* kokumin *were the Ochi, who hailed from the most southern part of Yamato. Like the Yagyū, they supported the Southern Court. Thus, even in Yamato Province, warriors of both courts faced each other on the field of battle.*

For more than half a century the country remained in turmoil, torn between the rivalry of the two opposing courts. It took until the end of the fourteenth century before peace was restored. That moment came late in 1392, when the Southern Court responded to an overture from Ashikaga Takauji's grandson, Yoshimitsu. In December of that year, some fifty years after Emperor Go-Daigo caused a rift in the imperial house by taking refuge among the Yoshino Mountains, the fighting parties finally came to a settlement. From then onward, the two courts were unified. Succession was to alternate between the two imperial lines.

It had taken half a century to end the war, and for half a century the weary populace knew peace. That period ended abruptly with the outbreak of the Ōnin Rebellion (1467–77). [2] *Once again the ancient capital became the scene of battle. In 1333, trouble had spread from within the imperial house; now it was a succession dispute within the ranks of the Bakufu that formed the seed of discontent. Again there were two factions, each seeking to further its own aims by backing different contenders to the imperial throne but neglecting the country at large.*

In Yamato, which had never known a provincial governor, the political situation was especially volatile. The contenders were mostly minor chieftains, virile and ambitious men belonging either to the kokumin *or the shuto. Unchecked by the tempering influence of central authority, longstanding rivalries reasserted themselves, and lingering sores erupted with a vengeance.*

The Yagyū at this time were led by Ieyoshi, the great grandson of Yagyū Nagayoshi, the hero of Mount Kasagi. In a last attempt to help restore central authority, Ieyoshi backed the governor of the neighboring province of Kawachi, Kizawa Nagamasa, who had long had his sights on Yamato. By way of foothold, he had built a huge castle on the crest of Mount Shigi along the mountainous border. And with the help of the Yagyū he now began to rebuild the ruined stronghold of Kasagi.

Yagyū Castle

Whenever Ieyoshi entered the gate of Yagyū castle he felt a smile spread across his otherwise solemn face. Though small, to him the castle was a magnificent stronghold. Its white plastered walls dazzled the eyes in the bright morning light. At every few yards, narrow loopholes enabled archers to cover the sloping stretch of land toward the Yagyū Kaidō and the Hakusa River beyond. Within the walls, at the center of a wide inner court with a well and stables, a two-storied donjon with a gabled roof purveyed the surrounding landscape. He was proudest of the large gate. Built in the *kōrai*-style, its main overhead beam had a framed roof, and so had the outrigger posts and their braces on the inside. It was a great improvement on the old gate, which had no roof and was always exposed to the weather. The new, massive doors hung on thick beams that swiveled in two large blocks of granite. Made from solid *hinoki*, they were crafted by the same master carpenters who had worked on the Kasuga Taisha.

Ieyoshi stretched out his hand to touch one of the door's nail coverings, which were cast in the shape of his beloved Yagyū crest. He looked up at the broad beams carrying the tiled roof overhead and a surge of pride rushed through his veins as he thought of what his father, Shigenaga, had accomplished. He had taken the bold step of moving the clan's headquarters from the Yagyū manor at the southern foot of Mount Kasagi to the center of Yagyū Valley, where it would get the full day's sun. It was also a more strategic position. Situated on an elevation along the Hakusa River, it controlled the traffic between Kasagi and Nara along the Yagyū Kaidō.

For several decades now the castle had been the Yagyū's proud abode. Ieyoshi could still remember how, as a young boy, he had helped in its construction, carrying mortar and plaster up to the workmen on the bamboo scaffolding along the rising castle walls. At the time the walls had seemed to pierce the sky above. It was only later, when he grew up, that he realized they were only five feet high, and without a moat as a first defense, they were too low for the dangerous times they lived in.

And so he had set about on a large-scale reconstruction of the castle. He had raised the walls by four feet so that they now stood nine feet tall. Behind the wall, at the height of the loopholes, ran a raised platform on which his archers could freely move around. Finally, he had raised the money to replace the old gate. All in all, it had been a costly affair. The massive doors of the main gate alone had set him back ten thousand *mon*, enough to support ten warriors for a year.

All this would not have been possible without the financial aid of Kizawa Nagamasa, who had made Kasagi temple his local headquarters. In return for Ieyoshi's help, he had carried half of the cost of the reconstruction of Yagyū castle.

Work on the two strongholds was completed just in time. In the winter of 1541, both came under fierce attack from a hostile clan from Iga. For a moment it looked as if Mount Kasagi would again fall when Iga *shinobi* set fire to the priests' quarters, some of the outbuildings, and captured the *ichi-no-maru* and *ni-no-maru*, the first and second defensive rings. The turnaround had come on December 15, when Nagamasa and Ieyoshi left the safety of their strongholds and crushed the enemy in a brilliantly executed hammer and anvil tactic. Less familiar with the terrain, Nagamasa had moved east along the Kizu River at the head of a large army of *ashigaru*. He had intercepted the enemy just east of Kasagi, where the road pincered between the mountains and the river. The two armies were equally matched. But then Ieyoshi, who had taken a small force of mounted warriors east through the mountains, had fallen on the bewildered enemy from behind, driving them into Nagamasa's phalanx of *yari*. Between them they had taken more than thirty enemy heads.

Now the Yagyū had to fend for themselves. It was already two years back that Nagamasa was killed in action at the Taihei temple. He had been fighting the Miyoshi, yet another clan who had their sights on the coveted price of Yamato Province.

Shinobi

On the first day of January 1544, Yagyū castle was brimming with secret activity, and it wasn't just for the New Year's festivity of O-Shogatsu. That evening Ieyoshi had convened a council with the headmen of his *shinobi*, the 'secret men.' Trained in the art of stealth, their main task was the gathering of information. For a clan the size of the Yagyū, intelligence meant survival. Ever since they had joined Emperor Go-Daigo's cause, the Yagyū had relied on intelligence rather than brute force to achieve their aims. Go-Daigo's defeat at Kasagi had taught them an important lesson: it had been the stealth of their night attack rather than their superior numbers that had made the enemy victorious.

The Yagyū were one of the few clans to have their own *shinobi*. Powerful chieftains simply hired mercenaries to do their dirty work—spying and winning by stealth wasn't part of their mindset. Proud of their martial prowess, they relished the challenge of testing it in battle and poured their heart in the strength and valor of their armies. The spies they hired were of low stock, shallow, unreliable men, who massaged their message to suit their client and were known by a large number of names: *rappa*, *suppa*, *toppa*, *dakkō*, all of them derogatory.

Being only a small clan, the Yagyū knew they had to rely on more than just military might. For almost two centuries now, they had maintained a small force of *shinobi*. Recruited from local clans, these men of stealth passed their skills on from father to son, forming a large regional network of spies who could be mobilized at the drop of a hat. They had proven their effectiveness in the recent battle for Kasagi-*dera* when they had helped both to anticipate and trace the attack from Iga.

The Yagyū *shinobi* had developed skills surpassing those of the average spy. Called *ninjutsu*, or hidden technique, it was a skill-set that embraced a great variety of disciplines. They were able swimmers, could go on next to no food for days on end, and could climb the steepest walls. To do this they used a so-called *uchikugi*, a small iron anchor attached to a long rope, which they would hurl over a defense until it caught. Even without it, they were able to scale a castle wall making use of the crevices between even the most tightly laid stones.

Unlike regular warriors, who had just one or two weapons of choice, *shinobi* used a large range of weapons, including the popular *shūriken* and *makibishi*,[3] but also a variety of farm tools like the *nata* (billhook) and *kama* (sickle). Their sword was the *shinobigatana*, long enough to hold its own against the regular *katana*, short enough to carry on one's back. Their favorite weapon was the *kusarigama*, the notorious chain sickle, after the piece of chain that connected the sickle to a small weight. Whipping the weight forward, they could entangle an opponent's weapon or limb and draw them in to strike with the sickle.

There was a strict hierarchy among the Yagyū *shinobi*, and each group had its own specialty. The secretive Kitanoyama, who lived among the mountains on the eastern edge of the Yagyū domain and had served them since the very beginning, specialized in *teisatsu*, reconnaissance. They could make their way into any stronghold and memorize troop numbers, weaponry, down to the place where a harness had been made. Only the *teisatsu* wore the typical dress of the *shinobi*, a dark, short-sleeved *uwagi* tucked into a dark *karusan hakama*, the *hakama* with trouser legs, but tapered down to fit tightly around the shins. In winter they would wear warm, padded garments, but never any form of armor. Nor did they wear the regular headgear. Instead, they wore a dark cowl, leaving only their eyes exposed. Their sinister appearance and exceptional ability to disappear soon gave rise to outlandish rumors that spread among a superstitious populace, who came to believe *shinobi* could fly through the air and walk on water. The last one had a kernel of truth, for one of their *shinobi* had once escaped by staying under water and breathing through a reed.

The Obo, who lived a few miles south along the road to Uda, were different. They had specialized as *kanchō*, spies who mixed with the troops of hostile clans, thus extracting valuable information on troop movement and influencing morale. The best of them were able to insinuate themselves into the highest ranks, gaining direct insight into an enemy's strategy. Their's was one of the most dangerous roles, but also the most valuable.

The Sakahara, whose village lay a few miles down the Yagyū Kaidō toward Nara, had developed a special talent for *kakuran*, 'agitation.' They were masters in stirring up resentment and spreading rumors among the subjects of enemy warlords. They were looked down upon by the other *shinobi*, but not by the Yagyū chieftain, who knew how to value psychological warfare.

Only the *shinobi* from Iga and Kōka rivaled those of the Yagyū in stealth and subterfuge. Yet, as the recent events at Kasagi had proven, when it came to a pitched battle, the Yagyū warriors amply made up for that.

Now their *shinobi* headmen had all gathered at Yagyū castle for an important meeting. A week earlier, Ieyoshi had ordered them to find out what they could about the Tsutsui. For more than a decade now the Tsutsui had been led by Tsutsui Junshō. Since his father's death in 1535, Junshō had worked tirelessly to strengthen his clan's power base in Yamato. He had only been twelve at the time of his succession but had already displayed all the qualities of a true clan leader. He was young, possessed of a razor-sharp intelligence, and driven by an unquenchable ambition. His headquarters of Tsutsui castle stood just a few miles south of Nara, on the western bank of the Saho River, which wound its way through the heart of the Yamato basin, the clan's traditional power base.

Ieyoshi was eager to hear what his *shinobi* headmen had to say. As always, the Kitanoyama headman spoke first. He related how, setting out at midnight, they had traveled to Nara along the Yagyū Kaidō. At Nara, they had left the main road and traveled southward until they had reached the treacherous marshes between the villages of Kōriyama and Tsutsui. Using maps from previous forays, they had crossed the marshes unharmed and reached the outskirts of Tsutsui unnoticed. Unlike Yagyū castle, Tsutsui castle had two moats, the outer of which encircled what amounted to a small castle town. They had swum across the wide outer moat and made it to the inner moat, but no farther. 'The town seems like a battle camp,'the headman concluded. 'Not a house isn't occupied by officers, not a yard by *ashigaru*.There are more than a thousand warriors encamped in Tsutsui—Junshō is clearly preparing for war.'

Now the turn had come for the Obo headman to speak. 'We haven't been able to infiltrate into the Tsutsui clan itself,' the headman gravely reported. Noticing Ieyoshi's disappointment, he quickly continued, 'but several of our members have been initiated as monks by the Kōfuku temple.They have proven an important asset, for the Tsutsui still entertain close ties with the temple.'He had Ieyoshi's attention now. 'Recently, Junshō's younger brother, Junsei, has been appointed *kanpu-shuto*. He is a loose-lipped man, and we have learned that Junshō has signed a pact with Tōchi Tōtada. Moreover, lately, there has been a flurry of messengers between the Kōfuku temple and Tsutsui castle.We intercepted one of them—they are building a second stronghold on Mount Ryūozan.'

'*Chikushō!*' Ieyoshi cursed.This was bad news. Until recently, Tōchi Tōtada had been one of Junshō's greatest competitors in the region. Now the Yagyū had one potential ally less.Tōtada's headquarters stood in Kashihara, some nine miles south along the Nara Kaidō. Mount Ryūozan lay only a few miles southeast of Junsho's power base, making its new castle essentially a *shijō*, a satellite castle, to Tsutsui castle. It was clear that Junshō wanted to project his power eastward, beyond Mount Ryūozan, into the Kasagi Highlands, toward Yagyū and Kasagi.

Listening to his *shinobi* headmen Ieyoshi realized Junshō posed the greatest threat to his clan. It was true that his former ally, Kizawa Nagamasa, had been crushed by the Miyoshi, but their power base lay in neighboring Kawachi province. Junshō's power base, by contrast, lay right at the heart of the Yamato basin. His castle was a formidable stronghold, protected from the north by marshes and from the east by his new allies, the Tōchi. There was just no way the Yagyū could hope to launch a direct assault on the castle without the help of a major warlord. Their strength had always been intelligence and insurgency, not the kind of pitched battles or sieges conducted by the great warlords. It was only a matter of time before they would have to confront Junshō's warriors like his ancestors had confronted the Bakufu's superior forces on Mount Kasagi some two centuries before.

Invasion

Proof of Ieyoshi's premonitions came within months of his council with his *shinobi* headmen. No sooner had the snow cleared from the mountains than news arrived in Yagyū that Furuichi castle had come under attack. Situated just two miles south of Nara's Tōdai temple, on the edge of the Kasagi Highlands, it was the first stronghold that stood in the way of Junshō's eastward expansion. It was the headquarters of the fiercely independent Furuichi clan. For more than two centuries they had maintained their autonomy, bound neither to the Kōfuku temple nor the Kasuga Taisha, let alone some land-grabbing warlord. Many times before their ancestors had clashed with the Tsutsui. Yet, as if wrought from the same sword steel that improved with each strike of the hammer, each time they had come out stronger. Like the Yagyū they had spent a lot of effort in reinforcing Furuichi castle, adding a second tier to an already formidable stronghold. Now that same stronghold was being besieged by a large force under the joint command of Tsutsui Junshō and Tōchi Tōtada.

At least the Furuichi had had some time to prepare. Following his meeting with his headmen, Ieyoshi had given them the news from his *shinobi*, keeping them informed of all hostile movements. He still felt powerless. There was just no way he could now help relieve the besieged clan. All he could do was to keep lines of communication with the Furuichi open in case they decided to fall back. That moment came toward the end of April, when, after several weeks of fierce fighting they set fire to their castle and withdrew high into the Yoshino Mountains, forsaking lands their ancestors had ruled for generations. It was another reminder just how quickly a clan's fortunes could change in a country at war with itself.

That same year, on the eighteenth of May, Junshō marched on Sugawa castle, which stood only a few miles south of Yagyū castle along the Yagyū Kaidō. The Sugawa had long been allied to the Furuichi. Through the Nakanobō, they were also connected to the Yagyū. And like the Yagyū they had fought alongside Kizawa Nagamasa, resisting Junshō's increasingly belligerent stance. Being a minor clan, their stronghold was only a modest affair. Sitting atop a shallow hill, it had bulwarks in all directions but stone walls only along its western perimeter. Within the first day, twenty Sugawa warriors had died. Another week of intense fighting followed. Then, on the 26th, their clan leader and his son fell in battle while trying to repel another assault. As was the custom, their wives and children committed ritual suicide. Only a few of their clan survived. With the help of the Yagyū they fled northward to Tō-o, a hamlet nestled deep among the hills of the Kasagi Highlands.

The Tsutsui and Tōchi, too, had suffered. The fierce resistance from the Furuichi and the Sugawa had depleted their numbers. Through his *shinobi* Ieyoshi knew that they had set out from Tsutsui at the head of some two thousand men. The month-long siege of Furuichi castle had cost them half of their men. By the time they had driven the Sugawa from their lands, their numbers had again been halved. Not that this put Ieyoshi at ease. Far from it. It would merely win him time. For a while the aggressors would withdraw to their strongholds. Nursing their wounded warriors back to health, they would create a fresh, perhaps even stronger army. They would do so by imposing heavy taxes on their peasants, especially those who worked the rice paddies in the domains they had conquered. Then they would march again, to gain yet more territory, extort yet more taxes, grow even bigger armies. It was the way of the world.

Last Rounds

The news the forty-eight-years-old Ieyoshi had long been dreading came in the summer of 1544. On the evening of August the fourteenth, a group of *shinobi* he had dispatched to reconnoiter the vicinity of Mount Ryūozan returned with the news that Junshō and Tōtada were marching north along the Yagyū Kaidō, at the head of a large force. They were expected to reach Yagyū castle by the dawn of the next day.

By nightfall, Ieyoshi had mobilized all the men in his domain. For two years he had worked feverishly to meet the growing threat. He had recruited every able-bodied man from his domain. And though he had managed to raise a force of several hundred men, he knew it would be a desperate battle, one in which the odds would be stacked overwhelmingly against them. Only some of his men were fully fledged warriors, from samurai families, hardened over generations in man-to-man combat. Once there had been many more such men in his domain, but over the years they had fallen on the field of battle, fighting alongside Ieyoshi's father and grandfather. Little more than a hundred of them now remained, the rest being inexperienced though well-trained men. Yet all of them were willing to fight for their independence or, if fate ordained it so, to pay the ultimate price for the safety of their families.

That night Ieyoshi and his brother, Shigeyoshi, spent doing the rounds of their domain, making sure none would be left behind. By the hour of the Tiger, four o'clock in the morning, all who dwelled in Yagyū Valley, women, children, and the old, had moved within the castle walls. There was no need to shore up supplies. Ever since hostilities had erupted, Yagyū castle had been in a state of alert. Large supplies of dried deer, boar, and other foodstuffs had been stocked up in its thick-walled and cool warehouse. A hidden underground duct carried water from the nearby Hakusa River to within the castle walls. All repairs to the castle wall had been done, and at its foot sharpened bamboo pikes had been planted deep into the soil in dense rows.

Ieyoshi had just made a final round inside the castle, when his *shinobi* headman rushed through the gate shouting, 'Junshō's troops have just emerged from the woods at the southern end of Yagyū Valley! I counted well over a thousand men!'

It was all they needed to know—everyone knew their role. The womenfolk withdrew to the main building, where they helped the men into their harnesses and prepared food and bandages for the battle to come. Outside, archers took up positions at their loopholes on the scaffolding along the walls, while young boys ran to and fro with food and water.

A Young Warrior

One among those gathered within the walls of the small

stronghold was especially excited at the prospect of battle. It was Ieoyoshi's seventeen-year-old son, Muneyoshi. Though he vividly remembered the time his father and the governor of Kawachi had battled with the forces from Iga, he had been too young to join them. To his great chagrin, his father had ordered him to stay at home and help his uncle secure the castle. Ever since that day he had craved the chance to make a mark, like his great ancestors on Mount Kasagi. One of his two most prized possessions was a copy of the *Kasagi engi-ki*, a long scroll recounting in colorful detail the Battle of Mount Kasagi, the arrival of Emperor Go-Daigo, his meeting with the great Kusunoki Masashige, and their heroic battle with the hated Bakufu forces. All this, he was sure, he would now relive in person, as he too would fight his way into the proud annals of martial history.

His sisters helped him into his new harness. Made by the best artisans in Nara, it was of the newest *hara-ate* type.[4] Unlike his father's *dōmaru*, which was a full coat of armor, it only consisted of a cuirass and cuisses. It was light and flexible, allowing for great freedom of movement without wearing one down by its weight. It had first come into vogue among Nara's *sōhei*, who fought on foot and had to travel light. So did he. This would be a defensive battle, fought from behind protective walls, not one out in the field on horseback.

His grandfather, Mitsuie, who had spent the best part of an hour donning his old and worn *ō-yoroi*, looked at him disapprovingly and grumbled, 'It's below a warrior not to wear a full coat of armor.'

Muneyoshi didn't hear the old man's mutterings: he was too consumed with himself. Suspended over his armor hung his second most prized possession: the Kasagi no Tachi. Forged by the great Masamune,[5] it was the very *katana* with which his great ancestor, Nagayoshi, had fought off the evil forces of the Kamakura Bakufu on Mount Kasagi. A prized family heirloom, his father had given it to him on the day of his *genpuku*, the festive ceremony celebrating his coming of age. A rush of excitement passed through the young man as he prepared for what could only be a glorious battle. Today he would show them what a true Yagyū warrior was worth.

Under Siege

For the first time in recorded history, Yagyū Valley filled with the clamor of armies in the throes of battle. All of the Yagyū men, warriors, farmers, thatchers, and carpenters alike, stood their ground valiantly in the scorching heat of that midsummer day. Led by Ieyoshi and his brother Shigeyoshi, they repulsed one attack after the other until, by dusk, the enemy was forced to withdraw to the hills to regroup and count their dead.

The next day saw even more intense fighting. Junshō's troops now concentrated on the main gate. While recovering in the woods, they had felled a tall Segovia tree. They had made a large number of slings to create a portable ramming rod his strongest men now brought to bear on the structure's doors. They pounded away at the iron-clad doors, hampered by the constant barrage of arrows, stones, and boiling water from a small group of men under Muneyoshi's command.

Only now did the wisdom of his father's costly investment reveal itself. The two massive blocks of granite on which the doors hinged were hewn in the shape of a raised threshold against which each rested, causing the impact of the blows to be absorbed by the granite rather than the gate's wooden structure. After several hours the doors and main structure were still intact, while Muneyoshi had lost only a couple of men. Not so the enemy. By noon most of the original span of men carrying the ramming rod had perished, forcing Junshō to replace them with less strong and battle-weary men. They lasted only half as long, so that by dawn a clearly exasperated Junshō had to order their retreat.

Drunk with excitement, Muneyoshi, climbed on top of the structure's roof, raising his *katana* and shouting, '*Kaere! Kaere!*' (Piss off!), as the enemy, retreated toward the woods. Turning his head, he proudly looked toward where the others were, along the scaffolding, when he noticed his father franticly pointing toward the enemy, vainly trying to raise his voice over his men's clamor of victory. Looking back toward the enemy, he had just enough time to notice how one of the retreating soldiers was wielding a slingshot—in it, gathering speed with each whizzing rotation, sat a large stone they had earlier hurled down on them. Then all went dark.

Captured

When Muneyoshi came to, he lay in a room he had never seen before. He had a massive bump on his forehead and a throbbing sensation his head was about to burst. It was still early morning; the cicadas hadn't yet started humming. By the dim light falling through the paper windows, he could vaguely make out the layout of the room. It was a large room, its floor covered with beautifully finished *tatami*. Overhead massive beams supported a paneled ceiling—it was obviously a guest room. Then his gaze fell on one of the huge steel nails, and the reality of his condition sank in. It hit him harder than the stone that had felled him. There, emblazoned in gold leaf, glimmering ominously on the nail's ornamented head, were the *mutsuboshi*, the 'six stars,' the mark of the Japanese apricot, one of the 'three companions of the deep cold,' and the crest of the Tsutsui clan.

Stumbling to his feet he reached for the paper window. But no sooner had he moved than it slid open and warriors on guard ordered him to stay put. The window closed again, and now he could hear orders being bellowed across the inner court he had just glimpsed. For a while it was quiet. Then he heard the guards again. With a slam, the sliding door at the room's other end slid open and a rotund, diminutive young man in a dark robe entered the room. He had a totally unwarrior-like appearance. His face was big and round, like that of a Chinese despot, with fat cheeks but thin lips. He had sardonic, olive-shaped eyes, crowned by thin, highly arched eyebrows, which gave his face an expression as if he were in a state of constant bemusement. Most remarkable in a man his age, was his natural baldness. It wasn't the only clerical aspect of his appearance. He was dressed in a monk's full garb, with draped over his left shoulder a *kesa*, the Buddhist's traditional outer garment. Unlike the *kesa* of old, which were patched together from bits of cloth in reference to Buddha's own impoverished garment, his was made of neatly arranged sections of the most exquisite brocade.

Without any ado, the man proceeded to sit down on the floor on his knees, flanked at each shoulder by a tall guard. Then, in a soft, deliberate voice, he said, 'I am the monk Tsutsui Junshō.'

Reading the expression on his captive's face, Junshō almost sounded conciliatory as he continued, 'There is no need for remorse. Indeed, you should be glad. Your capture has been the sole thing that has saved your clan. Had you fought on,' he added matter-of-factly, 'fire would have been set to your castle like all the others. All your people would have been killed, to the last man, woman, and child.'

Then, to Muneyoshi's astonishment, Junshō dismissed his guards. When they had left the room he began to smile and, leaning forward, whispered, 'You will teach me the Yagyū art of swordsmanship!'

Muneyoshi was struck by Junshō's arrogant self-assuredness. Though only a few years older than himself, he ordered men twice his age around as if they were mere boys. Yet in sharp contrast with his overall sanguine appearance was his left hand, which never sat still, its chubby fingers constantly fumbling a long string of black prayer beads, nervously counting them, one by one, as if in terror they might miss one.

Junshō made it no secret that he was pleased with himself. 'It's true: because of you, we have lost some men, but the Yagyū warriors will more than compensate for that. You see, your dear father, Ieyoshi-*dono*, has wisely submitted to Tsutsui rule. Indeed, we have already signed a treaty. Of course,' he added airily as he lifted the string of beads and studied them, 'to enforce it, you are to remain here at Tsutsui castle—just in case your father has second thoughts about his sense of commitment.'

Hostage

Muneyoshi hated being a prisoner to the man who had subdued his clan. Not that life as a hostage was harsh in itself; as the scion of a respected clan of warriors, he enjoyed many of the privileges Junshō was heir to. Thus he had his own living quarters on the grounds of Tsutsui castle, where he could pursue his studies and be visited by his sisters. He even had his own servant and—more importantly—was allowed to continue his practice of swordsmanship. And thus, being still young, with time, he reluctantly came to terms with his new life.

At least he was valued as a fencing instructor. Already at a very early age, he had learned the various Yagyū fencing techniques from his father. Every day he had gone through the various *kamae*, the basic stances from which one parried or launched an attack. Yet it had been under his uncle, Shigeyoshi, that he had really mastered the difficult art of swordsmanship. Like Muneyoshi, Shigeyoshi had displayed a talent for the *katana* from a very young age. He had traveled the width and breadth of the country on countless *musha shugyū*, in the course of which he had gained a deep understanding of many different schools of fencing, including the famous Shintō and Chūjō-*ryū*. Now Muneyoshi was forced to share his knowledge of his clan's proud tradition with the very man who had taken away their independence.

Luckily, there was little danger of the secrets of the Yagyū-*ryū* being stolen anytime soon, for Junshō was the worst student ever. He might be a brilliant strategist, but his physique wasn't that of a swordsman. The Yagyū-*ryū* required one to squat deep down on one's haunches throughout many of its techniques. When mastered it gave one's attack an added resilience and scope for evasion. Yet it required great agility and physical endurance, neither of which were present in the Tsutsui chieftain, despite his young age. Overweight and stocky, he was slow and stiff in his movements. When he did lower his huge torso, he could hardly get up, let alone wield a *katana* in the process. Another drawback was his hands. Used to the constant fiddling with prayer beads, they had a tendency to do the same with the *katana*, causing the weapon to never sit still in his hand—an absolute requirement if one were to make a decent cut. At times Muneyoshi found it hard not to laugh out loud. To him all this was second nature. Yet he always managed to keep a straight face, for he soon learned Junshō had a viciously vindictive streak.

Murder

Muneyoshi had spent two years at Tsutsui castle when Junshō invited the chieftain Hashio Tamemasa to his guesthouse in Hayashikōji, at Nara's center. Throughout much of the warring period, the Tsutsui and the Hashio had been allies. Situated some ten miles south of Nara, Hashio castle formed the first line of defense against southern clans, and Tamemasa's men had proven fierce and reliable warriors. It was a remarkable alliance, especially when one considered that the Hashio clan belonged to the *kokumin* and that they had once lost their castle to one of Junshō's ancestors.

It was early May, the time of the annual *takagi-nō* performance, an open-air performance of *nōgaku*.[6] The event, which dated back to the Heian period, was hugely popular among the warrior clans and attended by dignitaries from all over the province. It was closely connected to the Kōfuku temple, and the responsibility of hosting the event revolved among the *shuto*. This year it was Junshō's turn. Outdoing his predecessors, he had erected a wide wooden stage at his mansion's eastern wing so that the temple's magnificent five-storied pagoda formed a natural backdrop. It was a huge success. Staged at night and lit by huge fires, it featured a string of performances from Kyoto's most famous actors and musicians.

Muneyoshi, too, had been ordered to participate. He gave a so-called opening *enbu*, a performance demonstrating a number of techniques of the Yagyū school of swordsmanship. His performance was lackluster, distracted as he was by conflicting emotions. But then his eyes caught something. From the stage, he had a clear view of Junshō and his guest, who had been sitting on the raised veranda of his villa opposite the stage. He had just begun on his last technique when he noticed how Junshō beckoned his guest to follow him inside. For a while they were swallowed up by the dark. But then, just as he was about to finish, he saw how two of Junshō's retainers left the side villa's entrance carrying what seemed to be a long bale of straw, though it was obviously far heavier than that. His worst suspicions were confirmed when Tamemasa's attendants, who were unarmed, were arrested while the main performance was in full swing.

Within weeks of Tanemasa's murder, Junshō launched a full-scale assault on his clan's stronghold of Hashio castle. Driven by revenge for his father's callous murder, Tamemasa's son put up a good fight, but within days, he too had to concede defeat and flee the province.

Night Crawling

Not long after Tamemasa's treacherous death, Junshō fell ill. At first, his physicians diagnosed him with smallpox, but they were at a loss when he was struck down by terrible headaches. At times these grew so bad that he took to his room and had all the shutters closed. Often, at night, Muneyoshi could hear him scream out in terror, and servants told him that when their master could no longer stand it, he would lock his jaw onto the small, padded headrest. Among the monks of the Kōfuku temple, there was no doubt what had brought on the affliction: it was bad karma.

The attacks grew increasingly frequent. By the end of 1549, Junshō was given to violent mood swings while his slurred speech hampered his ability to conduct the affairs of his rapidly expanding domain. Only occasionally was he able to give a coherent order, but even then it was delivered in a string of spluttering and driveling bursts. The next spring, feeling his end imminent, he summoned his clan elders to his bedroom. During a long and painful meeting, frequently interrupted by paralyzing fits, he appointed his brother Junsei as regent to his two-year-old son, Junkei.

Fearful the news would unleash a power struggle, Junsei kept his brother's illness secret and ordered his public appearances to be performed by Mokuami, a monk from the Kōfuku temple. Though blind, the bald and corpulent monk looked like a twin brother to the afflicted chieftain, who passed away a few days later aged only twenty-eight.

For a while the scheme seemed to work. Restricting Mokuami's public appearances to a minimum, Junsei managed to uphold the appearance that his brother was still alive. Yet to all whose lives evolved around Tsutsui castle, it was clear that a profound change had taken place in their leader. For though they were each other's spitting image outwardly, their characters could not be more different. Whereas Junshō had been a paragon of frugality and never had any concubines, the monk knew no bounds and seemed to lust after all that was forbidden. Born into a life of stoic frugality, it seemed as if the blind monk wanted to make good on all the pleasures he had gone without, to feel the things he would never see.

Junsei, meanwhile, proved a far more lenient master than his brother. Muneyoshi's curfew was lifted and though he wasn't allowed to return home, he could travel up to Nara, albeit under escort, and visit his sisters, who worked as *maiko*, or shrine maidens, at the Kasuga Taisha. For Muneyoshi, it felt like a breath of fresh air. He was now twenty-three years old and though comfortable, his life at Tsutsui had been one of learning and practice—all work and no play. The tales of Mokuami's exploits stirred up a burning desire in the young man for some excitement; he missed the company of women. While still at home he had courted the daughter of the village chief. As was the custom, he had crept into her room at night and revealed his intentions. She had let him in and over the next weeks, they had regularly met. Her parent knew, of course. With time he would be 'caught,' and they would have to marry. That was more than five years ago now. There were no such temptations at Tsutsui castle. Junshō had been too young to have daughters of Muneyoshi's age, nor could a man of Muneyoshi's class afford to consort with handmaidens.

All that changed when Junsei and his entourage took up residence at Tsutsui castle. Though a cleric, he was married and had two daughters. And one of them, the eighteen-year-old Nabu, immediately caught Muneyoshi's eye. She was tall and slender and her laughter was utterly captivating. Bright and inquisitive herself, she sensed his interest and taunted him with provocative glances whenever she passed his quarters on some errand. When they met, she made light of his fencing skills, but encouraged him in his learning, challenging him with lines from literary works he had never heard of. With each encounter, his infatuation grew. By summer it had reached a point where he felt he would burst. One evening, at a family gathering at which Muneyoshi was present, Nabu heard something outside the window. 'Hear!' she said, 'a bell cricket!' Then, in that same irresistible voice, she recited those beautiful lines from Murasaki Shikibu's *Genji monogatari*, as she stole a forlorn glance at him across the room.

> Fain would one weep the whole night long,
> As weeps the bell cricket's song,
> Who chants her melancholy lay,
> Till night and darkness pass away.

That night, guided by the faint sickle of a waxing moon, Muneyoshi rose from his futon and slid outside. He felt his heart pounding in his throat as he silently made his way across the spacious inner court toward her sleeping quarters. He knew where she slept, for he had often seen her sitting with her sister on the wide veranda outside her window. Climbing the veranda, he slid open the paper window, stepped inside, and softly called her name. Startled she lifted her head from the wooden headrest and stared at him. For a moment he thought she would scream. Then she rose, moved past him and gently closed the window behind him.

Musha Shūgyō

Ten years had passed when, in the spring of 1551, Muneyoshi and Nabu married. Ieyoshi had long opposed but finally relented when Junsei vowed to make his son a free man. Junsei had just one condition: Muneyoshi was to become chieftain on his return to Yagyū Valley. Muneyoshi was dying to get away from Tsutsui castle, but he didn't want to return home yet: he wanted to travel and see something of the world. Specifically, he wanted to go on a *musha shugyō*, the age-old tradition of night errantry.[7] For centuries each new generation of Yagyū men had set out on their own *musha shugyō* to challenge other swordsmen and deepen their understanding of their art. His father encouraged him, reminding his son that, as hereditary custodians of the Kasuga Taisha, the Yagyū had a duty to master the art of *heihō* and uphold all that was good and important for their way of life. For five long years, captivity had kept him from realizing that ambition, though at least he had been able to continue his practice on the grounds of Tsutsui castle with fellow swordsmen.

49

More recently, on his visits to Nara, he had taken up practicing *sōjutsu*, the art of fighting with the lance, or *yari*. Junsei had introduced him to the brilliant Hōzōin In'ei, chief abbot of Nara's Hōzō monastery. In'ei, who had just turned thirty, was already its unchallenged master. He was a direct descendant of the Nakanomikado, a line of *sōhei* associated with Nara's Kōfuku temple. Drawing on their traditions, he had founded his own school, the Hōzōin-*ryū*. He was also adept with the *katana*, an art he had acquired under the tutelage of Toda Yosaemon, an exponent of Nenami Jion's Nen-*ryū*. It was said that, in total, In'ei had studied under as many as forty different masters of various weapons, chief among them the *yari*, the *naginata*, and the *taitō*.

Now Muneyoshi wanted to put all he had learned to the test. And what better company to have than his uncle Shigeyoshi. The latter had spent much of his life on the road. A genial and avuncular man, he quickly made friends and was always willing to share his insights with his much younger nephew—the perfect travel companion. He was also a well-seen guest at the strongholds of powerful warlords and had given demonstrations of the Yagyū-*ryū* at the courts of the emperor and Shōgun.

Shigisan Engi

It was already early autumn and both men had been on the road for several months when, on their way home, they arrived at the Chōgosonshi temple. It stood on the southern slope of Mount Shigi, marking the mountainous border between Yamato and Kawachi. There was a reason why Muneyoshi wanted to visit the temple. Nabu had told him that it housed the *Shigisan engi*, the picture scrolls of The Legends of Mount Shigi, which dated back to the illustrious Heian period. The temple's abbot was impressed by the young warrior's knowledge of the scrolls. That evening, shortly after they had attended service and the temple bell had sounded the last toll, he invited both men to the temple's main hall, where he reverently rolled out the three long scroll on the spacious floor. Stretching more than eight yards each, they depicted the fabulous tales of the Shingon monk Myōren, who had founded the temple many centuries ago.

The abbot's hands hovered over the paper as his equally parched fingers pointed out the various scenes on each scroll. 'These scrolls,' he began, 'tell three tales.' 'This one,' he went on as he rolled out the first scroll, 'recounts how Myōren lived on this mountain to worship Buddha. To sustain himself, he ate whatever he could find. Toward winter, when food grew scarce, he grew hungry. Having acquired spiritual powers, he sent his rice bowl down the mountain to beg for alms at the house of a rich farmer who lived at the foot of the mountain.' The old monk patiently pointed out the events he related at the scroll's various stages, each time carefully touching the relevant passage with the long nail on his pink. 'The farmer, a tight-fisted man by the name of Yamazaki, refused and locked the bowl in his storehouse. But no sooner had he done so, than the building began to shake vehemently. Lifting itself from its moorings, it flew up the mountain, toward the monk's receiving hands.'

Muneyoshi marveled at the detail in which the tales were told, the craft with which the artist drew the reader's attention to the next scene through the startled gaze of the characters who populated the scroll. They were real people, going about their lives in pretty much the same way as they did in his day. Yet they seemed to have lived in a happier time. There were no tears, no wounded warriors. Women carrying their babies on their backs were full of laughter, picking greens among the fields, while old men met and chatted on the road without fear of marauding bands of bandits.

Noting the young man's keen eye and sharp mind, the abbot nodded. 'You should really go and visit Shigisan castle, farther up the mountain,' he said as he raised his hand aloft. 'Only recently a new warlord had taken up residence. His name is Lord Matsunaga Hisahide. He hails from Kyoto, where it is said he has made his fortune as a tea merchant. He is an avid collector, and his abode is decorated with all kinds of art.'

Matsunaga Hisahide

It so happened that the new lord of Shigisan castle was in residence. Matsunaga Hisahide was a striking figure. Unlike most warriors, he wore his long grey hair loose over a long silk garment that reached down to his feet. He had a aquiline nose above a pensive mouth, and one eye seemed set in an eternal squint, as if he were listening out for something. He seemed keen to meet the two weary travelers. 'I have heard of the Yagyū and their style of swordsmanship,' he said as he received them in the castle's *goten*, the opulent audience hall. 'Please be my guests and do me the honor of giving a demonstration for me and my elders tonight.'

Muneyoshi's eyes marveled at the opulence of Hisahide's court. Growing up he had thought Yagyū was the paragon of castles. Living at Tsutsui castle had taught him that it was just a modest affair. On their travels, he had seen other, even more splendid, castles. Yet Shigisan castle was in an altogether different league. Not only was it impressive in its multiple tiers of defenses, but its interiors were like nothing he had ever seen before. The number of rooms seemed endless and no costs had been spared on their decoration. All the walls and *fusuma* of Hisahide's living quarters were covered with paintings by masters of the Kano school. They drew heavily on the three scrolls of the *Shigisan engi* he had just seen: the flying storehouse, the sword deity's visit to the emperor, Myōren's sister praying at the Hall of the Great Buddha in Nara's Tōdai-*ji*—all magnificently represented against a dazzling background of pure gold leaf. The pillars and lentils were partially sheathed in lead, which in turn too had been gilded, so that it looked as if the whole interior of the castle was made of gold.

That evening Muneyoshi and his uncle made ready to perform an *enbu*. Muneyoshi felt uncomfortable: somehow Shigeyoshi didn't seem himself. A hush descended on the spectators as both men took up positions at the center of the audience hall. They had agreed to do a standard Yagyū-*ryū* routine in which Muneyoshi would rush in and strike from above with a *raitō* technique. Shigeyoshi, rising from a sitting position, would parry the blow from below. It wasn't a difficult move, but it did require expert timing, as one had to draw a fully sheathed *katana* in an upward motion, ready in time to intercept the blow from above with sufficient force to deflect it.

Sitting down opposite his uncle, Muneyoshi waited until the assembly had fallen totally silent. Then, fixing his eyes on his uncle, he swiftly rose while drawing his *katana*. Raising it high above his head, he moved in and brought it down on Shigeyoshi's head, assured that it would meet the blade of the latter's *katana*, just about a few inches below the tip, or *kissaki*. From there it would rush down its edge until it would be deflected by the handguard, away from the body.

The moment he brought down his *katana* he knew something was wrong. Shigeyoshi was slow. Not too slow, but the blades met each other much lower, so that his *katana* hit his uncle's guard with such force that one edge broke off and hurled across the room to lodge itself in one of the richly decorated *fusuma*.

Muneyoshi was stunned. It was the first time he had seen his uncle make a mistake. Was it the glittering opulence around him that made Shigeyoshi falter? He cast a quick glance toward their host. Yet far from being annoyed, Hisahide acted as if the whole thing had been part of the performance. More than anything, he seemed impressed. '*Yoroshū de gozaru*' (well done!), he said as he smiled toward Shigeyoshi.

To Muneyoshi's surprise, his uncle seemed to have forgotten all about his mistake. He eagerly accepted the warlord's invitation to join him for a tea ceremony in his private tea house in the corner of the castle's inner court.

Tea

Later that evening, at the appointed hour, Muneyoshi and his uncle made their way to the gate to Hisahide's tea house. True to custom, the terrace in front of the gate had been watered for the sake of freshness. Leaving their dirty sandals on a wide stone, they stooped down low to enter the low gate—devised in this manner on purpose to make one discard one's pride. Muneyoshi was the last to enter and locked the gate from the inside. Then both men sat down and rested in an arbor set among a miniature forest. It had been exquisitely done incorporating a tiny red maple set among a collection of pines that threw its crimson leaves in sharp contrast. After some time they rose again and now walked along a paved path toward the thatched tea house, which was hidden from view by the miniature forest. There, in a rough stone trough into which fresh water was being conducted by way of a duct of bamboo pipes, they washed their hands. Finally, they removed their fans and *tantō* from their sashes and placed them in a delicate cupboard beside the house and one by one crouched through the tiny wooden sliding door set in the lower corner of the house's stuccoed wall.

Having sat down on their knees before the small alcove, they arranged their clothing and trained their attention on the narrow scroll with an autumn landscape that had been suspended in the alcove above a small maple branch cutting—another reminder of the change of season. At length their host entered through another tiny door on the inside of the house and, thanking his guests, took his place next to the small recess in the floor in which a couple of carefully placed pieces of *sumi* charcoal were already crackling with heat.

Sitting close together in the cramped space of the tea house, Muneyoshi had a good opportunity to observe Hisahide. He noticed how the warlord's eyes remained locked on his uncle as he leaned forward, took the tea kettle from the fire, poured some hot water in a precious bowl filled with tea powder, and proceeded to stir its green content with a few measured flicks of a bamboo whisk.

'I will not hide from you my ambition to spread my sphere of influence into Yamato Province,' he said as he passed the two bowls to his guests. 'Earlier today, I have had a long meeting with my *zōei bugyō* who oversaw the expansion of Shigisan castle. My plan is to build another castle on Tamonyama, the shallow hill on Nara's northern outskirts. It will be even more splendid than Shigisan and rival with the great fortresses of the realm: Himeji, Nijō, Osaka. More importantly, it will serve as a buffer against Yamato's unruly chieftains.'

'Nara,' he piously continued, 'must be preserved as a center of religious learning, be spared the terrible internecine warfare that plagues the rest of the country. To do this I need capable allies. I admire the *kokumin* and their traditions, but of late they have lost much ground to the *shutō*, especially to the Tsutsui. Indeed, didn't your clan also lose its independence at the hand of the Tsutsui?'

'Yes,' Shigeyoshi intoned. 'It is the bleakest moment in our long proud history.'

'Then would it not be marvelous for you to regain your independence?,' Hisahide almost whispered as he made Shigeyoshi another bowl of tea. 'What if you were to join me? Under my banner, you will not only regain your freedom—your estate will be tripled! Life under my rule,' he sighed, 'can be long and prosperous.'

While he was talking he drew away a piece of silk cloth covering a number of small boxes. In them were pine crickets. 'Even my crickets—' he said as he offered Shigeyoshi the filled tea bowl with his other hand, 'even my crickets live well beyond their normal age. All it requires is proper attention and good nourishment.'

A Choice

For the Yagyū Hisahide's offer presented a new dilemma. Once again they were faced with a stark choice. Should they continue to serve the Tsutsui in the hope of holding on to what they had? Or should they choose Hisahide's side and regain their independence? The dilemma was greatest for the young Muneyoshi. As the new chieftain ultimate responsibility for the clan's future now lay with him. Yet he felt compromised. For him, his marriage to the beautiful and intelligent Nabu had only been a blessing. She had set him free in more than just the physical sense. Through her wide reading she had introduced him to a side of his heritage to which his eyes had as yet been closed. And she had born him his first son, Shinjirō. Yet she was mistrusted by many of his clan members, who suspected she clouded his judgment.

So much was borne out at the first meeting of elders over which Muneyoshi presided. Chief among his wife's detractors was Shigeyoshi, who didn't mince his words as he addressed Muneyoshi: 'You, dear nephew, are clearly under your wife's spell. You may be happy to do the Tsutsui's bidding, but I for one am tired of risking my life on behalf a cursed *shutō*.'

Then he turned toward the rest of the elders. 'Lord Hisahide has assured us he favors the *kokumin*. And many of them—the Sugawa, the Furuichi, the Hashio—have already signed pacts with Lord Hisahide. It is time for us to join them!'

It was a powerful argument. All these clans had, like the Yagyū, been forced to subdue to the will of the Tsutsui. And while they too had reaped some benefits, it had come at a heavy price. Especially when one considered the way in which Hashio Tamemasa had come to his end.

'Hisahide's offer,' Shigeyoshi continued, 'gives us a golden opportunity to reclaim our place of pride among equals, to restore our sense of chivalry, our sense of honor, our integrity. We shouldn't miss it...'

Muneyoshi felt torn. Of course, his wife would be unhappy with such a move, but she would never try to change his mind. And while he too deplored how Tamemasa had come to his end, that piece of treachery had been Junshō's work, not that of his clan, who were now being led by the more moderate Junsei. He was also deeply suspicious of Hisahide. He had seen how he had stroked Shigeyoshi's ego, showered him with compliments, plied him with gifts of costly tea utensils on their departure. On their way home he had confronted his uncle with his poor timing during their demonstration, but Shigeyoshi had brushed it aside, retorting he had come in too fast. Had not Hisahide praised him for his swordsmanship? It was a ridiculous argument; one could never be too fast, only too slow. For the first time he had seen a side of his uncle he had never seen before, his vanity—it was a terrible weakness, the result of which was now painfully on display.

When Ieyoshi finally asked the clan elders to cast their vote, his fears came true: a narrow majority was on Shigeyoshi's hand. And thus, not wanting to go against the majority of his clan, and compromised by his marriage to a member of the Tsutsui clan, the young and inexperienced chieftain chose freedom. It was a noble choice. Yet it was also with a deep sense of foreboding that the next day Ieyoshi dispatched a messenger to Shigisan castle with a letter declaring the Yagyū on Hisahide's side.

Wounded

Hisahide, on his part, was delighted with the Yagyū's defection. They had a reputation on the battlefield that reached well beyond Yamato's borders. Moreover, they knew the local terrain among the eastern Yoshino Mountains and their *shinobi*'s talent for gathering intelligence was second to none. Aware of what a valuable asset they would prove in his efforts to topple the Tsutsui, he quickly made good on his promise. Their estate was tripled, and as one of his chief retainers, Muneyoshi received an additional stipend of two thousand *koku* a year.

It wasn't long after the Yagyū had gone over to Hisahide that the latter realized his plan by building a magnificent castle at Tamonyama. Neither cost nor labor was spared. The whole hill was reinforced with stones, while a tiled structure ran around its circumference, giving its defenders shelter from arrows and fire throughout. Like Shigisan it had a four-storied donjon, a feature only shared with Azuchi castle. Its wide inner court was graced with a number of luxurious buildings, including a huge *goten*, Hisahide's official dwelling when in residence. Its interiors were of such dazzling splendor that many claimed they surpassed even the beauty of the imperial court.[8]

As one of Hisahide's chief vassals, Muneyoshi was invited to build a residence within the walls of Tamonyama castle, where he could sojourn whenever he was called upon to attend a council of elders. Yet it wasn't long after his clan had joined Hisahide's side, that Muneyoshi began to have serious misgivings about his clan's defection. Somehow it seemed that, despite their sumptuous lifestyle and rewards, a dark shadow hung over anything they did. While he himself had been a prisoner at Tsutsui castle, his clan had fought many a battle on behalf of the Tsutsui to help pacify the region. Sure, they had lost men, yet it had always been in the knowledge that their overlord had done all he could to save lives. Now, fighting on behalf of Hisahide, they had lost more men in a year than they had lost in a decade on behalf of the Tsutsui. Often it was as a result of needless risks taken by Hisahide's generals, who seemed unable to persuade their master of the recklessness of his goals.

Nor did Hisahide's behavior in private inspire the warrior with much confidence. Suffering from palsy, the first thing on the warlord's mind each morning was to have his surgeon burn moxy on the crown of his head to relieve the symptoms. Much of the rest of the day he would spend in conducting elaborate tea ceremonies with dignitaries from the imperial court in Kyoto. Even when encamped for battle he kept up this extravagant lifestyle, spending hours with his beloved collection of tea utensils, leaving his generals to pour over the battle maps and work out the strategies by which his ambitious goals were to be realized.

It was on one such campaign that Muneyoshi and his men were crossing the Tōno Pass, deep among the Yoshino Mountains, when they were ambushed by a group of Tōda archers hiding among the dense woods flanking the narrow road. Muneyoshi, who was riding up front, was struck in the left hand. Frightened by its master's sudden jerk on the reigns, his horse buckled, throwing Muneyoshi to the ground, and leaving him exposed to the enemy, who were now rapidly descending from the slopes. For a brief moment his fate seemed sealed, when two of his men, Matsuda Genjirō and Torii Sagami, came to his rescue and managed to bring him to safety. It had been a close call, impressing on the young chieftain more than ever that fortune had left him.

CHAPTER 3

While the Tsutsui were deprived of a forceful leader, Hisahide rapidly fastened his hold over Yamato Province. The secret behind his rise to prominence was the powerful Miyoshi clan. At the beginning of the sixteenth century, they had embarked with a large force from their stronghold of Shōzui on the eastern shore of Shikoku and landed at the port of Sakai. From there they widened their sphere of influence by capturing and building castles throughout the region and doing battle with local potentates. It had been in one of these, the Battle at the Taihei temple, that they had routed and killed the governor of Kawachi, Kizawa Nagamasa, the Yagyū's former ally.

At that time they were still led by Miyoshi Chōkei. Though a warlord in the standard mold of the Warring States period, Chōkei had some redeeming qualities. He was a shrewd and able administrator, and widely respected. He had thrown himself up as the guardian of the infant Shōgun, Ashikaga Yoshiteru, and become one of the first warlords in the region to be converted to Christianity by the Portuguese missionary Caspar Vilela when the latter visited the capital in 1559. Chōkei's chief ambition was to bring the Home Provinces under his control, and one of the men instrumental in realizing his plans was his private secretary, the shrewd and wily Matsunaga Hisahide.

Hisahide had insinuated himself into his influential position by marrying Chōkei's daughter. In spite—or perhaps because—of his commercial background Hisahide displayed a remarkable talent for playing one chieftain out against the other, so that one by one their domains fell into his hand. In 1553, by way of reward, he was appointed keeper of Takiyama castle in the province of Settsu, the first Home Province to be brought under Miyoshi control.

That same year Hisahide helped Chōkei subdue Akutagawa castle, situated along the border with Kawachi. That province became the next field on the board of the Miyoshi's expansionist chess game. And here, too, he was successful; by the end of the decade, he had captured Shigisan castle. During the decade since it's founder's demise, the castle had laid derelict, falling prey to the encroaching undergrowth. Using his growing financial clout, Hisahide began extensive renovations, adding a four-storied donjon and turning the castle into one of the most prominent in the region.

Using Chōkei's good reputation, Hisahide began to dispatch secret missives to local chieftains, encouraging them to join the Miyoshi in their campaign to topple the Tsutsui from power and regain their independence. Joined by clans like the Yagyū, he crossed the border and launched a massive campaign into Yamato. Then, from his imposing new fortress of Tamonyama, he began to put pressure on the Tsutsui. His initial strategy wasn't to attack their castle outright, but to weaken them by subduing or winning over their vassals throughout the region.

Though effective, this strategy took time, but it was hastened when, in 1564, Tsutsui Junsei died at Sakai a broken and disillusioned man. His son Junkei, though only fifteen years old, did all he could to hold on to his headquarters of Tsutsui castle. But when, in the winter of 1565, it came under attack of Hisahide's forces, he fled and fell back on Fuse castle, in Katsuragi, a small town along the border with Kawachi.

All this was illustrative of the inexorable current of the times, of the frightening ease and ever growing pace with which one warlord deposed another, and of the depth to which the once so mighty institution of the Bakufu had sunk. In the same way, powerful Shōguns had reduced the emperor to little more than a mascot during the tenth century, ruthless and ambitious warlords had now reduced the Shōguns to mere pawns in their self-seeking schemes.

Hisahide's hegemony did sound in a period of relative calm for those who dwelled in Yamato. It was a period in which the local clans could recover, rebuild their castles, resow their crops, and replenish their stores for conflicts to come. It was also a time in which to perfect their art, an art honed and molded to new and more effective forms in the countless battles they had fought over the preceding two centuries.

An Invitation

It was with a raised eyebrow that, one early morning, in the early spring of 1563, Muneyoshi opened the seal of a letter that had just been delivered to him by a messenger on foot. It was a letter from his old teacher and friend Hōzōin In'ei, inviting him to a contest with a man by the name of Kamiizumi Ise no Kami Nobutsuna, a swordsman from the northern province of Kōzuke and the founder of the Shinkage-*ryū*.

Muneyoshi had never met Nobutsuna, nor seen the Shinkage-*ryū* in action, yet he was confident he would win; over the years he had engaged in many a contest and not once had he been defeated. His wounded hand still gave him some trouble, especially with techniques like the *byōbu-gaeshi*, in which the left hand guided the blade. Yet even with his current handicap, he could deal with this swordsman from Kōzuke—or any other swordsman from any other part of the country for that matter.

Early next morning, and in high spirits, Muneyoshi told his servants to collect his gear and saddle his horse. Spurring on his horse, he set out in a gallop along the Yagyū Kaidō, the ancient and meandering road connecting the village of Yagyū with the temple town of Nara. He couldn't wait to meet and— so he firmly believed—defeat this swordsman from Kōzuke.

The Duel

Muneyoshi wasn't the only local warrior who had been invited by In'ei. Dozens of warriors had already gathered in the wide courtyard of the Hōzō monastery.[1] Some of them were going through practice routines, others were oiling the blades of their weapons in quiet meditation, or conversing with each other in subdued voices. Most of them were warrior monks from affiliated temples, but there were also a number of swordsmen, some from as far afield as Kyūshū. One of them Muneyoshi recognized as a promising young swordsman by the name of Marume Kurando no Suke Nagayoshi. He was a practitioner of the Tai-*ryū*, and had been studying with In'ei for some months now. He had seen him practice and it was clear that only few could equal his speed with the *katana*. He was stunned, therefore, to hear that Nagayoshi had become one of Nobutsuna's followers after he had been squarely defeated in a *taryū shiai* with one of his companions earlier that morning.

'Muneyoshi-*dono!*' In'ei welcomed his old friend, 'come and join us for a cup of tea and meet master Izumi Ise no Kami Nobutsuna from Kōzuke.'

Nobutsuna, who had been standing on the temple's inner court with two other men, cut an impressive figure. He stood six feet tall and wore a long silk gown, quite similar to those worn by the Chinese merchants living in Sakai. Unlike most swordsmen, he wore just one *katana*, a four feet long *tachi*. Though already in his fifties, he was extremely handsome and exuded a natural confidence that undoubtedly made him popular with the opposite sex. He had thick, distinct eyebrows set over fierce eyes, whose whites stood out all the more against his bronzed tan. He had long hair, tied up in a neat knot at the top of his head. Muneyoshi could hardly follow a word Nobutsuna was saying, as he spoke in a thick Northern accent. Yet as they talked he warmed to the warrior, and wanted to know more about his style of fencing.

'I've come to Nara to brush up my skills with the *yari*,' Nobutsuna explained as the five men sat down around the small *hibachi* and had their cups filled by one of In'ei's acolytes.

In'ei smiled. 'Your skills with the *yari* need no brushing up, Nobutsuna-*dono*. Are you not known throughout the realm as one of the Nagano Jūroku no Yari, the Sixteen Lances of Nagano?'

Nobutsuna bowed politely and continued. 'Let me introduce my two companions, who have traveled down with me from Kōzuke. This here is Jingo Itō no Kami Muneharu...He is the son of a samurai from the village of Hachiōji, some twenty miles west of Edo...And this here is Hikida Bungorō Kagetomo... He hails from Ishikawa, on Japan's west coast...He is related to me through his mother, my sister-in-law.'

Listening to the warrior, it struck Muneyoshi that, though possessed of an imposing physical presence, Nobutsuna was a thoughtful and soft-spoken man—a man who clearly weighed his words before he uttered them and felt no need to ad force when he finally did.

Muneyoshi was all the more disappointed when, having looked him over carefully, Nobutsuna quietly turned to In'ei and said, 'I suggest you pit Master Muneyoshi against Bungorō.' Given his reputation as one of the Home Province's master swordsman, the thirty-seven years old Muneyoshi had naturally assumed that Nobutsuna would do him the honor of dueling with him in person. To have to defer to one of his disciples like the young warrior from Kyūshū felt like a snub, if not an outright insult. Moreover, Bungorō struck him as a bit of a ruffian. He wore his hair unkempt. Even on his neck it spread, dense and dark, all the way down to his bulging shoulders. He seemed a typical northerner, smelling like one and spitting freely in public after having quite audibly cleared his throat. Yet something in Nobutsuna's demeanor, a man almost twice their age, made Muneyoshi acquiesce and take up his position opposite the ruffian from Ishikawa.

It was immediately clear to Muneyoshi that he was dealing with a fundamentally different style of fencing. Instead of assuming the regular *kamae*, in which one held the *katana* at the center of the body, its blade upright, Bungorō held his *bokken* at the height of his right shoulder, the sharp edge of the blade facing outward, but its tip trained on Muneyoshi's throat as if drawn there by an irresistible force. He didn't bat an eye but remained still as if he were luring a fish to its bait. Muneyoshi felt a slight irritation well up inside of him as he sought to accommodate this exotic and strangely unsettling *kamae*, adjusting the angle of his *bokken* to parry a possible attack from the side.

Bungorō didn't change his stance. All that moved was one of his bushy eyebrows as he calmly said, '*Yagyū dono, sono kamae warushū de gozaru*,' (Master Yagyū, that is a poor *kamae*). Bungoro's words had the same effect on Muneyoshi as if he were struck in the face. Raising his *bokken* above his head, he brought it down with all his might on the head of his opponent. But the Kantō warrior swiftly moved aside as Muneyoshi's *bokken* hit the ground. Again Muneyoshi charged, but again the ruffian outmaneuvered him, this time striking him on his painful left hand, almost causing him to lose his grip on his *bokken*.

'*Matte!*' Nobutsuna's forceful voice rang out across the inner court. Summoning Bungorō to withdraw, he proceeded to take his place opposite Muneyoshi but did so empty-handed.

Frustrated by his embarrassing defeat at Bungorō's hands and vexed by the unassuming confidence with which the old man had intervened, Muneyoshi accepted Nobutsuna's challenge and charged forthwith. Again he raised his *bokken*, high above his head this time and bringing it down on Nobutsuna's left shoulder. Yet the very moment the wood was about to strike he felt the iron grip of the old man's hand wrest the weapon from his hands as he tumbled headlong into the dust.

Even before Muneyoshi had the time to recover and get up, Nobutsuna had moved in on him, not to attack, but to help him to his feet. Noticing the fresh scar on Muneyoshi's left hand he frowned and, almost as if to himself, noted, 'Any battle scar will injure one's ability with the *katana*.'

It was without any sense of glee that Nobutsuna led the dazzled Yamato warrior back toward the others for another cup of green tea. 'That,' he explained, 'was the *mutōtori*, a technique invented by Aisu Ikō...He hailed from Nansei, a small port on the Shima Peninsula, only a few days travel east from here. I studied under him as a young man...He is long dead now, but through me his Kage-*ryū* lives on, though I have had the audacity to rename it the Shinkage-*ryū*, or New Shadow school of fencing.'[2]

Muneyoshi was fascinated by the northerner—and even more so by his Shinkage-*ryū*. When he learned that Nobutsuna intended to stay in the area for the next few months, he immediately offered him and his companions to come and stay at Yagyū castle. There they could stay as long as they pleased. They could also—so he fervently hoped—give him a deeper understanding of the Shinkage-*ryū*.

Minowa Castle

Nobutsuna wasn't a man of many words, but over the course of the next months, as he and his two disciples enjoyed the hospitality of their grateful host, the old warrior gradually began to open up. Winter had already set in when, after a long day of training, Muneyoshi and Nobutsuna sat down to enjoy the warmth of the *hibachi*. Warming his hands on the small stove, the old man sighed and began to talk as he had not done before, only taking long pauses to collect his thoughts. 'Like you, I was once the master of my own domain. My ancestors belonged to the Ōgo, a clan of Ashikaga descent. They hailed from Tōtomi, on the east coast...The great upheavals of the Ōnin Rebellion caused them to move to Kōzuke, where they settled just north of Umayabashi. I myself was born and raised at Ōgo castle, at the southern foot of Mount Akagi.

'Being the head of only a minor clan, I owed allegiance to the Nagano, whose headquarters of Minowa castle stood on the other side of the Tone River[3]...The Nagano then were still led by Lord Nagano Narimasa, an experienced and able chieftain, who successfully withstood attacks by far more powerful clans.'

Nobutsuna paused for a while as he looked wistfully at the smoldering flames. 'All that changed in the summer of 1561, when Narimasa passed away, leaving his vast domain to his seventeen-year-old son, Narimori. The clan elders sought to keep Lord Narimasa's death secret...But word must have gotten out and reached Takeda Shingen, for early in January of 1563 he marched into Kōzuke and laid siege to Minowa castle.

'Luckily, news of Shingen's approach had reached us well before the end of the previous year. This gave us some two months to reinforce the castle's defenses, stock up on provisions, and rally our men...We had some great warriors among us—

men like Fujii Bungo, Akana Buzen, Terao Bingo, and Nagano Shuzen—all battle-hardened men who had served Narimori's father in numerous battles. I too abandoned Ōgo castle and put my men at Narimori's disposal.

'Minowa was a formidable castle. Yet it had one weak point. Built on rocks, it didn't possess a well and we had to draw water from a small brook from outside its walls…It wasn't long before Shingen discovered the stream and had it diverted, away from the castle, so as to deprive us of our most vital lifeline.

'For two months we held out like this, saving each drop of water we could spare. Had it been late spring, the rainy season would have saved us. In the end, we faced only two options: surrender or make a last stand…And thus, on February 22, Lord Narimori ordered the gates to be opened, and we all stormed out in a final attempt to break through the ranks of Shingen's forces.

'Almost immediately young Lord Narimori was cut down. Only a few of us were able to break through the enemy line, including my companions, Bungorō, and Muneharu…I myself was badly wounded. But with their help, we managed to reach the village of Kiryū, some twenty miles east of Umayabashi. There we found refuge at Kiryū castle, the stronghold of Kiryū Suketsuna, an ally of the Nagano clan.

'For several weeks we stayed at Kiryū castle, nursing our wounds…And it was then that I made up my mind to spend the rest of my life in *musha shugyō*.' Nobutsuna looked intently at Muneyoshi as he concluded, 'I am an old man now. Who knows how many years are left to me here on earth?…I want to put the time that remains to me to good use; to dedicate it to the perfection and spread of the Shinkage-*ryū*; to pass it on to the next generation: it has saved my life and will save the lives of all who master it.'

Inka

Nobutsuna remained Muneyoshi's guest for far longer than both men expected.[4] For both it proved to be a deeply rewarding period: for Nobutsuna in that he was able to impart his Shinkage school of fencing to such a talented pupil; for Muneyoshi in that he was able to absorb all the tenets and intricacies of this, to him, new and revolutionary school of swordsmanship.

Two years the two new-found friends had spent in intense training when, on the first day of April, 1565, during a small ceremony held at Yagyū castle, Nobutsuna granted his disciple a so-called *inkajō*, a formal document by which a master certified that his pupil had reached maturity in training. It read:

> Since my early youth, I have sought to master the arts of swordsmanship and military tactics, exploring the *okugi* of various schools. I meditated and practiced day and night, until the gods enabled me to found the Shinkage-*ryū*. When I traveled down to Kyoto in my quest to propagate my school of fencing throughout the land I unexpectedly met you. And you were solicitous and sincere in many ways, so that it is hard to find the right words to express my gratitude. I thus declare that I have, without any omissions, transmitted to you my full knowledge of the Shinkage school of fencing.

To celebrate the occasion, Nobutsuna bestowed on Muneyoshi the *tachi* he had been wearing during their first encounter at the Hōzō monastery. It was a beautiful and formidable weapon; forged by Izumo no Kami Naganori, its blade measured more than four feet, its hilt another two.

It wasn't long after, that Nobutsuna presented his friend with four scrolls. It was the *Kage-ryū no mokuroku*, a Catalogue of the Kage School of Fencing, in which he had recorded for posterity all the things his old master Aisu Ikō had taught him so many years ago. Opening the first scroll, Muneyoshi began to read. It revealed what had led the one-time pirate to turn his back on the sea and embark on a life of meditation and ascetic practice:

> When Ikō came to a province on the island of Kyūshū, there was a shrine called the Great Gongen of Udo. There, he confined himself for thirty-seven days in devout prayer that he might spread his school under the heavens. By thus deeply immersing himself in prayer, he achieved divine knowledge. On the seventeenth day, he was again immersed in prayer before the altar when an old man came to him, saying that east from there was a warrior whose name was Sumiyoshi and that he should slay him. Ikō, without further ado, went to the house of Sumiyoshi and stated his purpose. Sumiyoshi respectfully listened and desired to meet him in a duel, upon which Ikō, possessing the secret art attained in meditation, defeated him. By this then his name was known to the four winds and his fame spread throughout Kyūshū.

Engrossed in reading Muneyoshi suddenly felt Nobutsuna's hand on his wrist. 'I will be leaving you presently,' the old warrior said softly. 'The time has come for me to continue on my *musha shugyō* and spread my school to other parts of the realm...I have been invited by an old friend of mine, Master

71

Yamanashi Tokitsugu, to come to Kyoto. I look very much forward to seeing him again, for he is a man of many talents.'[5]

Nobutsuna's departure left a deep void among the members of the Yagyū clan, but not in Muneyoshi's heart. Reading his friend's *Kage-ryū no mokuroku*, he thought about his own clan's experience in an age of turmoil. Like Nobutsuna, his father had fought hard to maintain his independence. To regain it, Muneyoshi had chosen the side of Matsunaga Hisahide. Yet with every passing year, he had found his vassalage to Hisahide harder to stomach. Here was a man who spent his idle hours trying to lengthen the life of his pet crickets, yet at the same time had no qualms in shortening the lives of those poor peasants who couldn't pay his tax levies. It wasn't so much the penalty as the pleasure Hisahide derived from them that appalled the warrior. For he would have the hapless men put on a straw raincoat and had his men set it alight. Was it because of Hisahide's same creepy obsession with insects, he wondered, that he called it the *mino-mushi odori*? Yet how could one sit, drink, and cheer a man on as he writhed and contorted with pain in his final death-throws? Muneyoshi felt in the pit of his stomach that sooner rather than later he would be faced with another stark choice—or he and his clansmen too might be forced to join in Hisahide's macabre 'dance of the raincoat bugs.'

CHAPTER 4

In 1563, one year before his death, his health already rapidly declining, Miyoshi Chōkei appointed his eleven-year-old son, Yoshioki, as his sole and only heir. He made all his counselors, including Hisahide, promise to look after his son until he would come of age and could take over the reins of power. Yet soon after Chōkei's death, the young boy was struck by an inexplicable affliction to which he succumbed within days. Far from mourning the loss of his young lord, Hisahide seemed to delight in the boy's demise. As the most influential man among the Miyoshi leadership, he began to position himself to seize control of the Bakufu.

On June 17, 1565, following a feigned visit to Kyoto's Kiyomizu temple, Hisahide's son, Hisamichi, led a group of two hundred warriors toward Nijō castle, the residence of Shōgun Yoshiteru. Anticipating just such an attack, Yoshiteru had spent much of the previous year strengthening the castle's defenses, deepening its moats and reinforcing its walls. Only the huge gate doors were not yet completed. And it was through these that Hisamichi and his henchmen forced their way into the castle's compound and demanded an audience with the Shōgun. Even as the Shōgun's counselors were hurrying to and fro, Hisamichi's riflemen fired on the Shōgunal compound. Mortified at his failure to keep the assailants out, the Shōgun's head of guards disemboweled himself. Yoshiteru, who had practiced the art of swordsmanship under the great Tsukahara Bokuden, was determined not to go without a fight. Planting his best swords in the tatami *floor of his residence, he stood his ground until all around him had fallen. Finally, outnumbered and overwhelmed, he withdrew to his quarters where, along with his mother, he committed ritual suicide.*

Though perpetrated by his son, the plan had been hatched by Hisahide. It was a foul deed, made all the more contemptible by the threaths and intimidations to which Hisahide subjected those who had been close and loyal to Yoshiteru. The courtiers were so terrified that only a few monks from the Shōkoku temple were present at the former Shōgun's funeral. Hisahide's act of brutal treachery also lent ample credence to the stubborn rumor doing the rounds in Kyoto that Chōkei's son had not died of natural causes at all, but that he had been poisoned by one of Hisahide's henchmen.

Rumor seemed to turn to fact when, shortly after this gruesome episode, Hisahide had Yoshiteru's brother, Shūkō, murdered along with his page while on their way to the capital to visit Yoshiteru's grave. Only the Shōgun's youngest brother, the twenty-eight-year-old monk Kakkei, was left alive. He was placed under house arrest at the Kōfuku's Ichijō-in, the monastery he had entered when only five years old and of which he was now the head abbot.

Hisahide was anything if not shrewd. Though a fervent supporter of the rivaling Nichiren sect, he was well aware of the sway the Kōfuku temple still held over the clans in the Yamato basin; he had only been able to establish himself in Yamato by carefully steering clear from the temple. Were he to kill Kakkei now, he was bound to break his fragile peace with the Buddhist church. He knew such an act would irrevocably destroy the last notion among its patrons that his rule had any religious sanction, incurring the undivided wrath of all the clans that patronized the Kōfuku temple, as well as its large army of sōhei.

All these events put the Yagyū in an increasingly difficult position. As the direct descendants of the Sugawara, they had always sought to uphold the realm's two great pillars: the imperial court and the Buddhist church. Those pillars were now being consumed by the insatiable flames of endemic warfare. Ironically, it was in exactly such a lawless world, a world that imposed no constraints on those who lusted for power, that men like Matsunaga Hisahide did well for themselves.

Momiji Yashiki

Shortly after Nobutsuna's departure, Muneyoshi set about building a *yashiki* on the eastern side his domain. It was a labor of love, a spacious building, built in the *sukiya* tradition. It was skirted by a wide veranda that, on the southern side, gave way onto a small lake among the woods. Though in no way fortified, it used the latest *shinobi* countermeasures against intruders. To enter it one had to cross a large field of course gravel, alerting its occupants of someone's approach. The veranda's floorboards were not fixed but carried by metal hinges that emitted a squeaking noise whenever one stepped on one. There were many hidden doors, and each room had a secret armory stashed with weapons. He personally oversaw the building's construction, which helped to divert his mind from the absence of his new-won friend from Kōzuke.

There was another, more important reason why he had decided on its construction. Though the Yagyū now had their own *yashiki* on the grounds of Tamonyama castle, Muneyoshi only stayed there when he absolutely had to. He hated the place. Its opulence oppressed him, especially when he considered it had been built on the backs of a starving peasantry, many of whom were unable to pay Hisahide's heavy taxes. Their regular executions on the castle's wide forecourt cast a grim spell on the place, for the first thing that greeted one were the heads of these innocent victims—men and women alike—put on display in the scorching sun to warn all those who opposed his rule.

Having a *yashiki* away from Tamonyama castle gave Muneyoshi the sense that he had at least distanced himself from Hisahide and his evil ways. He had seen the corrupting influence the cruelty and opulence could have on those who served under Hisahide. Like, for instance, his uncle Shigeyoshi. As of late, he had become indulgent, spending less and less time in practice, and more and more in the pursuit of *Cha no Yū*, the Art of Tea. He had adopted the Buddhist name Shōginan and, like his idol, had begun sporting the outlandish garments brought by the Portuguese. It seemed that he cared more for a single tea utensil than the life of the Shōgun and his family. Most worryingly, he had gradually gone from being a proud warrior to a ruthless assassin, willing to do his master's bidding, no matter how depraved. Just recently, he had reached a point beyond redemption. He had abetted in the murder of the sitting Shōgun and helped to keep his successor from assuming his rightful position—merely in reward for material wealth. Now he had been put in charge of the men guarding Kakkei, the Shōgun's only remaining brother, who was being kept under house arrest at the Ichijō monastery, one of the many temples on the grounds of the Kōfuku temple.

How different it had been when Muneyoshi was still a young man, and Shigeyoshi and his father had taught him the art of swordsmanship. Time and time again Shigeyoshi had put Muneyoshi through the paces, first on the basics, then on to the more difficult techniques. How Muneyoshi had looked up to his uncle then, at that time one of the most accomplished swordsmen in the region. Then he had still worn a simple *karusan hakama*, topped with a plain *uwagi* and no *haori*, his tastes and talk as yet unaffected by the pernicious influence of men of wealth and power. Had it not been for Shigeyoshi's groundwork, the Yagyū-ryū never would have acquired the fame it now enjoyed, even with Nobutsuna's revolutionary influence.

Muneyoshi felt better by having some distance between himself and Tamonyama castle. For the time being, his new *yashiki* gave him a place to withdraw to. It was only a first step. Sooner or later he would have to decide what to do about his fateful pact with Hisahide. But he had to be patient. He had to bide his time, wait for an opportunity to present itself.

Set amid a section of the woods dominated by maple trees, he had named it Momiji (Maple Tree) *yashiki*. To reach it one had to walk down from Yagyū castle and cross the Hakusa River by way of the small bridge his father had erected when he had built Yagyū castle. Hidden among dense primeval forest the Momiji *yashiki* was a place of spiritual retreat, a place where he could spend weeks by himself, or in the company of friends. From there, he would go on long walks through the forest for quiet meditation, or he would retreat to his study overlooking the lake. There, at a small desk that had belonged to his great-grandfather, he would rub some ink on his old ink stone and take out a sheet of locally made *washi*, dip his brush in the black film of ink, and work on the *Gyokuei shūi*, the ancient family records of the Yagyū clan.

It had been partly to keep himself busy that, following the ambush at Tōnomine, he had begun on the record's compilation. By now the wound in his left hand had largely healed, but it had lost much of its strength. The handicap didn't affect him when fighting on horseback, when one brandished a *katana* in one hand, but on foot, when the *katana* was held with both hands, it diminished his ability to engage in man-to-man combat. When writing, he could rest his ailing left hand on the soft sheets of hand-made paper as the other wielded the brush.

For several weeks Muneyoshi remained at the Yagyū domain, seeking wisdom in meditation and study amid the stillness of his Momiji *yashiki*, enjoying its smell of new-sawn cedar and fresh *tatami*, the sound of the wind in the high trees, the wood's filtered light playing on the surface of the lake. Yet he still found it hard to find peace within himself, for his mind remained afflicted by the great dilemma that confronted his clan.

A Letter

It was while Muneyoshi was working on the *Gyokuei shūi* that, in the middle of August 1565, one of his servants came down from Yagyū castle with a letter. It was from Kamiizumi Nobutsuna. Since his arrival in the capital, the swordsman's star had rapidly risen. His friend, Yamanashi Tokitsugu, had introduced him at the Shōgunal court for a demonstration. A fervent practitioner himself, Yoshiteru had been impressed with Nobutsuna's art, so much so that he had presented him with a certificate of merit and expressed his wish to become a student of the Shinkage school of swordsmanship.

Now the Shōgun was dead, treacherously slain by Hisahide's henchmen. It was, in Nobutsuna's words, 'an unjustifiable and utter outrage.' Yet, even as he was writing his letter, efforts were underway to return the shogunate to Yoshiteru's one surviving brother, Kakkei, who was still imprisoned at the Kōfuku-*ji*'s Ichijō monastery. These efforts were led by Wada Koremasa, a member of the famous Rokkaku-shi from Ōmi province, a powerful clan that had long served the Ashikaga Shōgunate. Koremasa had only narrowly escaped Hisahide's henchmen himself, withdrawing to his hometown of Wada, some twenty miles north-east of Yagyū castle. From there he had won the support of other chieftains. Together they had hatched a plan to liberate Kakkei from captivity and escort him to the safety of Koremasa's Wadakan headquarters.

Nobutsuna wrote that he was well aware that Muneyoshi was one of Hisahide's vassals, yet implored his friend to help rescue Kakkei. The only feasible way to reach the Ichijō monastery was by way of the Yagyū Kaidō, the shortest route from Nara to Kasagi, which lay on the border with Ōmi. Nobutsuna and Muneyoshi had often walked it together since they first met in duel at the Hōzō monastery. Being a small and winding road, it was good enough for a small band of men to pass, yet narrow enough to slow down an army sent in pursuit. It would enable them to reach Nara unnoticed and smuggle Kakkei out of the Ichijō monastery under the cover of night. And here Muneyoshi's help was vital. For he held the key to Kakkei's escape: his uncle, Shigeyoshi; the man in charge of Kakkei's wardens. There would be no opposition from the Ichijō monastery. Kakkei was much loved by the Buddhist community, and its monks were bound to help in his release. They were aiming for the end of August, which was well before the season of the great typhoons, so they could be quite certain of a cloudless night.

Muneyoshi only had to read Nobutsuna's letter once to know what he must do. Involving his uncle wasn't an option; Shigeyoshi couldn't be trusted, not anymore. It pained him that he would have to betray a member of his clan. Yet had it not been for Shigeyoshi's adoration of Hisahide, they might never have been sucked into that vortex of internecine rivalry that was now bringing Yamato and the realm to the brink of ruin. The only way to make their plan work was to make sure his uncle was away from the temple on the night they would strike.

Luckily Shigeyoshi didn't take his assignment too seriously. Spending most nights in the pursuit of women and liquor, he usually left only a few regular soldiers behind to watch over the monk. Bored with the temple town's nonexistent nightlife, he often ordered his page to bring his horse in the late afternoon and set off for Kyoto to visit one of the many brothels around the famous Gion shrine. He would usually return late the next morning, disheveled and reeking from a night of carousing.

There were, Muneyoshi knew, a few days in August that Shigeyoshi was guaranteed to be in the capital: the days of the Rokusai Nenbutsu festival.[1] Celebrated throughout the realm in colorful parades, in the capital it had grown into lavish affairs that lasted to deep in the night. In Kyoto the festival fell on the eighth, the fourteenth, the fifteenth, the twenty-third, the twenty-ninth and the thirtieth of August. The festival of the fifteenth had just been held the day before. This meant there were still three days on which they could carry out their plan.

In his reply to Nobutsuna, Muneyoshi explained his plan and suggested that they pick the first best day the weather was fair, for the moon was already waxing.

Kakkei

On the hot and perfectly cloudless summer evening of August 23, 1565, a small group of determined men, all on horseback, reached Yagyū village. They were met by an elated Muneyoshi. To his delight, his friend Nobutsuna was among the party. Though in his fifties it seemed age had no sway over the Kantō warrior, for there was no trace of it in his demeanor, and his movements were as confident and smooth as the day they had met in duel at the Hōzōin.

'We have just this one chance,' Nobutsuna said as they set off along the Yagyū Kaidō.

'I know...' said Muneyoshi pensively. 'Are we to fail, Kakkei will almost certainly be moved to Tamonyama castle, from where there is no chance of escape.'

It was already five o'clock, well into the hour of the Tiger, that the small band of men reached the Kasuga Taisha on Nara's eastern outskirts. From there they made their way by foot through the woods to the grounds of the Kōfuku temple, which lay a few miles west of the famous shrine. Its temple grounds were vast. Enclosed by a high wall that ran for two miles on all four sides, it housed some fifty monasteries, as well as *yashiki* and pagodas. To complicate matters, the Ichijō monastery stood in the ground's far south-western corner. Once they had made their way across the grounds, they would have to negotiate a maze of interconnected and elevated passageways.

Their inside contact, a Yagyū *shinobi*, was already waiting at a small entrance at the southern corner of the compound's eastern wall. 'There are only a few guards on duty,' he whispered. 'Kakkei is waiting in his *yashiki*, dressed to travel.'

Muneyoshi and Nobutsuna slipped in and quietly made their way across the grounds. It was now well after midnight, and the temple's massive dark silhouette stood out sharply against a star-lit sky. There was no sign of life; the only sound the incessant hum of the summer cicadas. Soon the air would be filled with the bird's morning chorus. By then they should be well on their way toward Kasagi.

After a few tense minutes, they reached the Golden Hall, which stood on the southern end of the compound's central axis. Tracing its huge walls, they finally reached the western corner. It was only a few dozen yards from there to the small *yashiki* where Kakkei was waiting.

They could make out just two of Shigeyoshi's guards, posted at the *yashiki*'s entrance. Equally bored with temple life, they were sitting on the *yashiki*'s wide veranda, occasionally laughing as they boasted of their own nightly exploits during the previous Rokusai Nenbutsu. In an instant the two swordsmen were upon them, silencing them with a short but decisive cut across the throat with their *wakizashi*.

Freedom

That morning the massive roof of the Kōfuku temple seemed to glow as it was hit by the first rays of a glorious morning sun. By then the small band of men was already far away from Nara. They had safely reached Kasagi, from where they were being ferried across the restless water of the Kizu River.

Muneyoshi smiled to himself as he watched Kakkei board the small boat. How similar were the name Kakkei and the adjective *kokkei* (comical). And how apt! Only used to temple life, the stocky monk had cut a comic figure astride a horse as he bobbed up and down uncomfortably in his saddle, especially among the rough and lean-looking warriors. Yet he was clearly of noble blood, and proud of it too. As soon as they had left the temple enclosure, he had insisted on donning his Buddhist robes—he would travel as the future Shōgun, not as a fugitive monk.

Two days later, at the end of a makeshift ceremony at Wada Koremasa's Wadakan, Kakkei was proclaimed the fifteenth Shōgun of the Ashikaga Shōgunate under the name of Ashikaga Yoshiaki. It was only a symbolic gesture: there were no representatives from the imperial court to sanctify the investiture. Nobutsuna had sought in vain to convince his friend, Tokitsugu, to act as an envoy for the imperial court. The latter had declined. Living in the capital, he had already been prevailed upon by Hisahide's party to conduct various ceremonies on behalf of their protege, Yoshihide. Yet all who were present at that solemn occasion fervently believed it was just a matter of time before Yoshiaki would be formally recognized as the rightful head of the Ashikaga Bakufu. The huge question was how?

CHAPTER 5

Throughout 1566 the forces of Hisahide and his many enemies clashed in Settsu and Yamashiro. By the next year, everything pointed to a final confrontation in Yamato. By now Hisahide was not just facing his former allies, the Miyoshi, who had grown tired of his constant scheming. The Tsutsui, too, had joined the fray. Having fallen back on Fuse castle, along the border with Kawachi province, they held on tenaciously to their last remaining foothold in the province they once ruled. They were now led by the twenty-year-old Junkei, and of all Hisahide's enemies, Junkei's hatred toward the new Yamato warlord ran deepest.

A devout Buddhist, Junkei took great pride in his clan's traditional role as shuto *to the Kōfuku temple. At a young age, he had often visited his uncle, Junsei, when he served as* kanpu-shuto, *managing one of the temple's main administrative units, as his ancestors had done before him. On those occasions, he would take up residence in one of the Four Lodges. Situated in Nara's Seventh Zone, these grand and ancient buildings were reserved solely for the* shuto, *the clans that had grown out of the temple's* sōhei *and had been its staunchest patrons ever since.*

In exile, the Tsutsui clan's links with the Kōfuku temple had been rudely severed. To the young Junkei, steeped in tradition, it felt as if he had lost a limb. The pain forced the young chieftain to grow up fast, even more so as he saw his uncle grow increasingly despondent. It seemed that with every new atrocity by Hisahide, Junsei's grip on events in Yamato slipped, until at last his spirit and will to live had left him.

Picking up the reigns on his uncle's death, Junkei's first priority was to regain his family stronghold of Tsutsui castle, and it was here that the bold seventeen-year-old warrior-monk achieved his first victory. On June 25, 1566, following a siege of several weeks, he evicted Hisahide's forces from the castle, regaining a foothold in Yamato. For the Tsutsui, it was a victory of great symbolic significance, one that could not have been achieved without the help of Hisahide's former allies, the Miyoshi. Boosted by his victory, Junkei instinctively turned his sights on Nara, now the site of Hisahide's opulent headquarters of Tamonyama castle. If only he could drive the tyrant from Nara, he stood a good chance of regaining control over the whole province.

By the spring of 1567, the Miyoshi-Tsutsui alliance had grown to as many as ten thousand troops. They descended on Nara in the last week of May, setting up camp on a wide clearing on the town's southern outskirts. From there, they rapidly pushed toward the center. They reached Hayashikōji and were well within view of Junshō's former guesthouse when Hisahide's men set fire to the building. It looked like a one-off incident, but it had been done on Hisahide's direct orders. It set the tone for the next few months. One by one the imposing buildings that had graced the ancient temple town went up in smoke, sacrificed to Hisahide's ruthless scorched earth tactics. Some of the fires were caused by the negligence of his unruly troops, but most were deliberately started for tactical gain. More than a dozen of Nara's monasteries, temples, and temple halls were destroyed by fire, among them the ancient Kannon, Myōon, Myōkō, Tōkuzō, Konzō, and Hōtoku monasteries. With them had gone their libraries containing religious scrolls, paintings, and artifacts dating back a thousand years. At length, Hisahide's troops entrenched themselves around the Kaidan monastery, which stood at a stones-throw south-east from Tamonyama castle and on the eastern perimeter of the Tōdai temple grounds.

On the evening of June 1, Junkei's alliance pressed north toward the temple's towering Great Southern Gate where they exchanged fire with Hisahide's troops throughout the night. Junkei's allies were eager to occupy the grounds around the Tōdai temple, from where they could make a push for the castle. Junkei dithered. He well knew how sensitive the sects were about their hallowed grounds. Hisahide had turned the Kaidan monastery into a first defense for his precious castle, and its monks had been enraged, cursing all with the wrath of Buddha. Junkei wasn't a superstitious man but knew what it might do to their morale. Using his connections with the Kōfuku temple, he approached the head priest of the Tōdai temple and asked his permission to enter its grounds. He argued that he too had been incensed at Hisahide's blatant disregard of the temple's sanctity and promised to do everything in his power to desecrate its hallowed grounds. The priest obliged. On his invitation, a Miyoshi-Tsutsui contingent took up positions around the Daibutsuden, the towering Hall of the Great Buddha, which stood at the center of the temple complex and housed a giant bronze statue of Buddha.

Only a few hundred meters now separated the front lines of both camps. Yet despite the newly created frontier, the alliance made little further headway. At first, there were some victories on both sides, but then the fighting settled into a stalemate that dragged on for weeks and then months. And it soon became clear how far Hisahide was willing to go to save his precious castle.

Daibutsuden

Muneyoshi wasn't the nervous type, but the events of the last few weeks had gotten to him. For some reason, his left hand, which seemed to have healed just fine, had begun to act up with sudden, intense cramps, as if it refused to play a part in the sinister chain of events that had brought him here.

Chapter 5

It was November 10, and he and his men had taken up positions at the Kasuga Taisha. He had asked Hisahide to let them do so, partly because it gave him good access to the Yagyū Kaidō, partly because he could ensure the safety of the shrine his clan had so long patronized. From the shrine, it was just a few hundred yards to the Daibutsuden and the contingents of the Miyoshi-Tsutsui alliance, though they could not be seen from here. Set among dense forest that reached up to Nara's eastern outskirts, the shrine still seemed a blissful sanctuary amid the mayhem. The vast complex of structures was scattered among the forest over a large area of slightly undulating grounds as if they had been cast there by the gods. All that seemed to connect them was a web of narrow paths among the towering pines. Their hushed silence seemed to deny the battle that raged only a few miles away. If one didn't know any better one could be fooled into thinking the realm was at peace.

Today, his hand hurt more than ever. It couldn't be the cold. Though it was already November, the weather so far had been exceptionally mild. He sensed it had more to do with the war council at Tamonyama castle that morning. Hisahide had been in a foul mood. After six months of deadlock, the tyrant, used to getting his way, had become exasperated at the failure of his men to evict his enemies from the small temple town.

He had spent much of the time shouting down his generals, especially those who had allowed the enemy to reach the grounds of the Daibutsuden. Some had suggested launching an attack nevertheless. It had only made him angrier. 'Can't you see?' he had yelled at them, 'It is just what Junkei wants. Are we to move against them there, it will turn the temple—and its huge army of *sōhei*—agains us.'

He had been right, of course; if anything, he was shrewd. He had nevertheless insisted they enforce a victory, 'at any means.'

Just what those means should be, he didn't elaborate. Yet it was clear he was willing to sacrifice every last man—the whole of Nara—to save his decadent castle. Where was the logic in that? Even if Tamonyama castle remained standing, what would it preside over? A field of smoldering cinders?

Muneyoshi was roused from his musings by a dark figure approaching along one of the narrow paths among the trees. It was Nakanobō Morisuke, a descendant of the great Gensen, the brother of Muneyoshi's ancestor, Nagayoshi. Ever since the two brothers had taken up Emperor Go-Daigo's cause on Mount Kasagi, the two clans had remained close. Both had served the Tsutsui, and both had chosen Hisahide's side out of necessity. Morisuke, too, had attended that morning's council. He had long been Nara's *machi bugyō* and was just as appalled as Muneyoshi with the destruction that had been wrought on his town. 'How long can we go on like this?' he pondered out loud as both men sat down to warm themselves on the small fire Muneyoshi's men had made in the shrine's forecourt. 'There's just no way Hisahide can hope to enforce a victory—not as long as the Tsutsui remain entrenched at the Daibutsuden.'

Muneyoshi nodded. 'I'm not sure whether to admire or loathe Junkei's tactics,' he grumbled. 'Mind you, thus far it has worked. They say it is as if the great Buddha himself has taken his side, yet it feels more as if he has thrown himself on Buddha's mercy.'

'I don't think the Buddha approves of either man's methods,' Morisuke countered. 'Nor do I think he will protect Junkei and his men if Hisahide does decide to attack.'

'Well, whatever it is that Hisahide plans do next, I will no longer be part of it. There's been enough destruction already.'

'Come and join me then,' Morisuke said as if to lift the gloom. 'I am on my way to visit my old friend Eishun, the abbot of the Tamon-*in*. He is currently staying at the Ichijō-*in*.'

'Where is this Ichijō-*in*?' Muneyoshi, queried as he massaged his painful hand, careful not to reveal to his distant relative he knew exactly where the monastery was. It was only a year ago that he and Nobutsuna had rescued Kakkei from the self-same place. Thus far his involvement had remained a perfect secret, and he intended to keep it that way.

'It's just down the road from here, on the grounds of the Kōfuku temple,' Morisuke replied.

'In that case, let's pay your Buddhist friend a visit. Perhaps *he* can tell us what the Great Buddha makes of our errant ways.'

All seemed quiet around the Daibutsuden as the two men made their way toward the grounds of the Kōfuku-*ji* along the wide lane through the dark woods. It was an unsettling silence, pregnant with foreboding.

Eishun

Only in his late forties, Eishun already looked like an old sage. Living on an austere diet of pickles and rice, his parchment-like skin stretched over his bald head so thinly that one could make out every vein, every feature of his fragile skull. Yet his outward antiquity belied his youthful spirit. Only a pair of bright probing eyes and his lively demeanor betrayed the fierce energy that burned within, especially for his Buddhist church.[1]

'Look at what they are doing to our temples!' he cried as he met his guests at the eastern gate of the Kōfuku-*ji*. 'When I became a monk at the age of eleven, the Tōdai-*ji* was a pillar of stability in the region. Look at it now! Warlords are fighting out their petty feuds on its very doorstep!'

Eishun led his guests across the temple grounds toward the Ichijō-*in*, all the while talking and gesturing animatedly.

Muneyoshi felt ill at ease. He was familiar with the grounds and feared it might tell.

But Eishun was far too absorbed in his reveries to notice Muneyoshi's discomfort. 'The head abbot of the Ichijō-*in* has persuaded me to donate my private collection to the monastery. I've spent weeks carting my books, scrolls, paintings, and other religious documents over from the Tamon-*in*. Now I'm busy sorting them out and making sure they'll find their right place in the monastery's librar—'

The sharp crackle of musket fire rang out through the cold midnight air. It came from across the road, from the grounds of the Tōdai-*ji*. To the warriors, it was nothing new: every so often musketeers on both sides took potshots at each other. Yet it seemed to upset the old monk, who now hastened his steps toward the rear door of the Ichijō-*in*.

'At the time it seemed a good idea,' he continued nervously, 'now it seems the height of folly. I fear my collection will go the same way as those of Nara's other monasteries.'

He led the men into a small room in the corner of the monastery looking out over the temple grounds. On a low table near a finely latticed window lay a number of scrolls that, judging by their thickness, stretched for at least a dozen yards.

Fumbling the scrolls excitedly with his thin hands, Eishun sighed. 'As long as they don't destroy my *Tamon-in nikki*. For more than three decades now, I have been working on Yamato's history, a detailed chronicle of its events, its leaders, its men of culture. In my search, I have managed to uncover records dating all the way back to the Ōnin Rebellion.'

'Look here,' he said as he nodded knowingly at Muneyoshi and began to scroll through one of the completed scrolls. 'This is an account of the attack on Lord Kizawa Nagamasa at Mount Kasagi by the *shinobi* from Iga. It tells how they set fire to the priests' quarters and captured parts of the stronghold. And here,'he said as he pressed down the paper with a bony finger, 'I describe the heroic role of your father, Ieyoshi-*dono*.'

Muneyoshi cast a cursory glance over the passage, which was written in a wonderfully eloquent hand. He thought he knew all there was to know about the episode from his father, yet from what he read, he was impressed with the incredible detail in which the monk had rendered the account, even from within the safe comfort of a monastery in far-away Nara.

Eishun was eager to hear the latest news from his visitors. 'What are Hisahide's plans?' he queried. 'Will he dare move against the Miyoshi and the Tsutsui while they're encamped on the sacred grounds of the Daibutsuden?'

He had hardly finished his sentence when, as if in answer, a young novice, his face red with excitement, came rushing up the corridor and knelt down at the entrance of the small room: 'Master! Hisahide's troops have just opened the attack!'

Running back across the temple's wide grounds, the three men made their way to the five-storied pagoda on the eastern side of the Golden Hall.

Reaching the foot of the pagoda, Eishun threw open a small door and let the men in. Inside it was pitch black. For a moment the monk crouched in a corner. Then he held up a burning candle and the cramped interior bathed in a ghostly shimmering light. 'Up here,' he said as he pointed to a narrow staircase in the opposite corner.

Climbing the rickety stairs in circles toward the top tier, Muneyoshi wasn't as flustered as the monk and still able to marvel at the pagoda's ingenious structure. Unlike most buildings, there was no internal framework to give the fifty-yard tall structure rigidity. Instead, each story was loosely stacked on top of the other. Only a massive square pole made of the trunk of a giant tree and carefully poised at the length of its center prevented the tower from toppling over. It was a feat of architectural ingenuity, for it was this very device that had caused the building to withstand the many earthquakes that had hit the region since it had been rebuilt following a fire more than a century before. *Fire, always fire!* Muneyoshi pondered. How long would the beautiful pagoda survive this storm?

By the time they had reached the pagoda's top story, they could hear the distinct sound of bulb arrows. Stepping onto the narrow balustrade, the scene of battle unfolded before their eyes in full drama. Pouring through the temple's huge main gate, Hisahide's troops were attacking the entrenched Tsutsui and Miyoshi warriors. At some sections, they were already scaling the barricades and engaging in man-to-man combat with their enemy. One contingent had rounded the towering building, from where its archers were now firing incendiary arrows into the thatched roof of temple's grain store.

The three men looked on in horror as the fire, encouraged by a brisk easterly wind, spread from the grain store to the Hōkadō, the oldest structure on the Tōdai complex. From there it jumped from one building to the next until it had reached the roof of the Daibutsuden. Soon it seemed as if night had turned into day, as the huge torch lit up the deeply scarred temple town. For two more hour the men stood looking as if transfixed until, at the hour of the Ox, the massive roof imploded in peels of thunder, sending sparks high up into the cold midnight sky.[2]

A Dilemma

Muneyoshi felt as if he were being torn in two. Two years earlier, he had helped to liberate Kakkei in a bid to restore peace to the realm. And while he hadn't taken part in the fighting, now he felt he was abetting in Hisahide's atrocities. At least Nara had been spared further atrocities. Having failed to evict Hisahide from Tamonyama castle, the alliance had withdrawn: the Miyoshi back to Akutagawa castle on the border with Kawachi, the Tsutsui back to southern Yamato. To avoid a repetition, Hisahide had ordered his troops to set up camp on the grounds of the Tōdai and Kōfuku temples. He had ignored their abbots' demands to leave and imposed heavy fines on all of Nara's temples and monasteries to support his troops.

For the Tōdai temple it was a burden it could ill bear; most of its ancient buildings had been destroyed, among them two monasteries and two dormitories. Its greatest worry was the Daibutsuden, whose massive roof had completely gone up in flames. The heat of the inferno had been so intense that it caused the bronze head of the statue to melt away. When dawn broke the next day, all that remained standing were the walls and, amid their charred remains, the decapitated torso of the Great Buddha. It was a pitiful sight. In a world longing for peace and quiet, it instilled a profound spiritual unease, even in the hearts of the least pious of men.

For Muneyoshi the burning of the Great Buddha felt like the last straw: his service to Hisahide had become an unbearable burden. Most vexing of all was the blinding hypocrisy of the man. He vividly recalled how, only a few years earlier, in the spring of 1563, he had delivered a letter from Hisahide to the chief priest of the Tō-*ji*, the Shingon sect's head temple in Kyoto, which dated back to the eighth century. During a raging storm, the temple's five-storied pagoda had caught fire and been reduced to ashes. Standing taller than that of the Kōfuku temple it had been the highest pagoda in the realm. He had been present when the priest, still pale with shock, had read Hisahide's letter out to his acolytes so as to give them courage:

> ...no words to express the deep sorrow I feel at the burning of your temple's pagoda. Yet perhaps such events are just bound to happen, so do not grieve. We will all work together to rebuild this structure so that it may serve as a source of pride for future generations, and it is of crucial importance that the Tō temple itself, too, do its utmost to further its reconstruction.

Now much of Nara lay in ashes—and this after half a year of warfare in which the torching of religious buildings had been Hisahide's deliberate strategy!

Fortunately, the Yagyū had been able to extricate themselves from the fighting, yet Muneyoshi knew that before long they would again be called upon to play their part in some other vainglorious battle. The time was ripe to call a council of clan elders. Two years earlier, when he had furtively abetted in the escape of the Shōgun's brother, he hadn't dared to involve the rest of his clan for fear of internal dissent. Now, as they were witnessing one senseless battle after another being fought out in the cause of some nihilistic pursuit, they might be ready to consider a new way forward—even if it meant forsaking the privileges that came with their vassalage to Hisahide.

Divided

It was New Year's Eve and winter had finally arrived in Yagyū Valley. The mild Pacific winds of the previous weeks had veered west, introducing a bitingly cold frost from the Chinese continent. Outside the castle, the fields and forest were covered in a thin blanket of snow, though the water of Hakusa River refused to be tamed, still rushing under a crackling sheet of ice. Inside, at the center of the castle's main hall, a large fire occasionally popped, sending up sparks toward the aperture in the roof. It filled the room with a welcoming warmth and a pleasant fragrance of burning incense as the clan member filed in wearing their ceremonial garb, the wide skirts of their striped *hakama* rustling over the *tatami* mats. Sitting down according to their station, the wide shoulders of their freshly starched *haori* gave their movement added gravitas as they slowly placed their ceremonial fans in front of them. Then, in unison, they solemnly bowed toward the seventy-year-old Ieyoshi, who was now the most senior member of the Yagyū clan and thus took pride of place at the head of the room.

Muneyoshi looked around the room with some satisfaction. Unlike so many other clans, the Yagyū had successfully withered the storm, doing proud to their name. In spite of their differences, they had held together and all had shown up in a reassuring display of unity. Even Shigeyoshi was for once dressed in his traditional attire, instead of his outlandish Portuguese garments, though his hair was loose and disheveled.

Not that he had come willingly. Only with the greatest difficulty had Muneyoshi managed to persuade his uncle to attend the meeting. Ever since their alliance with Hisahide, their relationship had deteriorated. By now it had reached a point where they hardly spoke. Not that they often met. Where Muneyoshi spent most of his time at Yagyū castle and the Momiji *yashiki*, Shigeyoshi could usually be found at the clan's mansion on the grounds of Tamonyama castle—if he wasn't out carousing in Kyoto's notorious Gion district. For a while he had fallen out of favor with Hisahide over Kakkei's escape. But that was two years ago. Since then rumors had surfaced that Kakkei was holding up at Wada Koremasa's Wadakan in Ōmi and laying claim to the Shōgunate. Thankfully there were none about Muneyoshi's role in the escape, although some claimed his good friend Kamiizumi Nobutsuna had been a regular guest at the Wadakan. That news alone had been enough for Shigeyoshi to lose trust in his nephew. And while he had never openly questioned him about it, he eyed Muneyoshi suspiciously as they sat down opposite each other in front of Ieyoshi at the head of the assembly.

Muneyoshi was the first to speak. 'I sorely regret the burning of the Daibtsuden. Its destruction might not have been intentional, but not so the other temples and monasteries that have gone up in flames. Those fires were deliberately started,' he said to add weight to what he was about to suggest. 'The time has come for us to reconsider our alliance with Hisahide. He isn't from the region, let alone a warrior by birth. Indeed, I think we should seriously consider forging an alliance with the Tsutsui, whose roots do lie in Yamato. I have experienced their benevolence at first hand, and believe that under Junkei's rule we can reclaim our rightful place among the local clans.'

'Still tied to Nabu's bed string, aye?' Shigeyoshi snorted. 'How can you even consider crawling back to your former captor with your tail between your legs? Did the Tsutsui not rob us of our dignity by holding you hostage?'

There were grunts of approval from the *shinobi* headmen.

'Why do you not honor your oath of allegiance to Hisahide? At least I do!' he proclaimed as he struck his chest with a clenched fist in a dramatic flourish. 'Yet where were you when I and my men risked our lives last November? I went round to the Kasuga Taisha to call on your help. Yet all I found was a skeleton force with orders to safeguard the shrine...'

A disdainful smile spread across Shigeyoshi's face as he slowly rose, walked over to his nephew and bent over toward him. 'And where on earth were you on the night of Kakkei's escape from the Kōfuku temple two years ago?'

Muneyoshi immediately shot back as he stood up to face his uncle: 'And where were you? Sightseeing in Gion perhaps?'

He was about to go on when his father uttered a deep groan and shouted, '*Yamé*!'

Rising slowly to his feet, Ieyoshi cleared his throat. Then he spoke: 'Sixteen years have passed since we decided to ally ourselves with Hisahide. Then only a narrow majority was in favor. Looking back, it was a mistake. His arrival hasn't brought the prosperity we had hoped for. Moreover, the ease with which he makes enemies has brought much death and destruction.'

Ieyoshi looked at his son, who had sat down again. 'I admit that I am old and weary of all the treachery and fighting. Yet joining Junkei doesn't guarantee that things will get any better. He might be talented but he doesn't have the power to unify the realm. Only then will Yamato see peace again. Perhaps we should consider a different option. Perhaps we should go into exile, as many other clans have done.'

'No! I refuse to stoop that low!' Shigeyoshi said as he faced his brother—he was almost shouting now. 'I was born and raised a Yagyū and will not denounce you if you ever choose to do so, but neither will I betray my loyalty to Hisahide. From now on our ways will part.' Having spoken, he cast down his fan and left the room.

When the remaining members finally cast their vote the result was tied. For the first time in his life, Muneyoshi felt as if something inside him had broken. Never had his clan been so divided. Unity had kept them together through all the turmoil of the last two centuries, even in their darkest hour. Adversity had united his distant ancestors, the brothers Nagayoshi and Gensen. The two could not have been more different, the one a warrior, the other a Buddhist monk. Yet history and tradition had tied them together in a common cause, that of Go-Daigo and the Southern Court. Now his father and his uncle had fallen out. He instinctively felt his father was right: it was only their ability to adapt to the changing tides that would ensure their survival—an ability wholly lacking in his uncle.

At last, having decided to resume the council the next day, he and the other clan members made their way to the bell of the local temple to toll in the new year. All prayed it would be a better year—it could hardly be worse.

A Letter

It was amid this impasse that, on New Year's Day, 1568, the tenth year of the Eiroku era, a messenger arrived at Yagyū castle, this time carrying a letter from the warlord Oda Nobunaga.[3] There was no doubt the letter, made from the most exquisite Mino paper, was from the warlord himself. Written in an elegant, almost casual hand, it displayed a masterly use of ink Muneyoshi had seldom seen: never too thin; never too thick. To take any doubt away it bore Nobunaga's distinct, oblong red seal. Dated December 31, 1567, it read:

Chieftain Yaggyū Shinsaemon Muneyoshi-*dono*,

I intend to escort His Highness Ashikaga Yoshiaki to the capital. For this to happen it is of the highest importance that you show allegiance to Yoshiaki when the time arrives. In this connection, the first priority is for us to be on closer terms with Lord Matsunaga Hisahide of Tamonyama castle. I have already exchanged written pledges of support with both Hisahide himself as well as his son, and expect you to join his forces as a matter of urgency.

Nobunaga

Muneyoshi sighed. Finally the efforts of Kamiizumi Nobutsuna and his fellow conspirators in Ōmi were beginning to bear fruit. Almost two years had passed since he and his friend had liberated the rightful Shōgun from imprisonment at the Ichijō-*in*. Ever since, the contender had languished at the Wadakan and several other hideouts in Ōmi, constantly on the run and in search of an ally to help him achieve his aim.

It seemed Yoshiaki had finally found the kind of man who could help him do just that. Unlike Hisahide, Nobunaga was a warlord of immense power. Moreover, his stated ambition was to pacify all of Japan, not just a few provinces. That much was clear from the seal on the letter Muneyoshi was now holding in his hands. Printed in large, stylized Kanji it read *tenka fubu*, 'Rule the realm by force.' Since his famous victory in the Battle of Okehazama, he had made great strides in his quest to do so. The previous year, he had subdued the stronghold of Mount Inaba. He had renamed it Gifu castle and made it his new headquarters. The castle was of great strategic importance; Mount Inaba overlooked the Mino plain, controlling access to the provinces of Ōmi, Yamashiro, and the jewel in the crown: Kyoto.

Now Nobunaga had decided to move, but with the help of Hisahide! Nobunaga's reasoning was clear enough. As the party who had installed its own puppet Shōgun, the Miyoshi were his fiercest enemies. And they and Hisahide were now rivals, which automatically made Hisahide his ally—civil war indeed made for the strangest of bedfellows.

The Yagyū's role in Nobunaga's scheme of things, too, was perfectly clear. Expecting fierce resistance in Ōmi, the safest route to bring the Shōgun to the capital was not along the Tōkaidō but by way of a detour through Ise, Iga, and Yamato. That meant they would have to take the Iga Kaidō, which ran right through the Yagyū domains.

Nobunaga was, of course, chiefly motivated by self-interest. Yet he acted on behalf of Ashikaga Yoshiaki, the brother and rightful successor to the so treacherously deposed Yoshiteru. And if a man like Nobunaga thought it prudent to ally himself with Hisahide there was probably good reason for him to do so. Muneyoshi thought hard. To defect at this stage and abandon their obligations to the Shōgun was just too much to contemplate. If only for the sake of seeing the rightful successor become head of the Bakufu, no matter how weak that institution had become, the Yagyū had to sustain their support for Hisahide—at least for the time being.

CHAPTER 6

Nobunaga swiftly made good on his promise to install the rightful Shōgun. In the summer of 1568, he met Ashikaga Yoshiaki at the Ryūshō temple in Gifu, where the latter formally asked the warlord to escort him to the capital. One month later, on September 27, Nobunaga departed from Gifu at the head of some fifteen thousand men and began his march on the capital. By the time he set up camp on the eastern bank of the Aichi River in Ōmi, his troops had swelled to well over fifty-thousand as allied warlords prudently joined his cause. Others folded one by one, first at Mitsukuri castle, then at Kannonji castle, and finally at Akutagawa castle, from where the Miyoshi made a final desperate effort to bar him from reaching his goal. They were no match for his well-organized troops, consisting of teppō ashigaru, *armed with the lethal Western muskets. On October 20, they abandoned their stronghold and crossed the border with Kawachi.[1] Upon his arrival in Kyoto, Nobunaga immediately sent for Yoshiaki, who reached the capital by way of the route Nobunaga had outlined in his letter to Muneyoshi. Finally, on November 7, 1568, during a grand ceremony, the emperor appointed Yoshiaki the fifteenth Shōgun of the Ashikaga Bakufu.*

In true character, the opportunistic Hisahide was the first to show his loyalty to the new powers that be. Where only three years earlier he had coldly conspired to murder the sitting Shōgun, now he could not wait to show his allegiance to Yoshiteru's newly installed brother. No sooner had Nobunaga arrived in Kyoto than Hisahide sent his son to ply him with hostages and exquisite pieces of Chinaware. They were accompanied by an obsequious letter in which he welcomed Nobunaga and vowed to serve his interests in Yamato. He was rewarded for his show of subservience with the governorship of Yamato and the freedom to do as he wanted in the province.

That freedom had to be earned. Only a month earlier, Hisahide had raised a force of some two thousand men at Shigisan castle and crossed the border with Kawachi to defeat a motley assortment of sōhei and rōnin who were holding out against Nobunaga from a number of fortifications concentrated around the Ishiyama Hongan temple in the delta of the Yodo River, just north of Osaka.

It was at this juncture that Tsutsui Junkei decided to move. Again and again, his forces had been beaten back by those of Hisahide. Now, with Hisahide away, he saw his chance clear to regain a foothold in Nara. On the same day Hisahide crossed into Kawachi, Junkei entered Tōchi castle, stronghold of the clan who had remained loyal to the Tsutsui throughout their struggles with Hisahide. Situated near the town of Kashihara, some fifteen miles south of Nara, it had remained outside Hisahide's grasp. Then, on September 19, he once more marched on Nara, descending on the temple town's southern outskirts and setting fire to many of the grand yashiki in the Furuichi district. Joined by some five-hundred sōhei from the Kōfuku temple, he ensconced himself in the grounds of the Kōnin-ji, an ancient temple on the crest of Takahi hill, just southeast of the temple town.

Tamonyama Castle

Muneyoshi looked out over the inner court of Tamonyama castle and winced. In spite of its spaciousness, he felt incarcerated. It was late September, but the summer cicadas had lost none of their vigor, and the lingering heat made his tour of duty at the castle all the more oppressive. He longed for Yagyū Valley, where the cool mountain air would soon descend from the forest, soothing his beloved Nabu, who had only just told him she was pregnant again. Would it be a boy; would it be a girl? He didn't mind, really. Already they had been blessed with four healthy sons and six healthy daughters. All he wanted right now was to be with her, with his family.

Only with great reluctance had he again taken up his post at the Yagyū mansion on Tamonyama's castle grounds. Two and a half year had passed since he and his uncle had fallen out and Shigeyoshi had vacated the building. For a long time, it had stood empty. When he finally moved in he had spent weeks restoring the place to its original state, removing the tasteless and garish decorations introduced by his uncle. Parts of the building still stood empty. He couldn't get himself to sleep in Shigeyoshi's quarters, where the odor of stale *sake* and semen still lingered, despite the fresh *tatami* mats he had placed. He wanted no reminders of the dissolute lifestyle of his uncle, who was now living in Kyoto as Hisahide's 'envoy.' Muneyoshi could not suppress a sardonic chuckle at the thought—some kind of envoy: Shigeyoshi's residence stood right at the heart of the notorious Gion district.

At least he wouldn't have to face his uncle at that evening's banquet, where he was to meet with Hisahide's new local commander, Takeuchi Hidekatsu. It promised to be an interesting evening, for they would be joined by a group of Jesuits from Kyoto. Muneyoshi had never seen a Portuguese, though he knew that Eishun had met with Jesuits before and had been impressed with their learning.

Jesuits

Muneyoshi was fascinated by the Jesuits' appearance. All were dressed in long dark gowns of coarsely woven material held around their waist by a simple cord, and on their heads they wore odd triangular caps of the same material. Yet he was most struck their by their faces. Like himself, they had dark eyes, yet between them sat long aquiline noses, while much of the lower parts of their faces were covered in dense black hair. They were intelligent faces, and judging by the way the men conducted themselves, all of them were used to Japanese customs. At first glance, then, they were men of culture, though one wouldn't believe it when one went by one's nose, for a penetrating smell of body odor hung around them like it did around cattle.

They were being led by a handsome man in his late thirties, who was introduced as Padre Luís Fróis, head of the Christian church in Kyoto, and was made to sit near Hisahide.

'So, padre-*dono*, what is it that brings you to Nara?' Hisahide said as he beckoned his servants to bring in refreshments.

Bowing deep before the warlord, the Jesuit kept his face near the ground as he began to talk in long, surprisingly eloquent though somewhat overwrought sentences,' As your Lordship will know, our church had unfortunately been banned from proselytizing in the Kinai region on command of His Highness the Emperor. However, through the kind offices of Lord Vata-*dono* from Ōmi, who is, as you know, a baptized Christian and has since assumed the high office of Governor of Kyoto, His Highness, in his great wisdom, has withdrawn these restrictions, and we have again been allowed to rebuild our churches. As your Lordship will know, one of them is situated in your magnificent temple-town of Nara, and we are visiting our Japanese padres here to assist them wherever we can to

spread the Holy Gospel and, in doing so, bring salvation to
those who seek it.'

Muneyoshi perked his ears. So Wada Koremasa had been converted! He was sure the padre's 'Vata-*dono*' must be Wada, who
had indeed become the capital's governor. What was it with this
religion that made so many warlords turn to this foreign creed
and abandon their native traditions?

'And what do you make of Tamonyama castle?' Hisahide asked
as he raised both hands aloft and looked around him as if he
were overwhelmed by the splendor himself.

'I think there can scarcely be a more beautiful sight in the
world than Your Majesty's magnificent fortress,' the padre
replied, 'for it is a sheer joy to look on it. Indeed, to describe
the beauty of your palace, one would need reams of paper, since
it does not appear to be the work of human hands. Words simply
fail me to—'

'Yes, yes, that is enough flattery for now,' Hisahide said as he
signaled to one of his attendants standing in the wings.

Muneyoshi felt a growing antipathy toward the obsequious
foreigner. Yet the man certainly knew his customers. Had the
padre done anything but flatter his host, he might soon find his
head impaled on a bamboo spike at the castle's main gate.

'Let's have a debate!' Hisahide said cheerily as if to bring a
semblance of equality to the gathering. 'Let's have a meeting of
minds—of spirits, rather—on the great religions of our two
great countries. Let's see how your Christian doctrine holds up
against our ancient Buddhist teachings.'

Apparently, the whole thing had been arranged beforehand,
for Hisahide's servants now ushered in Eishun, who seemed to
have been waiting in one of the adjacent rooms.

It was an odd choice, Munenori reflected, considering
Hisahide was an adherent of the fanatical Nichiren-shū, a sect

105

violently opposed to the proselytizing foreigners. Eishun, by contrast, was an exponent of the Hossō sect, which had always been tolerant of other sects and religions. It was also an understandable choice. Only the year before, Asayama Nichijō, a fanatic exponent of the Nichiren sect, had engaged this selfsame Fróis in a similar 'debate,' presided over by non other than Nobunaga. Thoroughly trashed by the Jesuit, the monk had rushed to the corner of the room and grabbed one of Nobunaga's *naginata* determined to kill the Jesuit. It had only been through the intervention of Nobunaga and his vassals that Fróis had been saved. Clearly, Hisahide didn't want a repetition of this embarrassing episode.

'It appears,' Eishun began, 'that your religion is finding fertile soil among the people of our country, for you have won many converts, even here in Nara, far away from your main mission down in Kyushu. I happen to know one of them, master Takayama Hida no Kami, who is a vassal of His Lordship.'

The Jesuit bowed again, though only faintly this time and without looking in Eishun's direction. 'We are grateful for the blessings God has granted us in His infinite mercy. For we have come to your country to bring the Peace of God—to guide your people toward the road of salvation and eternal life, though we also endeavor to reveal to them His great Mercy by helping them with the more practical matters of everyday life.'

'Yes,' Eishun said, 'I have learned a lot about Western medicine from Padre Luís de Almeida, a very able surgeon, who visited Nara some five years ago and stayed at the Tamon monastery, as there was no church yet for him to stay. I was greatly impressed with his knowledge of the human body and his methods to cure its many ailments...'

'Yet why is it,' the monk said after careful reflection, 'that the black ships that have brought him and your honored selves to our shores so as to bring, as you say, solace and salvation to our ravaged people, also carry in their holds the weapons that bring so much death and destruction in the first place. And why is it that, on their return home, those selfsame ships carry the most destitute among our men and women in chains to serve as slaves to your own countrymen.'

Fróis looked nervously to his fellow Jesuits, then to Hisahide, then to the floor, as he searched for a fitting riposte to the monk's probing questions.

'And why is it,' Eishun continued, 'that now you have the ear of so many of our converted warlords, you use it as a conduit to fill their hearts with hatred toward the Buddhist church, even though we at the Tamon-*in* took in your brother in his hour of need, as is our custom? Why is it that you speak ill of us and our customs to your congregation? Why do you claim that your God is the only true god, that they will only find salvation through Him, and that those who do otherwise will perish eternally in the flames of—'

'Enough!' Hisahide said as he raised his right hand to silence the monk. 'Sadly, we have more pressing matters that need our attention. I must be on my way to my camp at Takayasu,'—and here he paused for dramatic effect,—'for I am to meet with my trusted ally, Lord Oda Nobunaga, at Tennōji tomorrow. I understand that you have met with him at Osaka castle?'

'Yes, Dajon-*dono*' the Jesuit replied, calling Hisahide by his official rank of Danjō, or Imperial Prosecutor, while he again bowed deep to the ground. 'It is almost a year hence since I met with the King of Owari and that we received from him many favors.' The Jesuit shot a poisonous glance at Eishun as he continued. 'Indeed, it is through the King's great benevolence that we have been able to open the first Christian church in the capital, despite the vehement opposition of the bonzes.'

'You are right, not all the *bōzu* are as hospitable as our friend Eishun here' Hisahide said, correcting the Jesuit's pronunciation of the Japanese word for monk and casting a sardonic glance at Eishun. 'As you may know, Nobunaga and I have our hands full at present with the confounded *sōhei* of the Ikkō sectarians holding out at the Ishiyama Hongan-*ji*. I'm sure you Jesuits have come to share our hatred of these sectarians. Yet, if the gods— whichever one you prefer—are with us, we will soon defeat this last pocket of resistance. For the time being, we will have to call it a day. My vassals, too, will have to rise early tomorrow, for they are to discuss pressing matters with Takeuchi Hidekatsu-*dono* here, who has just come down from Takayasu and will be acting as my representative at Tamonyama while I am away.'

A Man of Caliber

Muneyoshi was somewhat surprised when, the next morning, September 20, 1570, he entered the castle's main hall. He had clearly not been the only one to receive a letter from Nobunaga. All the clans who had joined Hisahide's side were represented— the Sugawa, the Furuichi, the Hashio. Across the room, he spotted his distant relative Nakanobō Morisuke. He was sitting almost next to the rear entrance, farthest removed from the *tokonoma*—a clear sign he had fallen out of favor. Like Muneyoshi, he had withdrawn from the fighting around the Daibutsuden three years before. And like Muneyoshi, he had escaped repercussions by laying low. But now he was forced to act, and not just because he too had received a letter from Nobunaga. The Nakanobō *yashiki* was located in the middle of Tsubai, the very district affected by the skirmishes; they simply could not afford to stand by and see their possessions go up in smoke.

Muneyoshi didn't envy the Nakanobō. The Yagyū, by contrast, were lucky. As the crow flies it wasn't that far to Yagyū Valley from where they were sitting, some five miles at most. On the ground it was different. The Yagyū Kaidō, the only road connecting Nara to the valley, led through mountainous and densely forested terrain. By foot, it took close to half a day to reach his castle, less so by horse, but not much, as one could not give the animal free rein on the narrow and cobbled track, for that it was simply too treacherous. And thus, despite its physical proximity, in the minds of most, Yagyū castle felt far removed from the ancient religious capital. That mental barrier alone had saved the Yagyū clan from many of the atrocities that had plagued the temple town over the centuries.

Takeuchi Hidekatsu seemed more like a scribe than a commander. 'Junkei is to be stopped from entering Nara at all cost,' he droned as if he were reading from a prepared script. You are to assemble all able-bodied men and report for duty by the end of tomorrow, for the day after we will drive the Tsutsui from Nara and thence from his stronghold of Takahi hill. However, there is to be no murder, raping, or looting of Nara's populace, no destruction of properties, nor any use of incendiary arrows. 'Above all,' and here he almost looked embarrassed, 'there is to be no repeat of the Daibutsuden…eh, incident.'

Muneyoshi snorted. Hidekatsu might be acting in Hisahide name, but he had clearly been instructed by Nobunaga, who was encamped at Tennōji, just a few miles from Takayasu where Hisahide had set up camp. Hisahide had never bothered about Nara's populace, let alone its ancient buildings. One could almost hear Nobunaga's reproach, despite the commander's attempt to gloss over the atrocity by calling it an 'incident.' What was Hidekatsu thinking? Had the fool not seen for himself how half of Nara had been reduced to cinders? He shot a knowing glance toward Morisuke, who seemed to read his thoughts, for he looked just as bemused as Muneyoshi.

Sensing the reaction among his audience, Hidekatsu closed by reminding the chieftains that 'Hisahide is now one of Nobunaga's allies; he is the appointed governor of Yamato; and he has the sanction of the sitting Shōgun, Ashikaga Yoshiaki.'

Muneyoshi felt oddly reassured by it all, albeit for none of Hidekatsu's reasons. Only two years earlier, he and Kamiizumi Nobutsuna had escorted the Shōgun to the capital. They had followed the river to Kizu, from where they had safely reached the capital along the Nara Kaidō. For much of the way they had ridden together, briefing each other on events and enjoying each other's company. Nobutsuna had told him how he had also accompanied the Shōgun on his visit to Nobunaga's court in Gifu. On Nobunaga's invitation, he had stayed on and given a demonstration of his Shinkage-*ryū* during a party in honor of Tokugawa Ieyasu, a Mikawa warlord and close ally of Nobunaga. The two warlords had discussed events in Yamato, and it was obvious that neither of them held Hisahide in high esteem. Because of his pact with Hisahide, Nobunaga had closely followed the pursuits of the Yamato warlord, and what he heard pleased him little. Recalling the meeting, Nobutsuna had laughed out loud, shaking his head as he commended Nobunaga for his astuteness. When Muneyoshi had asked him for the reason of his mirth, he had leaned over in his saddle and, mimicking the warlord's deeply sonorous voice, said, 'This is a man of whom we should be wary, for he has gained notoriety in this world for three crimes: the poisoning of Chōkei's son and heir, the assassination of the rightful Shōgun, and the destruction of the Great Buddha of the Tōdai-*ji*.'

His friend was right—Oda Nobunaga was indeed a man of caliber.

Takahi Hill

Nara's temple roosters hadn't yet crowed when, on the morning of September 22. Muneyoshi arrived at Tamonyama castle at the head of a small contingent of Yagyū warriors. Following the war council, he had returned to Yagyū castle and scrambled all the men he could muster. His oldest son too had come. It was the first time he was going to join his father in battle. Shinjirō, who had turned nineteen, had just gone through his *genpuku* ceremony and received his adult name of Yoshikatsu. As was the custom, he had also received his first *katana*. Muneyoshi had given him the longsword he in turn had received from his friend Kamiizumi Nobutsuna, so he could pass it on to his own son in time. Renamed the Yagyū no Ōdachi, it was a beautiful gift, but only a ceremonial *katana*, as it was just too large for a young warrior to handle. Instead, Yoshikatsu was wearing the Kasagi no Tachi, the sword with which his ancestor, Nagayoshi, had defended Emperor Go-Daigo. Muneyoshi had acquiesced reluctantly—the weapon had brought neither him nor Nagayoshi much luck.

Riding out from Tamonyama castle along Nara's main thoroughfare, they passed the destroyed Daibutsuden and reached Furuichi at the hour of the Dragon. Much of the damage had already been done; large swathes of the district now lay in ashes. Most of the fire had by now consumed itself, though in many places it still smoldered. The little good wood that remained had been dragged off by Junkei's troops, who had used it to throw up barricades on the narrow road through the paddy fields on Nara's southern outskirts. Beyond, faintly visible through the lingering smoke, one could just make out Takahi Hill, home of the Kōnin temple and Junkei's new stronghold. It was well chosen. Though shallow, the hill was covered by trees and vegetation too dense for an army to penetrate. The temple stood on the hill's eastern slope, though its main approach was on the hill's northern side, through a mile-wide valley.

At noon Muneyoshi rendezvoused at the western foot of the hill with Nakanobō Morisuke, who had led a small contingent of warriors down from Tsubai. He too had been joined by his son, Fujimatsu, who was just one year younger than Yoshikatsu.

'There is no safe way to lead our men through the valley,' Morisuke said as he took in the situation.

'No,' Muneyoshi agreed, 'Judging by the slow pace of his retreat, Junkei is sure to have posted men among the woods on both sides of the valley. They will try cut off our retreat once we have entered the valley.'

Still, the Yagyū and Nakanobō warriors pressed on. After a day of intense fighting, they managed to evict the Tsutsui from their makeshift defenses, driving them back up the valley to their stronghold on Mount Takahi, where their advance was halted by Junkei's rearguard. Among them were *sōhei* from Negoro and Kii, many of them armed with the fearsome muskets. Some of Hidekatsu's troops, too, were armed with muskets, but the Yagyū were still fighting in the traditional way. Their superior mastery of the *katana* still made them a force to be reckoned with, but only when fighting at close quarters. And thus Muneyoshi and Morisuke ordered their men to withdraw, content that for the moment at least they had reached their objective: to expel Junkei and his men from Nara. Strategically, it was a victory of sorts. But it would take a much larger force to evict Junkei from Takahi Hill.

Small though it was, the victory had come at a cost. In sheer numbers, the Nakanobō forces had suffered most, yet only few of either clan's warriors had escaped unharmed. And it was only now, as they counted their dead and wounded, that the two chieftains realized their sons were missing.

Chapter 6

Teppō

As was the custom, Yoshikatsu and Fujimatsu had both been put in charge of a small group of warriors. It was all part of their coming of age as chieftain's sons. Soon, they too would be leading their clans into battle. To test and hone their skills, sons were usually put in charge of an army's right or left flank. Now they had been ordered to stay behind. They were to guard the entrance to the valley and offer assistance in case the enemy sought to cut their fathers off.

'*Bakayarō!*' Yoshikatsu swore as he drew up beside his distant relative. He had been reared on accounts of famous battles in which heroic warriors engaged in man-to-man combat having declared their progeny for all to hear. Here was his first chance to follow in that proud tradition. Instead he had been ordered to stay behind and mind the proverbial sheep.

Fujimatsu echoed his sentiment; he was just as eager to make a mark as his distant relative. Then his face lit up. 'I grew up among these hills and studied at the Kōnin temple as a boy. I remember there is another route by which we can reach the temple. It's through a valley round the hill's southern slope. The path is only a narrow ridge among the paddies, so we'll have to go on foot. But if we approach them from there, we're certain to surprise the enemy, who will be focused on the main assault from the northern side of the mountain.'

It wasn't a valley, really, just a narrow strip of land flanked on both sides by hills covered with trees. And the closer they got to their goal the narrower the strip got. It was well into the hour of the Monkey and growing dark when they had rounded the hill. They could just make out the temple's thatched roof, when Yoshikatsu heard a buzzing near his left ear, not unlike a hornet's, but much faster. It was immediately followed by a sound like a thick branch snapping, mockingly echoed from the opposite slope. Then there were more, and looking up, high among the dense trees, he could see bright flashes, instantly replaced by angry bursts of smoke, as if from a horse's nostrils on a cold winter morning. In an instant it seemed as if it was hailing, as pellets of hot led buried themselves in the mud around them, sizzling as they hit the thin film of water on top. Then the first man fell. It was Fujimatsu. Hit in his right shoulder, he spun round in a haze of blood and, losing his balance on the narrow ridge, landed face-down in the paddy's shallow water. A man behind him stepped down from the ridge to help him up. Bending over, he reached for Fujimatsu's hand when two bullets struck him in the back, sending bits of his armor flying, and thrusting the man onto the wounded warrior with a grunt. He was dead.

Only now did Yoshikatsu see their terrible mistake. They had walked right into an ambush. Musketeers, at least two dozen, had entrenched themselves among the dense woods. They would not come out and fight in the open; and there was no way he and his men could reach them without being decimated. There would be no man-to-man duels, no proud declaring of pedigree, no taking of heads.

It only took him a split second to act. Shouting, '*kaere!*' he ordered his men to retreat as he jumped down into the paddy field next to his friend. Toppling the dead man away, he dragged Fujimatsu from the mud and, slinging his good arm around his neck, followed his men back along the narrow ridge to safety. It seemed their retreat had satisfied their enemy, for the firing from above began to lessen as they slowly moved away. Soon they would be safe from these confounded *teppō*.

They were almost out of range when something struck Yoshikatsu from behind. For a moment he thought he had been kicked in the back, only to realize he was the last man leaving.

Then he felt the wet warmness of blood oozing down his harness. A burning sensation crept up his spine as he struggled onward along the muddy ridge. Yet by some miracle—how he didn't know—he was able to push on and bring Fujimatsu and the rest of their men to safety.

That evening, in a small room in the corner of the Kōfuku temple complex, Eishun knitted his brows as he bent over Yoshikatsu's wound. Many a man had been brought in since the fighting at the Daibutsuden, and he had quickly learned the devastating effects of the fearsome *teppō*. He had seen men shot at close range. On its way through, the hot, half melted projectile had disintegrated, exiting the body with much of it's victims innards in its wake. Yoshikatsu, by contrast, had been lucky. Due to the distance, the bullet had lost much of its velocity by the time it struck him. This, combined with the protection of his harness, had saved his life.

Your son was lucky,' the monk said as he turned to Muneyoshi. 'The bullet hasn't made a large wound. Nor, thankfully, has it damaged any vital organs. But I can't remove it. It has lodged itself next to his spine, too close to touch without fear of damaging his nerves. He might still be able to walk, provided he doesn't die of infection.'

Independence

For more than a week Yoshikatsu's life hovered between heaven and earth. Wrecked by violent fevers, he remained in a state of unconsciousness as his body struggled to accommodate the foreign object, encrusting it with hard layers of tissue to protect his spine. Then, toward the end of September, the fever abated and the young man came to. One more month he kept to his bed, nursed by his two sisters. When he finally left his room, he had lost a third of his weight. The strong muscles on his shoulders had withered, and his wrists and legs were as thin and unsteady as those of his seventy-three-year-old grandfather. As he gingerly made his way around Yagyū castle, happy to be alive and make himself useful with daily chores, he did so with a slanted stoop, as if still carrying the wounded Fujimatsu to safety. Yet walk he could.

Muneyoshi observed his son with a mixture of pride and guilt: pride in his son's tenacity; guilt for his own failure to protect him. Why had he not kept him at his side? Why had he not saved his son from the same recklessness that had made him a prisoner of the Tsutsui when he himself had been young? At barely nineteen Yoshikatsu was his oldest son and had bourn a large part of the burden in the upkeep and defense of the Yagyū domain. That was now a closed avenue. Moreover, Yoshikatsu was also the first in line to succeed him in the not too distant future. That, too, now seemed unlikely. None of Yoshikatsu's brothers were of an age where they could replace him. Two of them, Yoshihide and Munetaka, had taken the tonsure. Assuming the spiritual names of Kyūsai and Tokusai, they had entered Nara's Kōfuku monastery. This left Muneyoshi with just his fourth son, Muneaki, who had turned five that year.

Muneyoshi himself had just turned forty-three, but he felt like an old man. Two years earlier he had fallen from his horse while out riding in the vicinity of Takahata. Thankfully, he hadn't broken anything, but somehow, compounded by the wound incurred at Tōnomine, it had affected his strength. With an aging father, six daughters, a five-year-old infant, a crippled son to care for, and his wife with child, his clan was in serious jeopardy. Somehow he had to find a path to safety, to a future where they could prosper—be a clan among clans.

One thing was certain: that path lay not through his vassalage to Hisahide. But breaking with him, too, was fraught with danger. He need only look how other chieftains had fared. A few months earlier, one of them, Ido Yoshihiro, had gone over to Junkei's side. He too had grown weary of Hisahide's despotic rule. Yet unlike Yagyū castle, hidden away among the mountains, his stronghold of Ido castle stood in Kōriyama, at the center of the Yamato plain—at such a strategic location there was no way he could take a neutral stance. Yoshihiro's was a brave, but fateful choice, for among the many hostages held at Tamonyama castle was his own daughter. As soon as Hisahide heard of Yoshihiro's defection he had her thrown in jail where she lingered for a month until Hisahide made up his mind and had her strangled with a rope. Her fate was shared by another hostage, the son of Matsuzō Kensuke. It was said that during their weeks in prison the girl, who was only eight years old, and the boy, who was twelve, had grown fond of each other. Hearing of this, Hisahide though it a nice touch to unite them in death and had them impaled on one long pole at the gate of Tamonyama castle.

Most worrying for the future of Yamato was Hisahide's fickleness. He might for now have allied himself with Oda Nobunaga, but already rumors were spreading around Tamonyama castle that he was in secret communications with some of Nobunaga's fiercest enemies. How could such a man be trusted? How could one build a future on someone as fickle as that? It was only a matter of time before Hisahide would turn on Nobunaga, start another conflict, commit his next atrocity.

Muneyoshi shook his head as he pondered all these things. How could he sustain his vassalage to a lord he had come to detest, even if he had the sanction of the sitting *Shōgun*. And what did that sanction mean if he had murdered the *Shōgun's* very own brother. It was clear to him now that the Shōgunate, too, had been reduced to a mere pawn in the greedy hands of ambitious warlords—another instrument by which they could further their cynical aims. He felt like retching. To think that only a few years ago he had still believed he could change things for the better by liberating Kakkei—the folly!

Muneyoshi knew what he had to do. There would be no clan council this time, no meeting of minds; he had made up his own: better to live and risk destruction than to live in shame. The Yagyū would be completely on their own, with just a small army of men to defend their domains. Only time would tell if they would live to tell the tale, but at least it would be a tale that could be told with some dignity.

CHAPTER 7

Tsutsui Junkei stubbornly persevered in his efforts to evict Hisahide from Yamato and reclaim his clan's former territories. It was one of those paradoxes of a country divided that Junkei, too, had formed an alliance with Nobunaga, contributing large numbers of musketeers to the great Battle of Nagashino.[1] But somehow Hisahide continued to get the better of him, both in his alliance with Nobunaga and in his ability to manipulate the Yamato chieftains.

Not that Hisahide did much to earn Nobunaga's favor. Time after time he betrayed the warlord's trust, but for some inscrutable reason, Nobunaga could not get himself to drop the Yamato warlord. In 1572, Hisahide conspired with Takeda Shingen to drive Nobunaga from Kyoto. The plan failed when, the next year, Shingen passed away, but Hisahide was pardoned. He only had to make one concession. To serve as a subtle reminder of his allegiance, he had to relinquish his cherished Tamonyama castle to one of Nobunaga's confidants. In 1576, Hisahide again tried to topple Nobunaga, this time by entering into secret negotiations with the Northern warlord Uesugi Kenshin.[2] Not long after, Kenshin gave up on the plan. But Nobunaga learned of Hisahide's treachery, and this time he had had enough. Incensed, he stripped him of his governorship of Yamato, bestowing it instead on Junkei. Hisahide's gamble had failed. Now he faced the wrath of Junkei, as well as Nobunaga, who had far more troops at his disposal. Junkei was elated; he champed at the bit to settle his scores with the treacherous warlord once and for all.

It took close to a year for Junkei and Nobunaga to raise sufficient forces to attack Hisahide's last stronghold of Shigisan castle.[3] Finally, early in November 1577, Junkei marched toward Mount Shigi at the head of a few thousand men. At the foot of the mountain, he was joined by a vast army of forty-thousand troops under the command of Nobunaga's eldest son, Nobutada.

Hostilities started in earnest on December 14, when the besieging force launched a full-scale attack on the castle. Miraculously, the day ended in a partial victory for Hisahide when one of his commanders sallied forth from the castle with two hundred men, causing many casualties among the Nobunaga troops. Being vastly outnumbered, however, it was only a matter of time before the castle would fall.

In a last attempt to turn the scales in his favor, Hisahide dispatched one of his confidants, Mori Yoshihisa, to seek reinforcements from the Ishiyama Hongan temple. Situated in Osaka's inaccessible river delta, the temple was the headquarters of the notorious Ikkō sectarians.[4] For seven long years, they had doggedly held out against Nobunaga's rise, clinging on to the power they had gained in the political vacuum of civil war. It was another example of Hisahide's turncoat nature. Only recently he had still been assisting Nobunaga in his attempt to root out this last bastion of religious fanaticism. Now, as he found himself at the receiving end of the warlord's wrath, he sought to enlist the help of the very monks he had been fighting.

Unbeknown to Hisahide, his last ploy to save himself spelled his very end. His envoy had once been one of Junkei's vassals, who had lost his position following the fall of Tsutsui castle. He had spent several years as a rōnin until, like so many other minor chieftains in the region, he had been coerced into entering Hisahide's service. Having returned with a small army of Ikkō sectarians, Yoshihisa took control over the castle's third tier. From there they began to shoot incendiary arrows upward, *setting fire to buildings on the second tier. A gusty wind blew toward the top of the mountain, fanning the flames and causing them to jump to the buildings on the first tier. Before long most of the castle was alight, only its magnificent donjon still towering above the flames.*

Aware that his game was up, Hisahide withdrew to the main tower and killed himself. He did so by detonating a cast-iron tea kettle filled with gunpowder. It was the tenth day of the tenth month, and the historical irony wasn't lost on Nobunaga's chronicler:

> *Nara's Daibutsuden, too, went up in flames on the tenth day of the tenth month. And it was this very same Matsunaga who reduced it to ashes without good reason, and along with it the entire temple complex known throughout the realm. Thus it was heaven's retribution when Lord Oda Nobutada pressed home the attack on Shigisan castle, a mountain so high that not even birds and beasts can find a foothold.*

Recovery

Ten years had passed since Muneyoshi had broken his pact with Hisahide. For the first few years, they had lived in fear of Hisahide's wrath. That threat had been more than real. He recalled how Hisahide had reacted to the defection of his other chieftain, Ido Yoshihiro. The sight of the two youngsters, their frail bodies impaled on a pole at the gate of Tamonyama castle, was still etched on his retina. Of course it hadn't ended there. The warlord had next turned on the stronghold of the girl's father. Marching south from Nara, he laid siege of Ido castle with a large force, determined to wreak his revenge. To drive home his message, he had ordered his men to bring along the impaled girl and boy and had them planted in front of the castle, for all its inhabitants to see. Like Yagyū castle, Ido was only a small stronghold. It fell after a month's siege, though Yoshihiro and most of his clansmen managed to escape. It was one of Muneyoshi's eternal regrets that he had been part of that siege, that he and his men had contributed to the misery of the Ido clan. Ties between them and the Yagyū had always been good. One of their clansmen, a stout warrior by the name of Matsuda Oribe no Suke, had spent a long time at Yagyū castle as a *deshi*, studying the Yagyū Shinkage-*ryū* at their *dōjō*, and gone on to found his own school of swordsmanship. For a time he had even courted one of Muneyoshi's daughters.

Thankfully, the Yagyū had been spared the Ido's terrible fate, partly because of their remoteness, partly because Hisahide had been pressed elsewhere. His death, almost three years hence now, had first brought relief, then uncertainty about Junkei's governorship. It had been Nabu, in the end, who had saved the Yagyū from reprisals. She was, after all, Junkei's cousin, though he had only been two years old when she had moved to Yagyū castle. But her mother hadn't forgotten her. She had plied her nephew to accept her and the Yagyū clan back into the Tsutsui fold. It had worked. Junkei had attended a grand reunion at the Kasuga Taisha, where the Yagyū had organized a *nō* performance in his honor. Following the performance, Junkei had struck a conciliatory tone, complimenting Muneyoshi on his good taste in women and the wisdom of breaking his pact with Hisahide. He had also vouchsafed that, as long as he was governor of Yamato, they wouldn't be harmed.

Only minor sporadic unrests had disturbed the calm that followed in the wake of Hisahide's death, and the many clans that populated the Nara Basin used the opportunity to repair their castles. Junkei, too, joined in. Following his appointment, he began on a large-scale reconstruction of Tsutsui castle to the tune of thousands of *mon*. Materials from Tamonyama castle were used to reinforce the stronghold's walls and to build a massive new northern wing. It was a huge project, taking a workforce of several hundred men three years to complete.

Ikkoku Hajō

That summer, on the seventeenth of August, in the eighth year of the Tenshō era (September 25, 1580), Muneyoshi was ordered to Tsutsui castle. He hadn't been the only chieftain ordered to do so. It was a blisteringly hot day, and all the Yamato chieftains, some fifty in total, had gathered in the castle's main hall. Many of the chieftains who had been forced from their former domains were in attendance—the Ido, the Sugawa, the Furuichi—though none knew what they had come for.

Though presided over by Junkei, most of the talking was done by an official, an old and gangly man. It was a senior emissary of Taikō Toyotomi Hideyoshi, the new lord of the realm. The air was filled with a silent tension as the man drew a piece of paper from his left sleeve and slowly began to read. 'I am here today on behalf of my lord and master, Taikō Toyotomi Hideyoshi, to proclaim, effective immediately, the *Yamato Ikkoku Hajō Meirei*, the 'Order for the Destruction of All Castles in the Province of Yamatō...'[5]

'*Nan da!*' (What is this!) Ido Yoshihiro bellowed when the emissary had left. 'Is this what it has come to? Is this what my clan has suffered for all these decades? Time and time again we have put everything at stake to save our clans. I lost my daughter, and for years my clan has had to live in exile. And I'm not the only one. All here have suffered, in equal measure.'

There were grunts of support from the rest as Yoshiaki continued, though more imploring now. 'Together we have finally brought peace back to Yamato. We have helped Nobunaga get rid of Hisahide. We have sworn allegiance to you, Lord Junkei. And how are we repaid? We are to tear down our castles!'

'I know!' Junkei said as he looked Yoshiaki straight in the eyes. 'I know you have suffered and understand your anger. Yet I too have suffered. I and my clan have lived in exile for many years. Yet I have no say in the matter. Nor do I have any recourse. As you know, Nobunaga has removed Yoshiaki from Nijō castle for conspiring with Takeda Shingen, and even the Emperor is now impotent in these matters.'

He now turned to the rest of the gathered men. 'If it is any consolation to you, I too will be tearing down my castle, for I am ordered to move my headquarters to Kōriyama castle, which, as you know, is a far less formidable defense. In fact, so as to set an example, I will start tearing down this castle at sunrise tomorrow.'

Junkei made good on his word. Pressing a large part of Nara's population into forced labor, he raised Tsutsui castle to the ground in just three days, using much of the rubble to fill in the moats. Just a few of its features were left intact, among them the main gate, which was re-erected in front of the castle's main *dōjō*. The old *dōjō* too was saved, but only because Junkei had it converted into a Buddhist temple under the name of Kōsen-*ji*.

Dismantlement

Muneyoshi, too, tried to salvage what he could. Wielding large wooden hammers, his carpenters dislodged the mortises and tenons with carefully aimed blows that echoed down the valley.

Then, collectively chanting, '*yuisshoo!*' a group of his strongest men hauled the massive *sugi* beams onto their shoulders one by one to carry them to a neat pile near the *yashiki*. The large tiles from the roof and top of the walls, as well as the cylindrical top tiles bearing the Yagyū family crest, were salvaged. They and the beams were used to build a large extension to the Momiji *yashiki*, which would now have to house the whole family.

Other parts of the building, including the walls, couldn't be saved, and teams of peasants went at the stuccoed surfaces with pickaxes, exposing the woven mats within them so they could be used for kindling.

Muneyoshi grew despondent as he watched them doing their dreadful work. Normally they would sing some popular folk song of love and woe when at work. Now they silently went about their dreadful task, the only sound that of their destructive tools. Even his grandchildren, still too young to fathom the enormity of it all, had lost their sense of play; they just stood by, shyly, wondering why they were losing their home. How different it had been when he was young. He recalled how proud he had been when, as a young boy, he had helped in the castle's reconstruction. He vividly remembered how he and his father had poured over the large drawings, how his father had pointed out the various improvements on the old structure. His father never showed much emotion—unless he was really angry— but he could still recall how his father had emphasized the new walls would be higher than any other in the region. He could still see the glint in his father's eyes, hear the satisfied grumble in his voice, which always dropped when contented. He had dreaded having to break the news, especially to him. The old man had taken it well enough, expressing his hope that they wouldn't need a castle under Nobunaga's rule. But the next day he had stayed inside, even though it was a beautiful autumn day.

Muneyoshi couldn't remember when he had last heard that grumble in his father's voice, seen the glint in his eyes.

Most of the work on the Momiji *yashiki* was completed before the winter set in. When it came, it brought icy cold winds, with lots of snow to cover the gaping wound across the Yahagi River. By the time they saw in the new year, it was as if Yagyū castle had never existed; having weathered more than two and a half centuries of civil war, the occasional fire, and a long drawn-out siege by Tsutsui Junshō's forces, Yagyū castle, the proud abode of the Yagyū clan, was no more.

It was a meager consolation that none of the Yamato chieftains had been exempted. Nobunaga's decree was executed with such rigor and at such a dazzling pace that almost all the castles that had graced the Yamato landscape were obliterated. Tamonyama and Shigisan, too, had gone. Similar proclamations had been issued in the neighboring provinces of Kawachi and Settsu so that by the end of 1581, only one castle remained per province, all the rest lay in ruin or were gone.

A Newborn

Only when he observed his children did Muneyoshi's mood lift. He now had six daughters and five sons. During the first year of their self-imposed isolation, in the spring of 1571, Nabu had given birth to another healthy son. They had named him Shinzaemon, or 'New Guard of the Left Gate,' a traditional and auspicious name.

It wasn't just because he was his youngest son that Muneyoshi doted on Shinzaemon. Ten years had passed since his oldest son, Yoshikatsu, had been wounded at Takahi Hill. Despite the severity of the wound, he had recovered well. Unable to ride

126

or join his brothers in practice, he spent much of his time outside, doing odd jobs near the *yashiki*, or visiting the womenfolk in the fields. It was how he had met his wife, the daughter of one of their *shinobi* headmen. She had given him a healthy son, whom they had named Monzaemon. He still went with a stilted gait, but outdoor life had given him a sinewy muscularity and healthy tan. And while they didn't deliberately avoid each other, Muneyoshi and Yoshikatsu were hardly seen together, as both felt awkward in each other's company. Only once had they talked about Takahi Hill. It had been a difficult conversation, interspersed with long and painful silences, but no reproaches—for that they shared too much guilt.

Muneyoshi poured much of his energy into his fourth son, Muneaki, who was five years Shinzaemon's senior. He was bright enough, and always cheery. He was also a good swordsman, but quite incapable of abstract thought. Muneyoshi had tried to stir in the boy an interest in literature, share his enthusiasm for his *Gyokuei shūi*, the ancient family records of the Yagyū clan. But Muneaki would invariably grow bored; his interests were always practical: horse tackle, sword gear—the like.

Shinzaemon, by contrast, proved a highly intelligent child, whose natural aptness for learning and fighting was paired with a cockiness quite lovable in a boy his age. Yet there was something more in Shinzaemon that inspired a sense of awe in Muneyoshi, despite the boy's youth, something he had only observed in men far more advanced in age and experience. It wasn't his general demeanor; he still loved to fool around, play tricks on his older sisters with his brothers. But every now and then something shone through, revealing a profound difference between him and his siblings.

One day, breaking in a new pony while out riding with his father, they were talking about the past. Unlike his older brothers, Shinzaemon was always full of questions: about Muneyoshi's past, how his life had been as a hostage, how he and Nabu had met, how their clan had come to sign a pact with men like Hisahide, and how they had come to break it. These were not random questions out of general curiosity about his background; they were always driven by some topic, some specific theme he wanted to explore and organize in that remarkable young mind of his. This time he wanted to know all about Muneyoshi's friendship with Kamiizumi Nobutsuna and the close ties the latter had entertained with Oda Nobunaga.

Muneyoshi told his son how he and the swordsman from Kōzuke had first met at the Hōzō monastery, how he had been defeated by Bungorō, and how Nobutsuna had been his guest for almost two years. Muneyoshi enjoyed talking about this episode in his life: next to his courtship with Nabu, it was among his fondest memories. He explained how it had been largely through Nobutsuna's close ties with Nobunaga that the two of them had helped bring the Shōgun to the capital.

As always, the boy listened attentively until his father had finished. For a while he remained silent, playing with his reigns as he weighed and connected facts. Then, knitting his thin brows, he looked up to his father and asked, 'Why then, father, did you not use Nobutsuna-*dono*'s influence to gain a position at Nobunaga's court?'

Muneyoshi laughed off the matter, explaining to his son that unlike his friend Nobutsuna, who was a *rōnin*, a free agent, he himself had been a chieftain with commitments. But later, pondering the same question in the privacy of his study, he wondered: what if, at that early and fertile stage, he had declared himself openly for Nobunaga? Would he now be among that small circle of men at Nobunaga's court in Kyoto, directly influencing affairs of state?

Chapter 7

Education

It was on Muneyoshi's insistence that, at the age of nine, Shinzaemon entered the Ichijō-*in*. Not to become a Buddhist monk like his two older siblings, but to study under Eishun. Since the burning of the Daibutsuden, the warrior and the monk had often met. There was a mercenary side to their friendship. For Eishun, who was still working on his *Tamon-in nikki*, each encounter was an opportunity to learn more about Yagyū and Kasagi. For Muneyoshi, who was working on his own clan history, it was an opportunity to draw from the monk's staggering repository of knowledge. Now he wanted his son to profit from it too—there was enough there to answer all the questions Shinzaemon could ever think of.

During his early years, Shinzaemon spent much of his time with the monks of the Ichijō-*in*, studying calligraphy, Buddhist scripture, and the Chinese classics. As Shinzaemon advanced, Eishun would increasingly call him to his study overlooking the temple grounds. Shinzaemon soon grew familiar with the routine. Called, he would sit down at Eishun's door, call out his name and, when answered, slide open the latticed door of the monk's study. Sitting down on the other side of Eishun's wide desk, he would take tea from the small cabinet along the wall, put some in a small ceramic teapot of red clay with a long handle, and pour on hot water from the cast iron kettle that perennially simmered on a small *hibachi* at the room's center. Then, at the right moment—Eishun hated tea that had been infused too short or too long—he would fill his teacher's cup, his own, and Eishun would begin to talk. He would begin slowly as if rummaging for an important old document lost in a vast library. Then, having retrieved it, his sentences would grow longer, his gestures more animated.

A whole new world opened up to the young warrior as he listened in rapture to the chattering monk, whose jaw had such trouble keeping up with the stream of word, that bits of spittle would gather on his lower lip, which he occasionally wiped away with a scrap of paper from his desk, then cast it in the fire. There was not a subject on which the monk wasn't informed. Such as the origins of the Kasuga Taisha and the Kōfuku-*ji*, and their historical importance to the region. Shinzaemon knew that both dated back to the time when Nara had still been the capital, that they had both been founded by the Fujiwara, the clan from which he descended. What he didn't know was that, because of their great influence at court, Yamato had never had a governor. Instead, it had been governed by the Kōfuku-*ji*'s abbot. Not even the Ashikaga had been able to appoint a governor—for that the resistance of the *kokumin* and *shuto* had been too strong. Junkei's appointment, then, had been a momentous one. Only time would tell if it was a good thing—whether it would bring the peace and prosperity everybody craved.

Katsujinken

Because of his studies, Shinzaemon hadn't traveled much yet. Once, when he was ten years old, his father took him to Kyoto to see the *O-umazoroe*, a grand horse parade celebrating Oda Nobunaga's victory over his many foes. It was a huge spectacle. There were the armies of his chief generals, Niwa Nagahide, Hachiya Yoritaka, and Akechi Mitsuhide. One after the other their warriors, all on horseback, marched down the wide main thoroughfare leading to the Imperial Palace. There, sitting on a high podium facing the vast horse grounds on the palace's eastern side, Emperor Ōgimachi looked on as they silently marched by. The largest army was that of Nobunaga—ten divisions, each led by a member of the Oda clan. For hours they watched them ride by. Finally, toward evening, the great warlord himself arrived. Sitting astride his white steed, he wore a tiger skin around his shoulders and strapped to his waist a large *katana*, its gold-plated sheath glittering in the sun. Immediately behind him, two warriors in full armor carried a huge banner carrying his motto: *tenka fubu,* 'Rule the realm by force.'

On his return to Nara, Shinzaemon's enthusiasm was soon tempered by Eishun. 'Does master Shinzaemon know,' he asked, suddenly far less animated than his usual self, 'that following his victory over the *sōhei* of the Enryaku temple on Mount Hiei, Lord Nobunaga's men burned all its temples, like Hisahide did in Nara? Does master Shinzaemon know that all its monks, servants, women, and children were butchered to death?'

For once the young warrior was lost for words.

'Lord Nobunaga,' the old monk mumbled, almost as if to himself, 'might perhaps be a man of impeccable manners—that much I have dared entrust to my diary—yet he is also a man of unsurpassed cruelty.'

Eishun's words set Shinzaemon thinking. The temples had indeed suffered greatly. The eeriest sight among the many ruins was the ghostly specter of the Daibutsuden. All that remained standing were the charred sections of its walls and the decapitated trunk of the once so magnificent Great Buddha. Whenever Shinzaemon set his eyes on the headless torso, protruding ominously from the macabre palisade of charred woodwork, a chill ran down his spine. It seemed as if even the benevolence of the Great Buddha had been exhausted by the constant warring. All that violence had come out of nothing, and had led to nothing. The only thing it had achieved was to inflict yet more suffering on an already starving populace.

In the course of Shinzaemon's years at the Kōfuku temple, he gradually opened up to the reality of the time he was living in. Growing up in the secluded setting of Yagyū Valley, he had been allowed to believe the world was a good place. He hadn't realized that, out in the wider world, there were at work evil, destructive forces—forces beyond one's control. Now, as he wandered Nara's ruined neighborhoods on errands for his teacher, he began to see their destructive power. With every year, he began to see more clearly, and finally with total clarity, the shortsightedness of many a chieftain's ambitions.

Not that he didn't believe in the superiority of his class. Far from it. Though warriors had wrought much of the destruction, they were also uniquely poised to undo it. From the moment he had taken up practicing at the small family *dōjō* in the woods behind the Momiji *yashiki* under his father's tutelage, there had been one thing that his father had returned to again and again. It was the duality of *setsunin* (taking life) and *katsunin* (giving life). Eishun taught him these were not new concepts. For centuries Zen monks had used them in their struggle to rid themselves of worldly desires. They were not necessarily about the physical act of killing and giving life. Rather, they were concerned with the spiritual realm, the good and bad within oneself. 'To give life to the good within us,' he had explained, 'we must first kill the bad within us. Only then can one hope to become enlightened.'

He knew it had been Kamiizumi Nobutsuna who had first adopted these concepts into the philosophy of his Shinkage-*ryū* by introducing the term *setsunintō-katsuninken*, or 'death-dealing sword' and 'life-giving sword.' And while one Yagyū technique was even named Katsuninken, Muneyoshi had stressed that the duality of *setsunintō-katsuninken*, underpinned all of the Yagyū Shikage-*ryū* techniques, and that it embodied everything the

132

Yagyū stood for—that it should always, always guide his actions. He must also never forget the profound importance of his position. They were a clan of warriors, they were *bushi*, and as a *bushi* Shinzaemon could decide over life and death, influence good and evil in an imperfect world. His *katana* was his divinely ordained instrument, and like its blade, it had two faces: that of *setsunintō*, and that of *katsuninken*. He could use it to root out evil by killing those who practiced evil with his *setsunintō*. By rooting out evil, and saving what was good, his sword would become a *katsuninken*. This, his father had impressed on him, was something Lord Matsunaga Hisahide had never understood. In his hands, the *katana* had become an evil force. It had been this awareness, more than anything, that had ultimately made him decide to break his pact with the warlord.

On such moments Shinzaemon venerated his father. At the same time, there was also something in his father that saddened the young warrior. He found it hard to put his finger on what it really was. His father never, ever bragged, and would always reproach him and his brothers whenever he caught them doing so, saying pride would be their undoing. Sometimes, when in a good mood, he would tell them of his adventures—how he and Shigeyoshi had gone on a *musha shugyō* and how he and Kamiizumi Ise no Kami Nobutsuna had first met at In'ei's Hōzō monastery.

Shinzaemon's favorite story was that of their daring rescue of Kakkei from the temple where he was now studying—how in the dead of night they had sneaked into the temple grounds and liberated Shogun Yoshiaki. He knew that it had earned them recognition. Though his father never mentioned it, his mother had told him how, two years before he had been born, his father had been invited to Nijō castle to demonstrate his skills before none other than the Shōgun himself. It had been on that occasion that Yoshiaki had granted Muneyoshi the honorary name of Tajima no Kami, the name by which he was addressed by all who served and knew him.

His father did tell him and his brothers at length of the honors granted to his great teacher from Kōzuke, recounting how he had been present when, on June 27, 1570, the Shōgun had raised the sixty-two-year-old Nobutsuna to the rank of Jūshi-i, or Fourth-Level Warrior Follower. Never in Japan's feudal history, he told them, had a swordsman been appointed to such high rank.

Shinzaemon had heard it all before, a thousand times. He always grew irritated when his father went on about the achievements of others while belittling his own. Why could he not take pride in his own achievements? Hadn't he helped to restore the Shōgun to his rightful place? He recognized the virtue in modesty, yet he hated the self-effacement. He was determined to do things differently. He did want to be like his father, he too wanted to make a change, be a force for good, but he also wanted to feel proud.

CHAPTER 8

late in June 1582 Oda Nobunaga was sojourning in the capital. He was making preparations to march for Bitchū, where his chief general, Toyotomi Hideyoshi, was laying siege to Takamatsu castle, a stronghold of the Mōri, a powerful clan from the west of Japan. The latter were offering fierce opposition, forcing his general to appeal for reinforcements. Always confident, Nobunaga went about his preparations with a degree of leisure. On the evening of June 21, he even found time to organize a tea ceremony at the Honnō temple, his usual abode in the capital. He was in high spirits that evening, regaling his guests with tales from his early youth. By the time he and his guest heard the stampeding of hoofs, it was too late. Aketchi Mitsuhide, one of his generals had turned against him. Nobunaga rushed out, shouting that Mitsuhide would 'never succeed,' but his retinue, though it fought bravely, was outnumbered. At length he withdrew into the burning building and committed seppuku.

Nobunaga's sudden demise propelled his chief general, Toyotomi Hideyoshi, into the forefront. He was up to the task. Though a man of humble origins, Hideyoshi was a brilliant general with an cunning way of winning powerful chieftains over to his side. Sensing the threat Mitsuhide posed to Japan's unification, he immediately launched a campaign to crush the rebel.

Tsutsui Junkei was now put in a tight spot. Ties between the house of Tsutsui and that of Akechi were close—it had been through Mitsuhide's offices that Nobunaga had granted Junkei the province of Yamato. And sure enough, facing Hideyoshi's wrath, Mitsuhide called on his friend to rally behind him. Junkei was reluctant to act. He did raise a small contingent, but when he learned that Hideyoshi was marching on the capital he balked and stayed put at his new headquarters of Kōriyama castle. He was unable to make up his mind: join Hideyoshi and live; join Mitsuhide and perish.

When Hideyoshi's and Mitsuhide's forces finally clashed at the strategic narrow of the Hora Pass, Junkei's reinforcements failed to appear. Instead he sent a missive to Hideyoshi's headquarters of Himeji castle in Harima. In it he pledged his allegiance to the general, vowing not to lift a finger against his troops. His gamble paid off; in return for his show of loyalty, Junkei was allowed to hold on to his governorship of Yamato Province and continue residing at Kōriyama castle.

In 1584, Junkei died following a short illness. Leadership over the Tsutsui was assumed by his twenty-three-year-old adopted son Sadatsugu, who was ordered by Hideyoshi to move his headquarters to Ueno in the neighboring province of Iga.[1] Some of the chieftains who had found peace with the Tsutsui chose to follow him to Iga. Among them was Nakanobō Hidesuke, the son of Morisuke and the new leader of the Nakanobō clan. Others preferred to hold on to their domains, and chose to serve under the new governor and lord of Kōriyama castle, Hideyoshi's stepbrother Hidenaga.

There were good reasons why Hideyoshi had made his stepbrother the new governor of Yamato. Together with castles in the other Home Provinces, it formed a line of defense around the capital, which was again the center of power. From Kōriyama castle, it was only twenty miles to the former site of the Ishiyama Hongan temple, where Hideyoshi had begun to build his new headquarters of Osaka castle, and on his way there he often stayed at his stepbrother's new headquarters.

It was during this period, while his power was at its apex, that Hideyoshi made the next great move in the campaign to pacify the country begun by Nobunaga. Retiring from his position as kanpaku *(regent) and assuming the title of* Taikō *(retired regent) he turned all his energies to conquer Shikoku and Kyūshū, and to subjugate the powerful Hōjō at Odawara castle in the Kantō.*[2] *Huge sums of money were required to finance these vast campaigns, and in a feudal age the chief source of revenue was the tax levied upon a plot of land's rice yield.*

To determine the tax that could be levied, it was of crucial importance for feudal lords to know the exact yield of the lands under their rule and that of their vassals. And here lay the great problem. A century of anarchy had thoroughly upset the pattern of land rights that had been in place under the Ashikaga Shōgunate. As the fighting had spread, so had the often conflicting claims by local military rulers over ever more fragmented pieces of land, until even they themselves were in the dark as to the size and yield of the domains under their control.

And thus, as he was nearing the completion of his predecessor's goal, Hideyoshi set about to conduct a nationwide land survey (kenchi). *Not surprisingly, the* Taikō Kenchi, *as it came to be known, was most rigorously executed in the provinces under his clan's control, especially Yamato, now under the governorship of his stepbrother Hidenaga.*

Gyokuei shūi

Since they had moved to the Momiji *yashiki*, partly to divert his mind from the loss of Yagyū castle, Muneyoshi had been spending much time on his life's work, the *Gyokuei shūi*. He was now fifty-eight, and he was determined to pass the work on to his offspring completed. He had just traced the distant relationship between the Yagyū and Nakanobō. It had been hard work. Though some of the documents in his clan went back to the Heian period, they were few and historically far between, shedding little light on this tumultuous but fascinating episode. To write it he had been forced to look elsewhere. For many months now he had been making the long climb up Kasagi Mountain to visit the temple's old library. There, among piles of ancient and dusty records dating back more than two centuries, he had spent countless hours painstakingly reconstructing the dramatic events of Go-Daigo's revolt and the strange spell it had cast on the fate of the two clans. Ever since that fateful summer day in the first year of the Genkō era, when Gō-Daigo had taken up residence on Mount Kasagi, the two clans had struggled to survive in an ever increasing vortex of violence. Why was it that they had so often found themselves fighting on the losing side? Was it simply that there was more evil than good in this fleeting world?

There were enough heroic episodes to take courage from. With deep interest he had read of the valiant roles of his distant ancestors, chieftain Nagayoshi and his brother, the warrior-monk Gensen. The records revealed that both of them had fought bravely. Both had paid a heavy price for their loyalty to the rightful emperor. He had learned how Yagyū Nagayoshi had been dispossessed and forced to throw himself on the mercy of the Kasagi temple. Having covered most of the intervening time, he now knew that it had been the only time his clan had ever lost their lands. Thankfully Nagayoshi had been allowed to stay on in his beloved valley, working a small plot of land belonging to Kasagi temple. It had been Gensen's close ties to the temple that had saved them.

How things had changed since then. Now Gensen's descendants, the Nakanobō, were gone. Giving up his clan's close ties to the region, Nakanobō Hidesuke had decided to follow the Tsutsui to the neighboring province of Iga. It had been a difficult time. He had been forced to abandon his clan's *yashiki* in Tsubai and start afresh again in Iga's capital of Ueno.

And while the Yagyū, too, had had their fair share of setbacks, at least they hadn't been forced to part with their beloved lands. For a small clan, their domains were considerable. Stretching from the southern foot of Mount Kasagi to the northern slopes of Mount Ittai, some five miles southward, they covered some twelve thousand acres. It was fertile soil that had sustained life ever since the dawn of man. The annual yield of the Yagyū *han* lay around 2000 *koku*, well above the yield of similar domains in more arid regions. There were also some *kakushida*, so-called 'hidden paddies'. They lay on the other side of the hills behind the Momiji *yashiki*, in an adjacent valley. The *kakushida* were a nice source of extra income, for they yielded much rice and, since they were hidden, no tax was levied on them by the Yamato governor. Muneyoshi didn't worry about them; no one but his own clansmen knew of them.

Kenchi

It was on his return from one of his trips up Mount Kasagi, in the fall of 1585, just as he was about to cross the Momiji bridge toward his *yashiki*, that Muneyoshi heard the stampede of hoofs. Looking southward down the valley he saw the dust rise behind a small group of men on horseback. For a moment his nerves tensed, then his muscles relaxed: they were governor Hidenaga's men.

As they drew closer they reigned in their horses, coming to a stop at the foot of the bridge. Still weary of his long climb up and down Mount Kasagi, Muneyoshi leaned on the bridge's wooden balustrade with one hand, using the other to block the sun, as he blinked at the men high on horseback. One of them was a senior official.

'I am Mashita Nagamori Saemonjō. I am Hidenaga's *kenchi bugyō*, and I have been commissioned with the survey of all the domains in the province of Yamato.'

Muneyoshi grew uncomfortable. He had faithfully reported the acreage of his domain—his official domains, that was. Were he to report his *kakushida*, he would be in deep trouble. Going by their modest appearance, the other men were Nagamori's assistants. One of them he knew: it was Matsuda Oribe no Suke, an Ido warrior who had once been among his *deshi*. They had remained close until 1558 when Muneyoshi had helped his then lord Matsunaga Hisahide to evict the Ido clan from their castle.

Oribe no Suke didn't meet Muneyoshi's eyes, nor did he respond to Muneyoshi's stammered words of welcome. He merely turned to the *kenchi bugyō*, pointed eastward, toward the mountains behind the Momiji *yashiki*, and coldly said, 'They lie on the other side of the mountains.'

Involuntarily Muneyoshi's other hand went to the balustrade, for he felt his legs might give way. Only shreds of Nagamori's words registered in Muneyoshi's numbed brain as he pondered the immense implications of the man's words: ...'assess the full extent of the Yagyū domains'...'tracts of land of unregistered or doubtful status'...'reassessment of effective rice yield'... 'redistribution of all lands'...'rightfully belong to the great Taikō Toyotomi Hideyoshi.'

Rōnin

The strange thing was that, afterward, Muneyoshi couldn't remember what had happened next; it seemed as if, from that point on, everything had happened as if in a blur. Had he accompanied the men around his estate? Had he gone with them and pointed out the *kakushida*? He had a vague recollection of his oldest son at his side, railing at Oribe no Suke, but being pushed aside by their horses.

It took Mashita Nagamori only a few weeks to arrive at his reassessment. That same month, the eleventh month of the thirteenth year of the Tenshō era, Governor Toyotomi Hidenaga issued a lengthy summons, which was delivered to Muneyoshi by a gloating Oribe no Suke. All of the Yagyū domains were confiscated forthwith. Their *yashiki*, too, was impounded. Their only solace was Muneyoshi's stipend of five *koku*, just enough to keep him and his family from total starvation.

Many times in his life Muneyoshi had faced difficulties. But each time he had found a way through. This time he saw no way through, no plan to fall back on. Long ago, on his return from Oki Island, Emperor Go-Daigo had restored his ancestor, Nagayoshi, to his rightful possessions. Now, the emperor could not save them; he was just a puppet in Hideyoshi's hands. Not even the Shōgun could help them. More than ten years had passed since Nobunaga had sent Yoshiaki into exile, bringing to an end more than two centuries of Ashikaga rule. Now Oda Nobunaga was dead, and the Yagyū had no connections to his successor, Hideyoshi, let alone his stepbrother Hidenaga. Nor could they fall back on Nabu's ties to the Tsutsui and move to Iga, even if they had wanted to. Their new leader, Hidetsugu, had little affinity toward his adoptive cousin. No—this time around it seemed nothing could save the Yagyū from reaching the pit of that terrible vortex.

The Yagyū were now true *rōnin*, with no castle to live in, no land to defend, no lord to serve. In a world in which everything depended on this inseparable trinity, the future of the Yagyū clan seemed doomed. Even their unsurpassed mastery of the sword, an art that had seen them through so many troubles, now seemed reduced to a useless anachronism, unable to hold its own against an art of warfare in which the *teppō*, the loathed foreign musket, took pride of place.

Enjō Temple

It was Eishun who helped the Yagyū find a new roof over their heads. Konoe Sakihisa, a close friend of his, had been rewarded large tracts of land in the wake of the Taikō Kenchi. They lay in the vicinity of Hirao, a hamlet, some four miles east of Nara along the Yagyū Kaidō. Eishun also entertained close relations with the abbot of the local Enjō temple, an old Shingon center that stood in the shadow of Mount Ittai near the village of Ōhirai. And it was there that Sakihisa allowed the Yagyū the tenure of a small cottage behind the temple including a small plot of land they could work to their own benefit.

For the fifty-eight-year-old Muneyoshi the humiliation was unbearable. Seeking to distract his mind, he tried to work on his *Gyokuei shūi*, but couldn't bring himself to commit his troubled thoughts to paper. Each time he took up his brush to write, he broke out into a cold sweat and his hand would begin to tremble involuntarily as he forced himself to concentrate on the events of the last few months.

Too old and frail to join the rest of his family in the fields, he preferred to steal himself away from the Enjō temple. Every morning, at the hour of the Rabbit, just after the sun had risen, he would take his staff and walk up the Yagyū Kaidō, directing his steps northwards. It was only three miles from Ōhirai to Yagyū Valey, a half-hour walk for his old legs. Though his lands now belonged to the governor, they were still tended to by the same peasants who had worked for him. Sometimes he would visit them, listen to their complaints about the governor's harsh regime, the high taxes he levied. More often he would go and visit the Momiji *yashiki*. Though it had been confiscated, no one had cared to use it. It just stood there, as they had left it, as if it wondered where its owners had gone. He would spend hours sitting on its wide veranda, listening to the song of the warbler in the woods above. Then he would wonder: how had it come to this; how would his children fare in such a hostile world; would they ever be able to return to their beloved valley?

Stone Vessel

For two years Muneyoshi kept up his daily walks to Yagyū Valley. Then, in the winter of 1587, following a short illness, his father, Ieyoshi, passed away. After that he lost interest.

Only once, shortly after his father's passing did Muneyoshi visit the Momiji *yashiki* again. It was on that visit, sitting on the building's old veranda, that Muneyoshi reflected on his father's life. It seemed that with his passing a whole generation had gone, like a coat of leaves, shaken off carelessly with the changing of seasons. What had it all meant, all that fighting, all that sorrow? His uncle Shigeyoshi, too, was dead, fallen with his master in the defense of Shigisan castle—another warrior who had fallen victim to his own vanity. Come to think of it, Muneyoshi realized he was little better than his uncle. At least Shigeyoshi had never pretended to be guided by any moral compass, but simply indulged his earthly desires. Yet deep down he knew he could never be like his uncle; he still had his conscience, however much it tormented him now.

Not that his father had done anything to cause that torment: Ieyoshi had never reproached him for the pact he had signed with Hisahide, not even his capture by Junkei's men. Yet no matter how often the old man had told him they would have lost out eventually, that his capture had saved them from a worse fate, he couldn't bring himself to see it that way. His stupid pride had got the better of him. He recalled how he had glowed with self-importance in his newly tailored suit of armor, made by Yoshida Gempachirō, the best artisan in Nara—how he had insisted, against his father's will to wear the Kasagi no Tachi, the family heirloom forged by the great Masamune. Yet what kind of heirloom was this? It was the *katana* his ancestor Nagayoshi had worn during the fall of Shigisan, it was the *katana* he himself had worn during the fall of Yagyū castle, and it was the *katana* Yoshikatsu had worn during his fateful attack on the Kōnin temple, leaving him crippled for life.

A sudden rage swept over Muneyoshi; he was sure now the Kasagi no Tachi was cursed. Ever since Yoshikatsu had been wounded he had fought against the idea, brushing it off as silly superstition. Still, he had anxiously kept the weapon away from Shinzaemon. Wanting to stop the boy from using the *katana*, but reluctant to explain why, he had hidden it under the floor of the *yashiki* during the renovations. Now he wanted to make sure the boy would never find it. Clambering to his feet he drew open one of the wooden shutters and pushed inside the house. Already the rain had found its way through the thatched roof in several places, leaving large stains on the *tatami* mats underneath. Swelling up they had begun to mold and rot so that, moving over toward the main room's alcove, he had to watch his step in the dark for fear of falling through the floorboards. Protected by the recess, the single, half-width *tatami* in the alcove was still in good shape. It came out in one piece when he pried it loose with his walking stick. Casting it aside, he looked down into the house's inner bowels. There it was! Glimmering ominously in its lacquered sheath, it was still tied with two silk ribbons to the beams supporting the floor. Untying the ribbons he took the cursed trophy. As if in a fever, he stood up and made his way outside, rushing now, toward the old willow beside the lake. There, below the tree's weeping branches, he drew the weapon one last time from its sheath, gathered all his strength, and cast it as far away from him as he could. With a muted splash it landed in the middle of the lake. Only a slowly widening ripple bore witness to his deed until they died among the reeds of the lake's shallows. Then all was silent.

Muneyoshi moved back from the lake, afraid to turn round, as if it too was cursed. A shiver went through the old man. It was growing dark, and cold mountain air was making its way down the snow-covered slopes. He looked down at the sheath in his left hand. It was beautifully crafted, lacquered with *urushi* throughout, and both ends were strengthened with *same*, shark skin, while the Yagyū crest was inlaid in mother of pearl at the middle and embossed on its silver tip. He muttered something to himself as he stared at it. Then he turned and walked up close to the raised veranda. Planting the lower end of the sheath into a gap among its thick floorboards, he tensed the muscles in his face as he gave the other end a hard tug. With a sharp crack the sheath disintegrated under his callused hands. Then, crouching down in the shelter of the house, he lit a small fire and fed the sheath's splintered remnants to the flames.

Five years later, in the second year of the Bunroku era, he told the Enjō temple's abbot he had decided to take the tonsure. From now on, he would do so under the name of Sekishūsai, or 'stone Vessel.' One more time he returned to his small study to take up his brush. Not to work on his history. He was done with writing. He had made up his mind on what he would do with the few years he still had. Then his hand began to move, as if directed by a higher power, a force beyond his control:

Without a means to live
I will make the art of swordsmanship
my refuge, my sad repose.
It is good for hiding places,
yet in strife it has no use.
For though I may win contests,
I am but a Stone Vessel,
unable to cross the sea of life.

CHAPTER 9

Having subdued the entire Japanese realm, Toyotomi Hideyoshi now launched his most ambitious and at the same time his most foolhardy project: the subjugation of the Korean Peninsula. For a long time he had entertained the idea of invading the continent, perhaps even to conquer China. As early as 1586, he had begun to build a large fleet of ships to ferry his troops across the Korean Straits. He had even sent across an assault force to test the Korean's strength. In its wake followed several embassies with ultimatums demanding their submission and participation in China's conquest. Now, at the apex of his power, and with thousands and thousands of battle-hardened troops spoiling for another fight, he decided to act.

On April 13, 1592, the first of nine divisions, under the command of Konishi Yukinaga, set sail from Ōura, on the island of Tsushima, halfway the Korean Straits. That same evening they landed near the port of Busan. On May 25, having taken Busan, they laid siege to the castle town of Dongnae, which fell within a day at the cost of three thousand of its inhabitants. The second division, under the command of Katō Kiyomasa, occupied the abandoned city of Tongdo and soon after captured nearby Kyongju. The third division, under the command of Kuroda Nagamasa, first captured Unsan, then Changnyong, then Hyonpung, then Songju.

Over the next few weeks, this pattern was repeated as Korean towns and cities fell one after the other. By May 11, the first four divisions had subdued the southern part of the peninsula and conquered the capital Hanseong (present-day Seoul), while four others had landed at Busan (one had remained behind on the island of Iki by way of reserve). By then, some one hundred and fifty thousand Japanese troops had set foot on Korean shores. Finally, on June 20, the northern town of Pyöngyang, the last major unconquered town on the peninsula, was captured. Not once did the Japanese suffer any serious setback.

Yet the campaign that began in a blaze of glory soon turned sour; exactly one year later the roles had been reversed. A large Chinese force had driven the Japanese troops back into the peninsula's southernmost provinces, while the superior Korean navy had decimated the invasion fleet. Hideyoshi's generals were in such difficulty that they felt obliged to sue for peace. Lengthy negotiations followed, and at last, the Ming court agreed to send an embassy to Japan.

Hideyoshi decided he would receive the Chinese embassy at Fushimi castle, conveniently situated close to the capital and the imperial palace. To accommodate such a grand occasion the castle needed drastic expansion, a project executed on the typical grand scale of despots. Six zōei bugyō, or 'construction magistrates,' were put in charge of renovations; the warlords whose forces were not stationed on the Korean Peninsula were required to provide a workforce of more than twenty thousand men to work on the project day and night.

Heritage

Two things kept the aging Muneyoshi going: his family and his art of fencing. Every morning, at the break of dawn, as the morning mist still lingered over the paddy fields around Ōhirao, he and Shinzaemon would retreat to their makeshift *dōjō* behind the Enjō temple. It wasn't a *dōjō*, really, just a patch of ground set off by a bamboo fence, its ground flattened and hardened like that of a *sumō* ring. There they spent hours in intense practice with the *fukuro shinai*. After a light lunch of rice, *miso* soup, and some pickles and a long break, they would resume their study, but this time concentrating on particular aspects of a technique they had practiced. Toward evening, as the sun's red disc began to sink behind the dark ridges of the surrounding hills, they would retrace their steps home. Having enjoyed the evening meal with the rest of the family, they would retire to the adjoining room, where they would reflect at length on the new insights they had gained, or Muneyoshi would expound on some of the concepts at the core of his teachings.

The most complex concepts were those of *shuji* and *shuriken*.[1] Derived from the term to describe the point where the neckline of a Japanese coat meets and overlaps, in the context of swordsmanship, the term *shuji* represented the mark to aim at when engaged in a duel. It was this principle that Muneyoshi had first observed in the exotic stance of Nobutsuna's disciple Bungorō during their memorable *taryū shiai* at In-ei's Hōzō monastery. The term *shuriken* derived from the esoteric tradition of 'cutting the nine ideographs.' In keeping with this Taoist practice, Muneyoshi and his son recited the *Kuji*, the nine magic words, at the start of each practice, forming the accompanying hand gestures as if in prayer: *rin-pyō-tō-sha-kai-jin-retsu-zai-zen* (Celestial warriors, line up for battle and proceed!).

Other concepts, like those of *suigetsu* and *shinmyōken*, were less difficult to grasp. Representing the reflection of the moon's light on the surface of the water, the term *suigetsu* had been used by Nobutsuna to describe the ideal distance between oneself and one's opponent. This insight was especially important when one approached one's enemy unarmed, as Nobutsuna had demonstrated with his *mutōtori*. Just as important was the concept of *shinmyōken*, the six-inch area around the navel, where the tip of the *katana*—either one's own or that of one's opponent—naturally settled.

'These laws,' Muneyoshi impressed on his son, 'are the core of our school of swordsmanship. Without them, our techniques are no more than a physical exercise, a collection of meaningless postures and movements without coherence, without a goal.'

Shinzaemon enjoyed his father's teachings. Five years he had spent under Eishun's tutelage at the Ichijō-*in* and by now his mind had little difficulty in grasping abstract concepts. He had learned so much in those five years, about temple life, about Yamato's history, about his clan's place in it all. In truth, he had been reluctant to return to his family following their move to the Enjō temple. Not that he had renounced his warrior background. Far from it; he was and would always be a warrior, that much he knew. He valued his clan's traditions, their way of life. No, it was just that he hated what had happened to them, the way they were living now. He yearned for the days when they had still been living at the Momiji *yashiki* when he and his father would go out on horseback to inspect their domain or visit a befriended chieftain. He could only imagine what it must have felt like when they had still been the proud masters of their own castle, their own army—a clan to reckon with.

Slowly but gradually Shinzaemon adapted to his new surroundings. In between practice he would go and visit his sisters in the fields, bringing them *onigiri* to eat. At times he would join Yoshikatsu on some errand, or help Muneaki groom the horses. Thankfully, they were still able to keep some. Recently, using all of his savings, he had bought a beautiful mare. She was all black, with just a narrow white blaze between her intelligent eyes. He had named her Ookage, after the horse of the famous

150

warrior Akechi Samenosuke Hidemitsu. Once, when blocked
by Toyotomi Hideyoshi's men at Ootsu, on the shore of Lake
Biwa, Hidemitsu had driven his horse into the waters and
crossed the lake's narrow by clinging on to the animal's manes.
Shinzaemon knew he courted danger in naming his horse thus.
Hidemitsu, after all, had been a retainer of Akechi Mitsuhide,
the man who had assassinated the great Oda Nobunaga. But he
despised Nobunaga and his successor, Hideyoshi, for what they
had done to the Yagyū; if it hadn't been for them the Yagyū
would still have their lands and castle.

He hated most what it had done to his father. Their daily
training routine had restored much of Muneyoshi's health, but
somewhere deep inside, at the core of his being, something had
broken. He never laughed anymore, nor did he indulge them
in those longs tales of past glories. Once, on a beautiful day out
riding to Kasagi, his mood had lifted, like the sun breaking
through the clouds. Crossing the bridge across the Hakusa River
had triggered his memory and he had begun talking about the
siege of the temple long ago, how the Bakufu camp along the
Kizu River had been flooded by the rising river. Getting into
his stride he had gone on to describe their night attack on the
mountain, how they had climbed its most dangerous face, how
the enemy had set fire to the buildings, how they had surprised
their ancestors Nagayoshi and Gensen. Then, just as he came to
the point where his ancestor's fortunes had been rerstored, his
voice faltered and he grew silent.

Genpuku

In the fall of 1580, Shinzaemon turned seventeen. He was eager
to have his *genpuku* ceremony. It had been embarrassing to have

to wait so long; all his brothers and sisters had reached adulthood at a much younger age—only peasants reached adulthood at such a late age. He had really expected to go through the ceremony on his return from Nara. But each time he pressed his father, Muneyoshi would tell him the time wasn't yet ripe, that he still had more to learn, more aspects of his role as warrior to master. At times it seemed as if his father wanted him to know every damn little thing, the meaning of each tawdry aspect of their customs, the relevance of each trivial detail of his clan's long history. And while he had little trouble in committing it all to memory, at times it felt as if his head would burst. It made him thirst for some space, some time to let it all sink in. Whenever he questioned his father on why he had to endure it all, why his siblings were spared, his father would grow irritable, reminding him that he should know all the laws that governed the life of a warrior.

Now, finally, after four years of waiting, the day had come. Shinzaemon felt elated as he and his family made their way along the Yagyū Kaidō toward Nara and the Kasuga Taisha. It was a glorious spring day, the maple trees on the slopes surrounding Ōhirao were all coming into bud and it looked as if the pines had been sprinkled with tea powder: it was the verdant time of *shinryoku*. However much he had hated learning all the boring detail, he did feel strangely empowered to know exactly what he would be going through, the meaning of each aspect of the ceremony, each gesture. The crisp white robe he was wearing, for instance, meant he was still a 'child of the *kami*,' as yet untainted by the blood of war. Soon he would be receiving his adult garment, a full coat of armor, including a helmet with the Yagyū crest! Being of Fujiwara decent, he would also receive an *eboshi*, the black-lacquered court cap dating back to the time when his ancestors still governed the realm. It was from this ancient aspect that the ceremony derived its name, *genpuku*: the head (*gen*) wearing (*fuku*) the *eboshi* for the first time, symbolizing one's rank and status in a warrior society.

That evening Shinzaemon was sitting under a starlit sky in front of the Kasuga Taisha. All the red lanterns along the long wide alley leading up to the shrine were ablaze and the small group of shrine musicians intoned a mournful tune on their *shō*, the ancient bamboo wind instruments. For close to an hour Shinzaemon had to sit still as the shrine's *kannushi* went through one invocation after the other, each phrase sanctioned with a swish of his *haraegushi*, the long wand with a thousand paper strips. Then the music fell silent and, ever so slowly, shuffling one foot in front of the other one by one, Muneyoshi, dressed in his full dress of a shrine official, moved forward until he stood facing his son. For a moment Shinzaemon wanted to look up, eager to accept his new headwear, but he checked himself and looked downward, faintly flushing as his father solemnly placed the lacquered *eboshi* on his head and pronounced his full adult name, 'Yagyū Fujiwara no Munenori.' It was clan tradition, too, that one of the two Chinese characters that made up his new name was taken from his father's name, in his case, the character *mune*, meaning essence, origin. But the second character was his own—*nori*: the ancient laws that rule the life of a warrior.

The next morning, after they had all returned to their refuge on the grounds of the Enjō temple, Muneyoshi was walking in the garden when he spotted Nabu on the veranda, her slender back bent over some item she cradled in her lap. His curiosity aroused, he approached her, silently, not wanting to disturb her in her musings. She had grown old beyond her years, and deep furrows now scarred her once so soft features. She looked up as he approached the porch, slightly startled to find him there. And for just a fleeting moment, through the mists of time,

Muneyoshi saw her as she had been long ago, that beautiful face looking up at him in amazement, when he had slid open that window and whispered her name. Then the moment was gone, and he was looking into her dark, sad eyes. They looked at him searchingly, fathoming his thoughts. She looked down again, smiling at a small bowl she was holding in her hands worn with wear. It was one of the few items she had held onto since she had left Tsutsui castle almost forty years ago: a small *kintsugi* bowl. He had never understood what she found so attractive about it. When he had first seen it, it had seemed the latest fad, a product of Yoshimasa's decadent court, for it had been purposefully broken, only to be glued together again, painstakingly, with gold lacquer, of all things, one shard at a time. At length she spoke, more to herself than to him, while her fingers traced the delicate golden cracks in the surface. Only a few words she muttered, and as always in riddles, '*Wareta tokoro de yori jōbu desu mono*' (It is stronger in the broken places).

Kuroda Nagamasa

Having reached adulthood, it was time for Munenori to go on his first *musha shugyō*. In the fall of 1591, as the first leaves were falling, father and son left the modest comforts of their dwelling at the Enjō temple and set out north along the Yagyū Kaidō, first to Kizu, and from there to Kyoto, Osaka, and Himeji.

For the young Munenori each day on the road was a treat. He could ride Ookage and put his techniques to the test in *taryū shiai* at the *dōjō* of other domains, or deepen his understanding of his art in quiet meditation during their stay at temples along the way. For him every day brought a new challenge, a new insight. For Muneyoshi it was a way to forget. On the road with

154

his son, riding along some forgotten country lane among the mountains, it seemed nothing had changed, that all was right with the world, that he might still return along the Yagyū Kaidō to find his castle intact.

It was on their return from Himeji, while staying in the capital, that the two men were invited to perform an *enbu* of the Yagyū Shinkage-*ryū* at the residence of Kuroda Nagamasa. It was Muneyoshi's ties to Kamiizumi Nobutsuna that had secured them the invitation, for Nagamasa had been an avid student of the northern giant. Nobutsuna was no longer alive; he had passed away when Shinzaemon was just six years old.[2] Yet Nagamasa had continued to sponsor his Shinkage school of swordsmanship and had made Hikida Bungorō *shihan* to the Kuroda clan at their headquarters in Nakatsu, on the southern island of Kyushu. Through Bungorō, Nagamasa knew that Nobutsuna had stayed at Yagyū castle, and he wanted to see for himself what this fusion of the Yagyū and Shinkage schools of swordsmanship was all about.

Called the Nyosuitei, the Kuroda *yashiki* stood less than a mile north of Nijō castle, and only a few blocks away from the Jūrakudai, the huge palace where the great Taikō Hideyoshi held court. Having lived for almost ten years in the cramped space of their small dwelling at the Enjō temple, Munenori marveled at the lavishness of the Nyosuitei. There were dozens of rooms, each with fresh *tatami* mats throughout, neatly stuccoed walls, and sliding doors decorated with monochromes of rustic land-scapes. At the center of the compound, framed on all sides by a wide veranda, was a small garden dominated a by beautiful copper maple tree that seemed to glow in the bright shaft of autumn sunlight piercing the inner court.

Muneyoshi, too, was impressed, but for different reasons. The Nyosuitei *yashiki* might be lavish, but not when one had seen the boundless opulence in which many of the warlords of his time lived. Compared to the decadence of Matsunaga Hisahide's palaces, the Nyosuitei was a paragon of Japanese sobriety. It reassured him. The only color that reminded him of the riches the Kuroda must have amassed through their incessant campaigning was the maple leaves' gold-like hue.

Nagamasa, too, inspired confidence. He struck Muneyoshi as a thoughtful, yet at the same time forceful man; a man 'deliberate in counsel and decisive in action,' as the old saying went. He was also hospitable, amiable even, and somewhat apologetic too: 'My father and I have spent much of the last decade campaigning, both at home and on the continent,' he said as he led the two men to their quarters. 'Yet we have tried not to lose touch with our humble origins.'

Muneyoshi smiled politely but knew better. The Kuroda might not be of high birth like the Yagyū, but they had clearly done a lot better for themselves.

Over tea in their room overlooking the inner court, he and his son discussed the routine for that evening.

'Let's demonstrate a *mutōtori*,' Muneyoshi said. It was the subtle technique Nobutsuna had used on him at Inéi's Hōzō monastery and which they had often practiced at Yagyū castle—it was a technique he cherished.

'It's not aggressive enough,' Munenori objected. 'We'll be performing in front of men who have spent the better part of their lives on the field of battle. How can such men be impressed by an old man wresting a *katana* from his son?'

'Besides, father,' he continued, but now more conciliatory, 'doing a *mutōtori* just between the two of us might raise suspicions. How can they know we're not faking it? No, we need to make an impression, raise the temperature a bit.'

Muneyoshi grunted. His son had a point.

Chapter 9

'Let's instead do a *raitō*!' Munenori suggested. He loved this technique, its tension. He loved to sit there—absolutely still—and wait, just wait, testing his father, challenging him, challenging his confidence: in his own ability, in his son's ability.

'*Yoroshiizo*,' Muneyoshi conceded with a sigh. He saw Munenori's reasoning but still felt ill at ease. His mind went back to that evening long ago when he and Shigeyoshi had prepared for the very same technique at Hisahide's court. He recalled how the opulence had cast a strange spell on his uncle, how he had almost failed to parry his *katana*. The same sense of foreboding now crept over him as he observed his son. Would he too be affected by the splendor around them?

That evening, father and son made ready to perform an *enbu* at the small *dōjō* in the northern wing of the compound. As he had done so many times before, Munenori sat down opposite his father, some five yards away. Then, as they calmly tied the sash of the sheaths to their *obi*, they waited patiently until the assembly had fallen totally silent. Fixing his eyes on his son, Muneyoshi swiftly rose and drew his *katana*. For a moment he faltered. Then he raised it high above his head and swiftly moved in on his son. As he did so he knew his son would dare him, as he always did, waiting just that bit longer, just enough to rile him, stir his anger, at his son's self-assuredness, his own damn insecurity. So he went in, with full force this time, not holding back, not wanting to shame himself or his clan before the great warlord.

With a deafening thud the tip of Muneyoshi's *katana* buried itself in the thick floorboards of the *dōjō*. His son was gone, behind him now, the tip of his *katana* trained at Muneyoshi's head. Like lightning his *katana* had shot upward, upward, to meet his father *katana* on its downward trajectory. There, high above his head, the razor-sharp blades had met, just a few inches below their tips. Munenori's *katana* hadn't stopped his father *katana*; there was no blunt bashing of metals. It had just touched it, ever so slightly, guiding it down on its original trajectory, as he himself swiftly moved aside with a stunningly executed *tsure-ashi*, a few small steps past his father, then swiveling round on his right knee to face him from behind.

'*Hora!*' Nagamasa was the first to break the silence. Hitting his lacquered armrest with his flat hand he stood up and said, 'I have heard much about the Yagyū-*ryū*, and am glad to have seen it in action. Our clan has long been practitioners of master Kamiizumi's Shinkage-*ryū*, and I can tell the extent to which the Yagyū-*ryū* has been exposed to the man's revolutionary teachings.' He grew pensive for a while. Then he continued, 'Indeed, I would be much inclined to hire both of you as fencing instructors, were it not that I and my men will be embarking for the continent. Regrettably, the Koreans have turned down Taikō Hideyoshi's latest ultimatum, and he has just announced we are to sail again come spring.'

A Visitor

It was a wet day, early in June 1594, as a lone traveler took shelter under the massive roof over the gate of the Enjō temple. The wet season had arrived early that year and rain was coming down thick and fast. The man was clearly a warrior. A huge *tachi*, at least four feet long, sat in a belt over a threadbare *hakama* that now clung around his stocky legs like wet rags. The man's only protection against the rain was a *kasa*, the wide straw hat worn by peasants working the fields throughout the country. From underneath its ragged rim a pair of menacing eyes, crowned by dense eyebrows that met in the middle, took in the

scene around him. Then he took off his hat and passed under
the roofed gate into the temple grounds and called out his name
to announce himself: *Ooi Hikida Bungorō dazo!*

Muneyoshi never knew whether he should be glad to see
Bungorō come or go. It wasn't just that he had once been defeated
by the northerner; it was the man's unbridled gruffness. Nabu
detested his coarse manners and had been more than relieved
when he and Jingo Muneharu—though the latter wasn't as bad—
had decided to move on shortly after they had arrived at Yagyū
castle with Nobutsuna. Still, Muneyoshi did admire the man's
ability, which at least from his perspective, was unsurpassed. In
a strange way he had even come to like him, his frankness, his
uncomplicated manner. He was pleasant company, too, full of
stories and jokes—as long as he didn't touch any *sake*. And
towards Muneyoshi, at least, the northerner bore a warm heart.

Bungorō had visited the Yagyū several times since his arrival
in the capital. For three years, now, the Kuroda had been fighting
one campaign after the other on the Korean Peninsula. It had
very much put him out of work. Ever since they had departed
the Kuroda *dōjō* had stood empty. And thus he had returned to
Kyoto, hoping to find employment there, though he had had
little luck so far.

Bungorō looked boastful as he said, 'I have just come from
Higashiyama, where the Taikō-*sama* is expanding Fushimi castle,
on the northern bank of the Uji River.'

'Really?' Muneyoshi said, curious what would come next.

The northerner shook his head in disbelief. 'It's a sight to
behold, I tell you. Some twenty-thousand laborers are working
on the moats, walls, and buildings day and night. It is going to
be a magnificent castle. They say its rooms will be clad in gold.'

'I heard,' Muneyoshi said, 'that the Taikō-*sama* seems in a
hurry to get the castle ready for the Chinese embassy. They've

even dismantled parts of Kōriyama castle to build Fushimi's five-storied donjon. But what brings you all the way here?'

'Actually, I've come to bid you farewell, as well as bring you some good news, for I'll be leaving for Maizuru in Tango Province tomorrow. My *rōnin* days are over. I'll be entering the service of Hosokawa Fujitaka, the lord of Tanabe castle. He has offered to hire me on a stipend of one hundred and fifty *koku*. I know it's not a king's ransom, but neither is it a pauper's alms.'

'Congratulations,' Muneyoshi said, 'but what is the good news?'

'I was going to come to that,' Bungorō said somewhat offended. 'The fact is, I met Fujitaka while giving a Shinkage-*ryū* *enbu* for a number of warlords encamped around the capital. One of them was Lord Tokugawa Ieyasu, who is currently encamped at Takagamine, on the northern outskirts of the capital. He is a close friend of Lord Kuroda Nagamasa, and it seems Nagamasa has recommended you to him.'

'Really?' The ruffian now had Muneyoshi's serious attention, though he didn't show it.

'Of course, he asked me about you too,' Bungorō continued, throwing his broad shoulders backward and inhaling deep through his wide nostrils. 'I told him you were a pretty good swordsman in my opinion, though I didn't tell him I beat you hands down at the Hōzō-*in*.'

Muneyoshi remained silent.

'Anyway, I've come to bring you this,' Bungorō said as he pushed a letter toward Muneyoshi with the Tokugawa seal.

Muneyoshi broke the seal and read the few short lines of cursive script—It was an invitation for him and Munenori to give an *enbu* for Ieyasu at Takagamine before the month was out.

'Don't put your hopes up too high, though,' Bungorō said airily as he rose. 'Ieyasu-*dono* is a hard man to please. I too gave a demonstration before the warlord, but I don't think he appreciates the superiority of the Shinkage-*ryū*, so why on earth should he value your Yagyū Shinkage-*ryū*.'

Stepping outside, Bungorō snorted and spat hard on the ground, as if to rid himself of a bitter taste in his mouth. Then he bowed slightly, turned, and left the way he had come.

Muneyoshi didn't really mind Bungorō's jibe. Obviously, his encounter with Ieyasu hadn't been a pleasant one, but then again, neither had their first encounter at the Hōzō monastery been. Indeed, could an encounter with Bungorō ever be pleasant? He wondered how the warlord had reacted to his friend's gruff manners. It irked him that he knew so little about Ieyasu. What was he like? Then he recalled his old friend Nobutsuna mentioning the meeting between Ieyasu and Nobunaga, how both warlords had condemned Matsunaga Hisahide's excesses, and suddenly his mood lifted.

Mutōtori

It was June 21, 1594, when Yagyū Muneyoshi and his son Munenori rode into Ieyasu's camp at Takagamine. For weeks it had been pelting down incessantly, but for once the rain had cleared, revealing a beautiful spring morning. As was the custom with men of high rank, Ieyasu's quarters were encircled by a high curtain, emblazoned with the triple hollyhock Tokugawa crest and held up by a row of pikes placed at regular intervals. As they entered the enclosure, Muneyoshi's eyes immediately fell on a stout man sitting outside his tent on a low chair covered with a deer hide. It was Ieyasu. Next to him sat his son, the thirteen-year-old Hidetada, and round him, in close attendance, were his *hatamoto*, his most loyal bannermen, many of them renowned swordsmen. Ieyasu looked in his early fifties, with tanned features and a few days' grey stubble of a beard gracing his furrowed chin. He was wearing a thin silk crimson *haori* above a *karusan hakama* and wore his hair in a tight knot behind his head.

'*Yōkoso!*' Ieyasu welcomed them cheerily when the two swordsmen were led into his presence. 'Now this is a welcome break from the tedium of building-duties.' Jumping up from his stool, he addressed them by their honorific names as he invited them to follow them to the center of the encampment where a clearing had been prepared for the demonstration. 'Kuroda Nagamasa-*dono* told me of your *enbu* at his *yashiki* the other day. Now, you may know that I myself am a practitioner of master Ono Jirōemon Tadaaki's Ittō-*ryū*, but I'm always open to the insights of other schools. However,' he said as he looked Munenori over, 'I don't want you to perform an *enbu*; I want to have a personal bout, with you young master Munenori.'

For a moment father and son's eyes met. Then Muneyoshi nodded: the time had come for Munenori to prove himself.

Munenori lost some of his usual cool as he and the warlord sat down to greet each other formally. He felt the man's prying eyes on him, following his every move as he untied the sash by which his sheath was attached to his belt, drew his weapon from his *hakama*, held it vertically in front of him, lowered it until the tip of the sheath touched the ground, and then gently laid it on the ground in front of him. Countless times his father had made him go through the routine until he had finally got it right.

Ieyasu had also removed his weapon from his belt, though he held the weapon aloft horizontally in the style of the Ittō-*ryū* before he too placed it gently on the ground in front of him.

Munenori felt how the warlord kept watching him as they both slowly bent forward toward their *katana* and greeted. It almost felt as if he were not there to demonstrate his dexterity in his school of fencing but his mastery of etiquette.

Rising slowly, Ieyasu took a *bokutō* presented by one of his men and placed himself at the middle of the enclosure. All the while he closely watched Munenori, who also stood up and took a *bokutō* offered by one of the bannermen.

No sooner had he taken up his position, than the warlord charged, raising his *bokutō* high above his head and uttering a *kiai* at the top of his voice as he brought the weapon down toward the young man's head. Yet instead of parrying the blow, Munenori cast his *bokutō* aside and moved in upon Ieyasu. They were about to clash when he stepped left of Ieyasu's right foot and, swiveling round on the ball of his left foot, firmly seized the hilt of Ieyasu's *bokutō* from below with his left hand, causing the warlord to lose his balance and tumble forward, leaving his *bokutō* behind in the left hand of the Yamato warrior.

A nervous silence descended on the encampment as Ieyasu rose and brushed the dust from his summer tunic. Then he began to laugh. '*Sasuga!* Nagamasa-*dono* was right. Well done! I must confess I had my doubts about the Shinkage-*ryū*, but you have convinced me otherwise. Only recently I had a similar bout with a fellow by the name of Bungorō, but I wasn't impressed. The man might be a great swordsman but he doesn't have a clue how to behave among superiors. He even reproached me on my *kamae*! Can you believe it?' Ieyasu shook his head at the recollection. 'No, Bungorō is a *hippu*, a course man, practicing *hippu no ken*. You, young master Munenori, by contrast, are manifestly a man of good breeding who knows how to conduct himself. And you understand your craft!'

Turning to Muneyoshi now, the warlord's tone dropped as he said, 'Would you be willing to let your son move to Edo? I would like him to join my retinue of *shihan*.'

Bewildered, yet at the same time deeply honored, Muneyoshi accepted. The full portent of the offer hadn't yet sunk in. It only hit him when Ieyasu called his scribe and made him draft a written pledge vowing 'not to divulge to anyone what I have learned, be they my own parents or children, before I have received my *inka*.'

It was a remarkable reversal of fortune that the gods had granted the aging Yamato swordsman. Close to two-and-a-half decades he and his family had spent in obscurity, not knowing what setbacks the dawning of each new day would bring. Now, overnight, his son had become a fencing instructor on a stipend of two hundred *koku* to one of the most powerful warlords in the realm—a warlord whom even the great Taikō Hideyoshi had deemed it prudent to keep an ally.

Takuan

Though in Ieyasu's service, to the young Munenori it felt as if he were on paid leave. Consumed by his many commitments and engagements, the warlord had very little free time and only occasionally called on him for practice. The rest of the time Munenori was free to do as he liked. He had been provided with his own modest *yashiki* in Kyoto until work on Fushimi castle was completed and they would move to Edo. It was nothing like the Kuroda *yashiki*, but compared to their small dwelling on the grounds of the Enjō temple, it was a palace. His father meanwhile had returned to Ōhirao, and for the first time in his life Munenori was free to do as he liked. He reveled in Kyoto's life, especially its night-life, which was full of temptations. He was now twenty-three years old and, coaxed by his fellow *shihan*, he soon found himself frequenting the capital's pleasure quarters. Of course, he carefully hid this side of his life from his father, whenever he visited him back in Ōhirao. He couldn't count the times the old man had warned him of the capital's temptations, how they had ruined his great-uncle Shigeyoshi. His father had shown him where the man had lived, right on the edge of the Gion district. The place had since been turned into a *sake* house where commoners made merry and drank away their meager earnings. At least his father needn't worry he would end up being a drunk: he detested the taste of *sake*.

Whether it was to atone for his sins he couldn't tell, but he continued to pursue his Buddhist studies. Having lots of time on his hands, he often visited the famous Daitoku temple to study under the temple's recently appointed abbot, Tōho Sōchū, a profoundly cultured man who had studied the art of tea under Sen no Rikyū and entertained close relations with powerful western warlords. Built during the first half of the fourteenth century, the Daitoku-*ji*, the 'Temple of Great Virtue,' was one of the main centers of the Rinzai Zen sect. Go-Daigo, the emperor on whose behalf Munenori's ancestors had fought so hard, had been the temple's patron. It's founder, Shūhō Myōchō, whose name began with the same character as Munenori's given name, had received from Go-Daigo the title Daitō Kokushi, 'National Teacher of the Great Lamp.' Ever since that time, the temple had maintained close ties with the clans who had been loyal to the Southern Court. With the fall of the Ashikaga Shōgunate, the ties between the temple and the warrior clans became even deeper. It was the temple where Nobunaga was buried and where Hideyoshi had drunk tea with Sen no Rikyū.

Hundreds of acolytes studied under Sōchū, but one in particular made an immediate impression on the warrior. His name was Takuan. He clearly was from a poor family, for his robe was pale and frayed at the sleeves. Yet it wasn't Takuan's outward appearance that struck Munenori, but his big wide eyes. Instead of looking out onto the world, it seemed as if they looked inward. What he saw must be mesmerizing, for the words that came out of his mouth left Munenori spellbound. And though two years his junior, it felt as if Takuan had already surpassed him by many years.[3]

Eager to introduce Takuan to his father, Munenori invited the monk to go and visit his father at the Enjō temple. Early next morning, he had gone to Takuan's quarters but found that the monk had blocked the sliding door by placing a stick on the lintel in which it rested. Suspecting something awry, Munenori lifted the door out of its lintel, only to find the monk sitting on the floor in *zazen*, stark-naked.

Takuan seemed unperturbed and said, 'I just possess this one robe. I want to make a good impression on your father, so I've spent the night repairing and washing it. It now hangs outside to dry, but he sun is out, so it will be dry by the time we leave.'

Like Munenori, Takuan descended from a clan of samurai. Both their fathers had been reduced to *rōnin* and both had spent their youths studying at temples in the countryside. Their shared background and excitement at being at the forefront of political change quickly drew the two young men together. It was Munenori's destiny to be a warrior, yet he had a deep interest in religion; Takuan's destiny was to be a monk, yet he had a deep interest in the Way of the warrior. For the next two years, they saw each other almost daily, studying together and spending long evenings discussing their futures in a country racked by turmoil.

Then, in the spring of 1596, with Fushimi castle nearing completion, Ieyasu was promoted to Minister of the Center and allowed to return to Edo castle. Being part of Ieyasu's retinue,

Munenori, too, was required to move to Edo. Yet whenever his duties led him back to Kyoto, he would visit the Daitoku temple to seek out his Buddhist friend. Like all great friendships, that between Munenori and Takuan endured, though time and circumstances were to test it in various ways.

CHAPTER 10

Edo had once been the home of a warrior from Musashi by the name of Edoshirō, founder of the Edo clan during the late Heian period. His clan had gone on to play an important role in the exploits of Minamoto no Yoritomo, but lost its power in an uprising during the early fifteenth century. Edoshiro had ruled from a fortified hill on the Sumida River. It took until the middle of the fifteenth century before Edo castle arose at the hands of the warrior-poet Ōta Dōkan (1432–86). Dōkan took great pride in his creation, even composing a poem to celebrate the occasion:

> *This abode of mine*
> *Adjoins a pine grove*
> *Sitting on the blue sea*
> *And from its humble eaves*
> *Commands a view of soaring Mount Fuji.*

Edo castle was a modest affair, its interiors far from grand; just one main building, the Honmaru, flanked by two lesser structures, the Ni-no-maru and the San-no-maru. Wide moats framed the castle, yet no water filled them and grassy embankments had to make do as defense walls. The castle and its environs hardly changed over the next one-

and-a-half century. When Ieyasu first inspected it following his appointment as governor by Hideyoshi in 1590, it was in a bad state. Board roofs protected the main buildings, but the thatched outbuildings leaked profusely, causing the mats inside to stain and smell of mold.

The town itself was just a fisherman's hamlet on Edo bay consisting of a few hundred dwellings. Only the many shrines and temples, scattered around the town, lent the place some grace. It was in one of these that Ieyasu and his family took up residence when he set about doing up his new headquarters. Toward the north lay Kanda hill; toward the south stretched a reedy swamp that flooded during high tide. Beyond lay the vast plain of Musashinō. Stretching all the way to the Pacific coast, it took someone on foot several days to cross and made those on horseback disappear amid the ever restless and rustling pampas grasses.[1]

Too busy with the affairs of state, Ieyasu spent little time on his new headquarters. First he had the defensive moats filled with water. Then he had the castle's thatched roofs mended, its rooms cleaned, their floors covered with fresh tatami, but he did not touch the main structure. Even the entrance, an earthen floor with three steps made from the beams of old ships, was left untouched. He was more concerned that his retainers should have a roof over their heads. Most of them were stationed in one of the surrounding villages, but never farther than a day's journey from Edo castle. He ordered the village headmen to quickly construct additional buildings suited for retainers and his families. When on duty for extended periods of time, they could come and stay at the houses of townsmen or, if necessary, in makeshift barracks.

Shihan

Munenori found it hard to get used to his new home. Together with the other *shihan*, he had taken up lodgings in a house not far from Edo castle. It was a modest affair, nothing like his *yashiki* in Kyoto. In fact, it was more like their abode at the Enjō temple, worse even, as it had been the dwelling of a fish merchant. He had obviously used it as storage, for the smell of dried *bonito* greeted one as soon as one entered the earth pit after one had managed to open the rackety door. Being from the interior, Munenori had never developed a taste for fish and was put off all the more by the pungent odor that permeated its *tatami*, its crumbling walls, even the worm-eaten beams supporting its poorly thatched roof. It wasn't much different outside. Rotting nets and stinking baskets littered the small back yard.

The hovel's one redeeming feature was its view. Situated on a slightly elevated headland in Shinagawa, only a few miles south of the castle, it commanded a magnificent view of Edo Bay. Munenori could sit for hours on the small porch he had built from scrap wood scattered around the yard and enjoy the hustle and bustle of the hundreds of boats big and small that plied the waters of Edo Bay. Most of them were just *bekabune*, the small crafts of fishermen gathering seaweed or tending to the long fyke nets in which they trapped eel—the delicious Edo eel, the one fish he really enjoyed. Occasionally he saw *chokkibune*, ferrying samurai or their womenfolk from one end of town to the other. Increasingly he also saw *besaisen*, large cargo vessels that plied Japan's coastal towns. He had seen them at Sakai and Osaka, too, hundreds of them, carrying timber and other precious cargo from the farthest corners of the realm.

Most of his time Munenori spent at the O-Keikoba, the huge training hall that had been erected on the grounds of Edo castle. Measuring fifteen by thirty yards it was one of the largest *dōjō* in the country. Only the former *dōjō* of the Ashikaga in Kyoto could rival in size with the O-Keikoba.

Munenori wasn't the only fencing instructor at the O-Keikoba. Befitting a warlord of his position, Ieyasu's retinue included a host of martial arts experts from all over the realm. One of them, Okuyama Kyūgasai Kimishige, had, like Munenori's father, studied under Kamiizumi Nobutsuna and like Muneyoshi had founded his own derivative school, the Okuyama Shinkage-*ryū*. Then there was Arima Ōi no Kami Mitsumori, a practitioner of Iizasa Chōisai's Shintō-*ryū*, whose relative, Arima Kihei, had dueled with the legendary Miyamoto Musashi. All of them were great swordsmen in their own right, and all of them were fiercely competitive.

Chief among the Shōgun's *shihan* at the time of Munenori's arrival was Ono Jirōemon Tadaaki, propagator of Itō Ittōsai's famous Ittō-ryō. Unable to compromise and lacking any sense of diplomacy, Tadaaki was the very opposite of Munenori, and yet the two men got on well from the start. Being Munenori's senior by six years, Tadaaki took him under his wing, introducing the Yamato warrior into Edo martial society. And while he didn't spare him when they were sparring, when out on the town he was like a friend, albeit a mischievous one.

Having never visited eastern Japan, Munenori had great difficulty understanding the course dialect spoken by Edo's dwellers, let alone their customs. But bit by bit he attuned to their odd inflections, their sense of humor, their lack of reverence. And bit by bit, too, he came to like the towering brute, who seemed to epitomize all the qualities that made the Kantō men such fearsome warriors.

Like Munenori, Tadaaki had been born into a small clan struggling to survive the vortex of civil war. He hailed from Isumi, a hamlet on the eastern side of the Bōsō Peninsula. His clan had served a local chieftain, whose castle had come under attack from a local potentate bent on territorial expansion. His father had died in its defense and so he had set out on a *musha shugyō*. The next three years he had traveled the Kantō region, making a name for himself with daring exploits. His name had still been Mikogami Tenzen then. He had only assumed his present name after he had entered the service of his current master, Tokugawa Ieyasu.

Secretly, Munenori envied the Kantō warrior. The man had been only eighteen years old when he had dueled with the great Itō Ittōsai Kagehisa, who had been on a *musha shugyō* when he passed through Isumi. Of course Tadaaki had lost; he had been lucky to get off alive, really. That was probably why he was even proud of it, openly boasting of his encounter with the traveling swordsman, who had beaten him with no more than a piece of discarded wood. Tadaaki was a man of immense stature—and not only physical. His *dōjō* at his family *yashiki* in Edo's Surugadai district attracted hundreds of followers, and his reputation was only paralleled by the great Tsukahara Bokuden. Not a man inclined to etiquette, Tadaaki had little regards for his patrons and regularly got into trouble by insulting or even injuring their precious offspring.

Munenori made good use of Tadaaki's flaws. Where Tadaaki was gruff, he was polite; where Tadaaki was impulsive, he bided his time; where Tadaaki made enemies, he made friends. Indeed, making friends was one of Munenori's great talents, especially among the more powerful Daimyō. Ever since Munenori and his father had given a demonstration at the *yashiki* of Kuroda Nagamasa, the Yagyū had been welcome guests. His modest father had obliged local warlords with the occasional demonstration, but he never really enjoyed all the attention. Not so Munenori. He loved the attention and made the most of their overtures. Some, like Hosokawa Tadatoshi, were genuine aficionados of the martial arts. Others pursued less lofty interests. Men like Mōri Hidenari, for instance, a notorious womanizer and inveterate drinker, who, by virtue of his father's achievements, was ranked among Japan's most powerful. He and Munenori would spend whole nights carousing among Edo's *ageya*, indulging in wild dancing and usually ending up in some disreputable establishment. At times he couldn't remember the next morning where he had been the night before.

Hawking

In spite of his large retinue of fencing instructors, Ieyasu hardly ever used them. He did practice. He was a keen archer. Each day, shortly after dawn, he would go out into the castle grounds and shoot a dozen arrows into a number of tightly packed straw bales he had placed on a stand against the inner castle wall. Or he would fire a couple of rounds into a target in front of a wall of sand with one of his newest matchlocks. Munenori would often watch Ieyasu. He noticed Ieyasu's capacity to concentrate. He also noticed how his master took pleasure in being watched and wasn't fazed by onlookers in the slightest—not once did he catch his master missing the mark.

Much of the rest of Ieyasu's spare time was taken up with hawking. It was his one true passion. Munenori couldn't count the times he had been out with Ieyasu and his retinue as a guard on long forays into Musashi and Shimōsa. These were huge outings in which the warlord brought along most of the ladies of his court, insisting they went on horseback instead of being carried in palanquins. Munenori wasn't a poor hawker himself, and it wasn't long before he was put in charge of the large number of hawks that were kept at Edo castle, all with their own names and qualities. And whenever Ieyasu went out hawking, he would call on Munenori to bring out this or that falcon so that it could jump on his gloved hand.

Ieyasu's son, the seventeen-year-old Hidetada, was different. Unlike his father, he spent most of his time around the castle, either in study or practice. Short and remarkably muscular for a young man of his status, Hidetada had a natural ability in the martial arts. He seemed keen, too. He would often visit the O-Keikoba where Munenori and his fellow *shihan* practiced and taught. Being only seven years his junior, Hidetada preferred to spar with Munenori. Munenori willingly obliged, yet he would always try to steer their practice to a more abstract level, seeking to instill in his student a more comprehensive knowledge, an insight into the complex combat situations that had spawned the techniques he practiced.

Hidetada struck Munenori as an odd mixture of restraint and abandon. Even more than his father, who was known to be more than hard on himself, Hidetada had an iron discipline to a point where he cruelly expected it in others. He never winced when hurt in a bout, nor was he easily flustered. It was said that once, when he was just thirteen years old, an ox had broken loose and crashed through the latticed window of his study. Hidetada had simply remained seated, asking his attendants to remove the beast and his teacher to proceed.

Yet somewhere within, Munenori could sense a deep-seated insecurity, driving the future potentate to pursue his objectives with a single-minded determination that sometimes bordered on the insane. In this he differed profoundly from his father. Where Ieyasu was flexible and patient, Hidetada was rigid and easily vexed; where self-control caused the father to catch the right moment, it caused his son to miss it. When practicing, Hidetada would endlessly repeat a move to correct a minor flaw, unable to let it rest, and incapable of either comprehending or accepting that with time it would mend itself.

It wasn't the only way in which father and son differed.

One hot day Hidetada and Munenori were practicing hard when, his curiosity stirred by his son's bellowing *kiai*, Ieyasu entered the O-Keikoba. For a while he sat and observed them sparring. At length, he stood up and called the two young men over to his side. Some thirty men were practicing that day and they had all dropped their *bokken* and bowed toward their lord in reverence. He didn't tell them to continue, as he was want to. Instead, he raised his voice as he turned to his son and, out of the blue, said 'Why do you think I hired Munenori instead of Hikida Bungorō? Was not Bungorō a direct *deshi* of the great Kamiizumi Nobutsuna? So why did I choose master Munenori over the older and more experienced Bungorō?'

'Because of his ability,' Hidetada replied.

Ieyasu looked around the O-Keikoba questioningly. 'Are these not all able men?'

Hidetada looked at a loss. He seemed embarrassed to have to state the obvious, but challenged by his father he did: 'Well, did he not beat you at Takagamine?'

Ieyasu laughed and shook his head. Making a dismissive gesture with his hand toward his son, he addressed all the men assembled: 'Master Munenori did indeed beat me at Takagamine, It is true. Yet what you don't know, my son, is that when Bungorō was still young, he beat Munenori's father at the Hōzō-in. So I cannot contest he has a great ability in fencing. Yet the man cannot discriminate between those who need such skills and those who don't. A lord of the realm, or even a Daimyō, by contrast, need not cut people down with his own hand, for when he takes part in a battle he can call on his men to do it for him. What he needs first and foremost is the ability to judge the capacity of the people in his service.'

Then, turning to his son again, he said, 'A general does not need to fight in hand-to-hand combat. Rather, he must know how to avoid risks. Killing people isn't something with which leaders should tire themselves. Not that one can expect to win a battle sitting on one's campstool gazing at the backs of one's men. No, one has to be a man of action, charge with the greatest boldness and vigor, and pray fortune will do the rest.'

It wasn't long after that Munenori was raised to the position of senior *shihan*, bringing him on the same level as Ono Jirōemon Tadaaki.

The Envoys

Munenori's first official function came on October 22, 1596, the day Taikō Hideyoshi would receive the Chinese embassy. Like all of Japan's great chieftains, Ieyasu was expected to be present when Hideyoshi would sign his treaty with China, but not at Fushimi. That fall, only shortly after Ieyasu had returned to Edo, a large earthquake had struck the vicinity of Fushimi. It had caused the keep of the just completed castle to collapse. Hideyoshi, who had been in residence, had escaped into the courtyard, but some seventy high ranking ladies and their maids had been buried alive under a toppled wall. With no time left, Hideyoshi had decided he would receive the envoys at Osaka castle. Ieyasu was allowed just one attendant to accompany him and, wanting to make a good impression, his eye had fallen on the handsome and cultured Yamato swordsman.

Munenori was excited when, on October 21, the day before the envoys were to arrive, he and Ieyasu crossed the wide bridge across Osaka castle's moats and entered its imposing Sakura gate. From far away he had spotted the towering five-storied donjon, its roof covered with blue tiles, its walls with gold leaf. Drawing closer, he had marveled at the roof-tiled buildings that graced the lengths of its walls, the double ring of wide moats, the huge, steel-plated gates that kept commoners out. The castle really was a town in itself, with many streets running in the four directions of the winds between walls that seemed to touch the heavens. When they had finally reached the central courtyard, they came upon beautiful gardens arranged according to the four seasons.

Hideyoshi personally showed them around the castle, and if anything, its interiors were even more extravagant than its exteriors. As they neared the center of the building, the rooms grew in size, each one more lavishly decorated than the other. All the while Hideyoshi was talking, affably, occasionally chatting to a young girl at his side dressed in costly robes, who casually carried his *katana* on her shoulder. On each room they passed, on every item it contained, the Taikō felt the need to comment, often stating the obvious in a show of ostentation: 'this room is clad in silver,' or 'this room is clad in gold,' or 'this room is filled with bales of silk,' or 'these rooms contain costly *katana*.'

Munenori was struck by the stark contrast with the down-to-earth mood he was used at Edo castle. Throughout the castle servants stood in attendance, their heads bowed, ready to scurry away at the Taikō's slightest gesture, and bumping into each other in their reverent confusion.

In one room stood the strangest piece of furniture Munenori had ever beheld: a wide, box-like construction filled with padded quilts. It was crowned with an elaborately ornamented canopy supported by four posts and draped from top to foot with damask curtains. All the men marveled at the structure, wandering in vain as to its function. Only Ieyasu had the temerity to ask. Pleased with having perplexed his audience, Hideyoshi laughed heartily, 'This, my friends, is a vessel on which the Westerners pass the night.'

After yet more rooms, passages, and stairs, they reached the top of the donjon. There the Taikō invited them to step out on the balcony, where he proceeded to show them the castle ground's layout, pointing out the fortified palisades atop the castle walls, the countless turrets at their corners, and the storehouses within, filled to the roofs with provisions for lengthy sieges. There, gathered on that balcony with these powerful men, taking in the panoramic view of the Taikō's realm, Munenori was left speechless—who in his right mind would ever think of laying siege to such a citadel!

All of the next day, Munenori sat in attendance as Ieyasu and the other governors of the realm were seated in order of rank in the castle's main hall. The reception of the Chinese mission was an opulent affair, made almost theatrical by Hideyoshi, who made his appearance in a Chinese costume with forty of his pages donned in matching attire. An eerie silence fell on the gathering when, at the climax of the ceremony, the chief Chinese envoy gracefully placed his emperor's patent of investiture on a large lacquered table in front of Hideyoshi.

The Taikō seemed pleased enough and was all laughs and smiles. So were the envoys. Only when he failed to kneel before the document did a flash of disapproval cross the chief envoy's face. It evaporated when one of Hideyoshi's interpreters blamed it on a boil in the Taikō's knee. At that moment it became instantly clear to Munenori that the Taikō didn't understand a word that was being said in Chinese. Having enjoyed his study under Eishun's tutelage, Munenori could follow most of what was being said. And from what he heard it was clear the Chinese envoys did not regards the Taikō with the same esteem as his subjects.

Two days later, Ieyasu was again called to Hideyoshi's side, and this time Munenori wasn't allowed to attend: the Taikō had convened a meeting of his chief generals. But the next day, as they were riding home, Ieyasu called out to Munenori, who was leading his large retinue of footguards, beckoning him to come and ride beside him. 'Did you know the whole thing was a grand fiasco?', Ieyasu snorted.

Munenori looked surprised, but his master didn't seem to notice. 'Turns out that, following the audience with the Chinese, the Taikō-*sama* had the treaty translated by Saishō Shōtai. He is a Zen priest who has spent much time in China and is an expert on diplomatic texts. He showed us the document yesterday and—surprise, surprise—it wasn't what he expected. The Taikō-*sama*, in his great wisdom'—and this time Ieyasu shot a mischievous glance at Munenori—'thought that, having magnanimously withdrawn his troops from Seoul, he could hang on to half of Korea. Ha! He even thought that the Ming emperor might offer him the hand of his daughter! And guess what the Chinese response was?' Ieyasu said as he turned in his saddle to see Munenori's reaction.

'They refused to accept his conditions,' Munenori said, not sure whether he had just risked his career.

'Right!' Ieyasu shouted as he hit the pommel of his saddle. 'Our friend the Chinese emperor regards the Taikō-*sama* as a mere tribute-bearing vassal! There is to be no partitioning of Korea, and there certainly is to be no marriage to his delectable daughter! Ha! And guess what? In response, the Taikō-*sama* has now ordered us to prepare for a second invasion!'

Munenori was stunned. Not because Hideyoshi had ordered a second invasion—that surprised him little: the Taikō couldn't brook being belittled. No, what surprised him was that Ieyasu would talk to him about such sensitive matters. Ever since he had entered Ieyasu's circle he had noticed how, bit by bit, the warlord had warmed to him. Could it be that he was entering that small circle of Ieyasu's closest confidants?

Ulsan

It was in the autumn of 1598, four years into his son's service for the Tenka-*dono*, that Muneyoshi celebrated his seventieth birthday. For the old man, it had proven a period of remarkable recovery—of incredible reversals. From afar he had followed with satisfaction how his youngest son quickly made his way in Edo society, how he won the hearts of his fellow *shihan* and finally Ieyasu's favor. He couldn't deny the pride he felt when he heard his son had been promoted to senior *shihan*. Yet nothing, nothing could compare to that sweet moment in the spring of the previous year, when, through Ieyasu's petitioning with the Taikō-*sama* on their behalf, he and the rest of his family were allowed to return to Yagyū Valley.

It had taken his son Yoshikatsu the better part of a year to restore the Momiji *yashiki* to its former glory. The roof was newly thatched, rotten beams replaced, and all the interiors were freshly stuccoed and matted. Muneyoshi still couldn't believe it when each morning he drew back the thick wooden *amado* and looked out on the pond with the willow beside it, that weeping willow, a reminder of the Yagyū fate, for, besides all the joy, there was sorrow in his heart too.

It hadn't been long after their return to the Momiji *yashiki* that they had received dreadful news. Yoshikatsu's oldest son, Kyūsaburō, had fallen in the Korean campaign. He had served in the regiment of Katō Kiyomasa, the general in charge of the defense of the southern Japanese stronghold at Ulsan.[2]

It consoled Muneyoshi to know that Kyūsaburō had died a true warrior. At the same time it seemed that his grandson's life, like the lives of so many promising young men in these years of turmoil, had been lost in vain, cut short only fifty miles from where they had landed almost a year before. His sentiments were obviously shared by the generals in charge of the invasion force. After several more months of senseless slaughter, they sued for peace. Hideyoshi's grand plan for the conquest of Korea and China had run its course—the dream was over.

One other thought tempered Muneyoshi's grief over the loss of his grandson: he need not worry about the future of his remaining offspring. Yoshikatsu and his wife and children were now living with him and Nabu at the Momiji *yashiki*. Nor did he have any worries over his two other sons in line, Kyūsai, and Tokusai, who had long since taken the tonsure and entered the Kōfuku temple. As such, they posed no financial burden, except for the seasonal contributions to their temple's upkeep.

His fourth son, Muneaki, too, had seen action on the mainland. During the early nineties, he had entered the service of Kobayakawa Hideaki, a young but influential warlord from Kyūshū. Following the campaign, Muneaki had remained in Kyūshū, continuing to serve his young lord at his stronghold of Najima castle.[3]

All Muneyoshi's hopes and ambitions for his clan now rested on Munenori. All his time and effort he had spent in getting Munenori ready for the heavy task of leading his clan. About his son's ability as a swordsman he didn't worry. What troubled him was the self-evident air of superiority with which his son imposed himself on others. He acted as if he were born to greatness, though little in his circumstances justified any such ideas. In a way, Muneyoshi admired his son: his disarming brashness opened doors that might have remained closed to a man less confident. Yet it also made him friends that spelled trouble.

Takuan, for instance.

His son's friendship with the monk worried Muneyoshi. Only recently, Ishida Mitsunari had invited Takuan to come and stay at his Sangen-*in*, a monastery erected for the repose of his deceased mother. But Mitsunari was one of Ieyasu's fiercest opponents. At every turn he had sought to thwart Ieyasu's rise, forging secret alliances with fellow western chieftains. The hotbed of descent was Mitsunari's headquarters of Sawayama castle. And it was there, of all places, that the monk Takuan now lived. As yet, Munenori was safe: preoccupied with the affairs of state, the Tenka-*dono* had no time to concern himself with his *shihan*'s friendship with some monk, whatever his affiliations might be. But Muneyoshi had lived long enough to know that such diverging allegiances could spell serious trouble if his son would ever come to occupy a position of influence.

CHAPTER 11

In the summer of 1598, feeling his strength waning and realizing his nearing end, Hideyoshi summoned Ieyasu and the other great warlords to a council at Osaka castle. There he made them sign a written oath by which they solemnly pledged allegiance to his natural but infant heir, Hideyori. Then he called into life the institutions that would ensure they would keep their word. Drawing on the organs of state of the Ashikaga Shōgunate, he formed two councils of five men each. The board with most authority was the go-tairō, the Council of (five) Regents. Its members were Tokugawa Ieyasu, Maeda Toshiie, Mōri Terumoto, Uesugi Kagekatsu, and Ukita Hideie. These men, his most trusted vassals, had to safeguard continued Toyotomi rule.[1]

The second organ of state was the go-bugyō, the Council of (five) Commissioners. Its members were Ishida Mitsunari, Asano Nagamasa, Maeda Geni, Mashita Nagamori, and Natsuka Masaie. They were in charge of the administrative and day-to-day affairs of government and directly responsible to the tairō. Still not satisfied his son's succession was secured, Hideyoshi called Ieyasu to his bedside on September 5 and made him swear once more that he would obey his every injunction. Ieyasu complied. Two weeks later the Taikō was dead and the future of his heir in the hands of Ieyasu and the other tairō.

Ieyasu had dutifully complied with all of Hideyoshi's wishes, as had all the other warlords—to do otherwise was to court certain disaster. Hideyoshi never questioned Ieyasu's loyalty. He had made him Hideyori's guardian, with instructions to ensure the boy's appointment as kanpaku *when the time was ripe. Ieyasu on his part seemed (at least for the time being) content with the arrangement. The death one year later of Maeda Toshiie, the new lord of Osaka castle, made him the most powerful warlord among the five* tairō, *a position he underscored with characteristic decisiveness when he moved into the western wing of the vacated castle, forcing the other* tairō *to recognize him as the Tenka-dono, the undisputed 'lord of the realm.'*

Meanwhile, Ishida Mitsunari plotted toward a major confrontation. Ever wily, he forged secret alliances with other western warlords without giving his opponents any direct cause to accuse him of double-dealings. Ieyasu desperately needed a pretext, a ploy to expose Mitsunari's treachery for all to see.

That opportunity came in the spring of 1600. Ieyasu was at Osaka castle when his informants in the Kantō told him that one of his fellow tairō, *the northern warlord Uesugi Kagekatsu, was hatching a revolt in the province of Aizu. He had begun to build a new castle at the center of the Aizu Basin, issuing secret orders to his vassals to prepare for war. Like his adoptive father, Uesugi Kenshin, Kagekatsu had always been a nuisance, but with only half his talent and far removed from the center of power, he never posed a serious threat to Ieyasu's designs. Now, he gave Ieyasu the pretext he was looking for. Already Ieyasu had repeatedly summoned Kagekatsu to come down to Osaka castle and explain his conduct. Yet the belligerent warlord blatantly ignored the summons and continued to build up his forces around his headquarters of Aizu Wakamatsu castle—the time had come to act.*

Ieyasu traveled up to Edo castle. From there he prepared to march on Oyama in Shimotsuke to move against the rebellious warlord Uesugi Kagekatsu. First, however, he called at Fushimi castle, situated halfway Osaka and Mitsunari's Sawayama castle. Having taken stock of its condition, he *left Torii Mototada and some fifteen hundred warriors in charge of the castle's defense: he did not want to pit his men against those of the rebellious warlord and be pinned down in the north with his rear vulnerable to attack; he just wanted Mitsunari to show his colors and move against Fushimi castle—that was all he required.*

Oyama

Munenori wasn't tired when, on the first day of September, he and his master rode into Oyama. On the contrary. Ieyasu had brought a few thousand foot soldiers with him and the going had been slow. Oyama was no more than fifty miles from Edo; a forced march could have brought them here in a day. But Ieyasu didn't seem to be in a hurry. They had stopped at three post stations along the Nakasendō, and at each he had sojourned in great leisure. The only sign that something was afoot was the constant comings and goings of messengers.

Being on his trusted Ookage, Munenori felt even more rested than had he been forced to use the worn bucks provided by the post stations. He felt sorry for the wretched animals, whose backs were so worn by the heavy pack saddles that on some the spines lay totally bare. Others had holes on their backs into which one could put one's hand. No wonder the animals were so notorious for their obstinacy. It was another reason why he preferred riding his own horse.

Munenori had never been north of Edo and had enjoyed the three-day journey along the Nakasendō. They were not yet among the mountains, but he could already sense the cooler clime of the northern provinces. A stiff breeze was coming down from the mountains. Drawing it in through his nostrils he could smell the fragrance of autumn. Already some of the leaves on the maple trees were turning; soon the whole region would be awash with color—far sooner than back home in Yamato.

A large host of warriors had descended on the small hamlet. They were led by Ieyasu's staunchest supporters: Kuroda Nagamasa, Hosokawa Tadaoki, Ikeda Terumasa. There were also those whose support was less certain, but just as important, as many of their domains were strategically positioned along the Tōkaidō and Nakasendō. Were they to join Mitsunari's western alliance, they would pose a serious hurdle toward the capital. It was to force them to take sides that the next day Ieyasu convened a meeting with all the warlords present. Already Torii Mototada had sent word that, on August 27, Mitsunari had laid siege to Fushimi castle with some forty-thousand troops. Mitsunari had shown his hand; now the other warlords had to show theirs. Mitsunari, he argued, was only acting out of self-interest. Only he, Hideyoshi's chosen man, could bring unity to a divided country. Moreover, were they to choose his side, they would be amply rewarded.

Not a stone was left unturned by Ieyasu to achieve his aim, even if it required him to bend the truth a little. And it worked. Fukushima Masanori, who controlled Owari along the Tōkaidō, was the first to declare himself, but only after much cajoling on the part of Kuroda Nagamasa. Acting on secret instructions from Ieyasu, Nagamasa had assured the staunch Toyotomi ally that Mitsunari was acting on his own—that he hadn't even cared to send a missive to Hideyori at Osaka castle.

Not all the warlords present were as forthcoming. Sanada Masayuki and his son refused to declare themselves and withdrew to their stronghold of Ueda castle, which stood not far from the Nakasendō. Munenori knew why. Fifteen years earlier, in the summer of 1585, Ieyasu himself had attacked the castle with a force of seven thousand men. After a siege of more

186

than three months, he had withdrawn his troops without capturing a single stone. Clearly, Masayuki hadn't forgotten.

But Ieyasu was satisfied. Almost all of the warlords present had chosen his side and declared themselves against Mitsunari and his western allies. All were aware of the gravity of their commitment, for they were up against a mighty foe. Among the warlords who had chosen Mitsunari's side were Mōri Hidemoto, Ukita Hideie, and Kobayakawa Hideaki, all western warlords, and all men who could muster large armies. They and their fathers had obeyed Hideyoshi, but they had done so reluctantly. They resented the influence the Kantō warlords had come to exert, first over Kyoto, then over the Home Provinces, and finally even over Japan's western provinces. In a way, Ieyasu was happy. He had always been wary of warlords from the west of the realm, their reluctance to recognize his authority, their attempts to thwart him at every turn. Now he could finally face them in a true meeting of strength. The victor in that contest would decide the fate of the country.

The Errand

Four more days Ieyasu stayed at Oyama—days in which he set out the strategy by which he intended to counter Mitsunari's challenge. A number of warlords were to return home to their domains to raise yet more troops. The majority would lead their troops down the Tōkaidō to Kiyosu castle, just west of Nagoya. There they were to await the arrival of the others, as well as Ieyasu's son, Hidetada, who would lead the rest of Ieyasu's troops down the Nakasendō.

On September 6, Ieyasu called Munenori to his side. 'I have an important errand for you.' He looked sideways to his scribe, who was holding a letter, folded and sealed with the Tokugawa seal. 'This letter,' he continued as he took the letter and handed it to Munenori, 'is of the utmost importance. It is your task to ensure it is delivered without fail.'

Munenori was stunned; it was addressed to 'Yagyū Sekishūsai-*dono*,' his father. What did Ieyasu have in mind? What role could his old man still play in Ieyasu's plans to unite the country?

He wanted to ask, but already Ieyasu had stood up from his camp stool and walked over to the horses. Taking the reins of Ookage, he patted the animal on its neck and said, 'Never ride over dangerous ground. It may not matter for people of rank, who have spare horses brought along behind them, but a man who has to rely on just one mount must spare it as much as possible. A man who only thinks about the journey and doesn't consider his horse will end up injuring its legs. And then it won't be able to carry him when he really needs it.'

Orin

Impressed by the importance of his mission Munenori traveled as fast as he could. Only the endurance of his horse, Ookage, forced him to make the occasional stop at one of the Tōkaidō's few post stations for food and water. Even by the shortest route, the journey from Oyama to Yagyū covered three-hundred miles. Luckily, most of the domains through which he passed were under the control of Ieyasu and his allies. Yet one could never be sure where danger lurked, especially in Mino, where the western warlords could count on the support of Nobunaga's descendants at Gifu castle.

Only once did Munenori stop to rest. He did so at Kuno castle, in the province of Tootōmi. Situated on a shallow hill overlooking the vast rice fields along the Pacific coast, Kuno castle was a modest affair. Its master was Matsushita Shigetsuna, a close ally of Ieyasu. Shigetsuna had only recently ascended to the chieftaincy of his domain, for it was only two years since his father, Yukitsuna, had passed away. The old man had been a warrior of great stature. A descendant of the famous Rokkaku-shi, he had attracted able warriors from all over the region. One of them had been a young upstart by the name of Kinoshita Tōkichirō. Then still only a stable boy, he had steadily climbed the ranks and gone on to become the great Taikō, Toyotomi Hideyoshi, undisputed master of the realm. With Hideyoshi's ascendance, the Matsushita clan had rapidly risen in status. Their domain had doubled to six thousand *koku* during the eighties. By the time Yukitsuna passed away toward the end of the nineties, the Kuno fief had exploded to a staggering one-hun-dred-and-sixty thousand *koku*, all granted by a grateful Hideyoshi. Following Hideyoshi's death, the Matsushita had joined forces with the Tokugawa to do battle with the likes of Takeda Katsuyori.

Munenori's junior by eight years, the new master of the Kuno fief was more than welcoming, reverential, even. Once, accom-panying his father on one of his visits to Edo castle, Shigetsuna had seen Munenori in action at the O-Keikoba. An avid swordsman himself, he had been deeply impressed with the Yagyū Shinkage-*ryū*, the low stance from which its techniques were executed, the perfect balance between patience and swiftness. It had been then that he had invited Munenori to visit Kuno castle on his next trip down south.

Shigetsuna's sister, Orin, also was interested in the young warrior from Yamato. But not for his ability with the sword. It wasn't often that warriors from the Home Provinces made their way to Kuno castle; most who called were men from the

Kantō, course and far from couth. Munenori was different. He showed an interest in literature, painting, and poetry. She sensed a sensitivity in the young warrior, an alacrity, a mind attuned to all the things that stirred her tender soul. She couldn't help looking at Munenori, despite his disheveled appearance. Having arranged a splendid dinner for their guest, she instructed her maids to prepare a hot bath for the weary traveler.

It was already late when she showed their guest to his quarters, his bed already made by her maids for the night. She was about to turn and leave when Munenori caught her sleeve and made her stop in her tracks. He looked deep into her face, his eyes dark and mysterious. Then his lips began to move and the most beautiful lines began to spill from them:

> Fain would one weep the whole night long,
> As weeps the bell cricket's song,
> Who chants her melancholy lay,
> Till night and darkness pass away.

The words didn't fail to hit their target. She just stood there, nailed to the floor, as if struck by a bolt of lightning. She almost fainted with excitement as she felt herself being drawn into his room. She couldn't resist—wouldn't—as he reached over her shoulder and silently closed the *shōji* behind them.

Call to Arms

The rest of Munenori's journey passed without incident. Including his one-night stay at Kuno castle, he had covered the huge distance in only five days. Late in the afternoon of September 11, utterly exhausted, he drew up his horse outside the Enjō temple. Having dismounted and rushed into the temple gate on his last strength, he found his father in the garden, raking up leaves. Leaning against one of the pillars on the temple's porch, Munenori watched his father hold up to the light the unfolded piece of paper and absorb its content with grave solemnity.

Written in his fluent but bold hand, Ieyasu's letter was brief and to the point:

To master Yagyū Tamba Nyūdō

I implore you to assemble as many local *rōnin* and other warriors you can muster and, at the earliest opportunity, put yourself at the disposal of Lord Tsutsui Sadatsugu, the governor of Iga.

September 6
Ieyasu

Munenori filled his father in on the rest. 'Lord Ieyasu has sent two large forces down the Tōkaidō and the Nakasendō to crush Mitsunari and his allies in battle. Where and how it will take place I don't know, as the war council itself was conducted in great secrecy.'

Munenori frowned; it was a frown his father knew all too well. 'What's the matter?' he asked.

'Well, I remember Lord Sadatsugu was at Oyama, but for some reason, he suddenly left on the eve of the war council. It can't be that he has deserted Ieyasu: in that case, Ieyasu wouldn't have written—'

'No, that's not it,' Muneyoshi interrupted his son. 'He had to save his castle. When Lord Sadatsugu departed for Oyama, he left Ueno castle in the care of his brother. But shortly after he left, Mitsunari's allies marched into Iga and laid siege to the castle and drove his brother from the castle.'

Munenori wanted to speak, but his father continued, 'There is no need to worry,' he said as he folded up Ieyasu's letter and put it in the pocket of his left sleeve. 'Thankfully Lord Sadatsugu returned well in time before the enemy was able to firmly establish themselves and was able to recapture the castle without much trouble.'

Munenori sighed with relief.

'Yet we are far from out of the woods,' the old man went on. 'While you were on your way here, Fushimi castle fell to the enemy. Torii Mototada and all his men are dead. They certainly put up a brave fight, for they managed to keep the enemy at bay for more than a week.'

'*Naruhodo,*' Munenori frowned again. 'Judging by the number of chieftains who joined Ieyasu at Oyma, I would guess his combined force is close to a hundreds thousand. Yet he still needs more troops. Only then can he hope to subdue Mitsunari and his allies, whose combined strength well exceeds a hundred thousands.'

'Indeed,' his father nodded gravely.

'I see Ieyasu's reasoning now,' Munenori said. 'The last time I visited cousin Nakanobō Hidesuke-*dono* at his new abode in Ueno, I was impressed with the ability of Lord Sadatsugu's warriors. I'm not surprised he managed to regain his castle as quickly as he did. I believe that together we should be able to assemble several thousand well-trained warriors.'

'Indeed,' Muneyoshi nodded. 'But now you must rest. Tomorrow you have to rally all our warriors. The day after, we will cross the border into Iga and put ourselves under the command of Tsutsui Sadatsugu, lord and master of Ueno castle.'

CHAPTER 12

On September 12, Ieyasu crossed the bridge over the wide moat of Edo castle and entered the imposing gate to his eastern headquarters. Following the council at Oyama, he had ordered his northern allies to keep Kagekatsu in check. Now he had returned home to ready himself for the final confrontation with Ishida Mitsunari.

Events were now unfolding in rapid succession. On his arrival, he learned that four days earlier Fushimi castle had fallen after ten days of intense fighting in which Torii Mototada and all his men had given their lives. A week later news reached Edo castle that, having captured Fushimi castle, Mitsunari and his allies had proceeded eastward along the Tōkaidō and reached Ōgaki castle. On September 17, they took the small stronghold without encountering any resistance. It appeared they wanted to entrench themselves in Mino, where they could count on the support of Oda Hidenobu.

These tidings did not perturb the Tenka-dono in the least. He had given his two great armies enough time to reach their destinations—something confirmed by the news, shortly after his arrival, that the force that had marched down the Tōkaidō had reached the stronghold of Kiyosu according to plan. Ieyasu himself did not move from Edo castle. First he wanted to ascertain the loyalty of his commanders in the field—a loyalty that could only be proven by bold military action.

And such was the purport of a message delivered to the gathered forces at Kiyosu on September 26. It had the desired effect. Two days later, a contingent of five thousand men under the command of Ikeda Terumasa crossed the Kiso River upstream to attack Gifu castle in force. They came under dense musket fire from Oda Hidenobu's troops across the river, forcing them at first to retreat. The next day the scales tipped. A second large eastern contingent, under the command of Fukushima Masanori, had crossed the river farther downstream with a flotilla of small boats under the cover of night. The Oda forces continued to offer fierce resistance, but when they were threatened with being cut off, Hidenobu ordered his men to retreat to the castle.

At early daybreak on September 30, the Ikeda and Fukushima forces launched a massive attack on Gifu castle. Within hours Masanori's men forced one of the gates and made their way into the castle's second tier, the main line of defense protecting the keep where Hidenobu and his family were holding out. Not much later Terumasa's men breached the first tier, setting sections of the castle ablaze and hurling their banner into the keep shouting 'today, we are the first to breach the enemy's castle.' High up in the keep, Hidenobu prepared to commit ritual suicide. He would have done so, had not his retainers prevailed on him to surrender and go into seclusion in Gifu's Entoku temple. Hearing that Gifu castle had fallen, the master of nearby Inuyama castle also surrendered, removing the last barrier toward Ōgaki castle.

Mitsunari was stunned by the swiftness with which Ieyasu had turned the scales on him. In his plans, the castles of Ōgaki, Gifu, and Inuyama had featured as a barrier to guard the gateway to the capital and the western provinces. It had also seemed the perfect base from which to launch his intended strike against Ieyasu's home province of Mikawa and the Kantō beyond. Those plans had now been rendered futile. Within only a few days, the eastern army had captured two of his Mino strongholds. They now threatened to do the same with the castle where he and his allies had gathered. Mitsunari panicked; he ordered his troops to press forward, toward Gifu, to throw up a line of defense along the eastern shores of the Nagara River. The strategy backfired. Instead of throwing back the advancing eastern troops, Mitsunari saw himself forced to withdraw to Ōgaki castle at the cost of many casualties.

Seeing the huge force arrayed against him, Mitsunari now frantically began to write letters to befriended warlords, luring them with the promise of more territories and higher status. His efforts seemed to bear fruit: over the next few weeks one warlord after the other led his troops into Mino and set up camp in the vicinity of Ōgaki castle. Among them were powerful men like Ōtani Yoshitsugu, Ukita Hideie, Mōri Hidemoto, Kikkawa Hiroie, and Natsuka Masaie. Their combined forces comprised some thirty-thousand men, bringing the total of the western forces to eighty-thousand, twice the number arrayed against them. Even warlords of doubtful allegiance made their appearance, among them Kobayakawa Hideaki, who arrived with some eight thousand men in tow.

The eastern army, meanwhile, pitched camp at the post station of Akasaka, some three miles northwest of Ōgaki. There were some twenty contingents in all, varying in number from a few hundred to several thousands, the largest being that of Kuroda Nagamasa, who had put well over five thousand warriors in the field.

Tsutsui Sadatsugu, too, pitched camp. With the help of Yagyū Muneyoshi and other local chieftains, he had managed to raise close to three thousand men. They had departed from Ueno castle toward the end of September and joined their northern allies shortly after the fall of Gifu and Inuyama castles.

Yet there was still no sign of Ieyasu, nor of his son, Hidetada, who was leading the second great force along the Nakasendō.

Finally, on the afternoon of October 20, the Tenka-dono arrived and pitched camp at Akasaka. He had led a contingent of thirty-thousand troops down the Tōkaidō, bringing the total number of eastern troops close to eighty-thousand, almost the equivalent of those assembled under Ishida Mitsunari.

Sekigahara

It was no weather to lift the spirits when Ieyasu dismounted his horse and strode up to his tent to receive the first reports from his commanders in the field. It was fall, the time of year when fierce hurricanes swept in from the southern Pacific to hit the Japanese islands with their relentless force. It seemed that this was exactly what lay in store for the gathered warriors, for the wind was picking up fast. Already a thick veil of rain hung over the wide plain, subduing the vivid colors of their armor, the silk banners, and the bright sparkle of the long lances.

The air of gloom at Ieyasu's headquarters lifted when scouts reported that all of the enemy forces were still stationed near Ōgaki castle, leaving unprotected the two-mile-wide strip of land that ran westward toward the old barrier town of Sekigahara.

The news seemed too good to be true. From Sekigahara, the massive Ibuki Mountains stretched northward, all the way to Tsuruga, where they plummeted into Tsuruga Bay. Southward ran the Yōrō Mountains, an equally long and impenetrable stretch of mountains, right into the heart of the mountainous Ise Peninsula. Situated at the point where both mountain ranges met, Sekigahara was the gateway between east and west Japan. He who controlled Sekigahara held the keys to the realm.[1]

'How can Mitsunari have failed to seize the advantage?' Ieyasu exclaimed. 'Does he not appreciate the barrier's historic importance? Or is it something else? Is it perhaps the weather? Has the unrelenting rain gotten to these westerners?'

But Ieyasu's scouts detected no exceptional movements among the enemy. Only a small group of mounted warriors loomed up out of the haze to harass some troops stationed along the Makuse River. It was no more than a provocation, and the dreary day drew to a close without any further engagements.

That same evening Ieyasu convened a council of all his commanders in the field. 'Tomorrow,' he told them, 'we will press eastward, and try to pass the barrier. We'll leave behind five thousand men—too few to defeat the enemy, I know, but enough to keep them preoccupied for the remainder to pass the barrier into Ōmi province. From there we will attack the strategic castles of Sawayama, Fushimi, and Osaka. It is a bold plan, certainly, but if it works the realm will be ours!'

Hidetada

The Tenka-*dono* was in a foul temper when, early next morning, Munenori led two messengers to Ieyasu's tent. They brought disturbing news. During the previous evening, while he and his generals had been mapping out their strategy for the next day, a huge contingent of Mitsunari's army had broken up camp and begun to march eastward, into to the plains of Sekigahara. Caught in a blinding rainstorm they had temporarily lost their way, but shortly after midnight, they had reached the foot of Mount Sasao, where they had taken up positions on high ground.

For a moment it seemed that the Tenka-*dono* had been masterfully outwitted. The mounted warriors who had come down from Ōgaki to harass his soldiers the previous day had been sent with a purpose: to distract the attention of his scouts from the larger troop movements farther afield. As a result, Mitsunari now occupied high ground. His forces were more numerous, too, albeit by a narrow margin.

And it was the numbers that irked Ieyasu most. 'It should have been the other way round!' he shouted as he kicked a tent pole. 'Close to forty-thousand men I have entrusted to Hidetada's command. Why does it take him this long to get here? Given that he's departed on the first of October—a week before us—he should long since have arrived!'

Communications along the inland route of the Nakasendō were poor: the last news they had had from Hidetada was that he was tied down in Shinano, where he had laid siege of Ueda castle, the stronghold of the shrewd and redoubtable Sanada Masayuki—a stupid and unnecessary diversion, as Ueda castle lay not along the Nakasendō, but on a side road, into Echigo and the northwestern provinces.[2]

In the six years since he had entered Ieyasu's service, Munenori had never seen the Tenka-*dono* in such a temper. His mind went back to that hot summer day when Ieyasu had visited his son at practice at the O-Keikoba. He recalled how Ieyasu had cautioned his son that a true general must know how to avoid risks. It seemed that, by taking on the Sanada at Ueda castle, Hidetada had forgotten an important lesson.

The seasoned commander soon recovered. Stepping outside his tent, he began to issue orders. 'All troops are to immediately depart for Sekigahara and take up positions opposite the western forces as best they can. I will follow close behind with my own troops. Ikeda Terumasa and his men are to remain behind and cover the rear. Not all of Mitsunari's allies might have departed yet from Ōgaki—we might still cut them off!'

Battle Formations

It was five o'clock in the morning before the Tenka-*dono* set up his field headquarters at the foot of Mount Momokubari. His twenty contingents had failed to intercept the enemy; they had run into such dense fog that they had to halt for fear of losing their way, leaving them stranded on the low-lying fields below

Mitsunari's position. Meanwhile, the brunt of Mitsunari's allies had joined him around the Ikedera pond. Only a few of their contingents, among them those of Mōri Hidemoto, Kikkawa Hiroie, and Natsuka Masaie, had lagged behind. But even they had taken up positions on high ground, a few miles south to where Ikeda's men were stationed.

Munenori and the other Yamato warriors who had joined Tsutsui Sadatsugu's army were among the first to take up their positions opposite the enemy. They were now on the very front line, just east of the junction between the Nakasendō and the Hokkoku Kaidō. Even as they took up their positions, one by one the other contingents began to arrive, a huge clatter of armor, metal, and the nervous whinnying of horses. Flanking them were the Tanaka and the Katō; behind them those of the Ii, the Matsudaira, and the Miyoshi. From where he stood it was less than a mile to the enemy lines. It was still dark, but already apprehension and relish vied for control of Munenori's heart as he and his fellow warriors awaited the break of dawn.

By eight o'clock, the unrelenting rain of the previous night had somewhat lessened, though shrouds of mist still streaked the low-lying plain. The troops were so closely dispersed in the narrow valley that many, including those of the enemy, could be seen through the haze. It seemed as if the whole valley was alive with movement as close to two hundred thousand warriors readied themselves for the moment of truth.

From where he stood, just over the crest of a hillock, Munenori could clearly make out a black banner with a white cross, the colors of the Shimazu clan. Immediately behind them, at the foot of Mount Tenman stood the troops of Konishi Yukinaga, several thousand in all. Farther still, more toward the south, an even larger contingent, that of Ukita Hideie, faced Ieyasu's left flank under the command of Fukushima Masanori.

Turning his gaze northward, Munenori could make out yet
more allied troops, the Hosokawa, the Katō, the Nagaoka. And
beyond them, at the foot of Mount Maru, right opposite those
of Mitsunari, stood the forces of Kuroda Nagamasa, the man
who had played such an important role in the recovery of the
Yagyū clan. Now, Munenori realized, was the time to repay
Nagamasa and Ieyasu his debt of gratitude, by fighting to the
hilt—if need be to lay down his life.

Munenori noticed how, at less than a mile, the troops of
Fukushima Masanori were closest to the enemy. It was a position
he envied. Being the first to see action, the commanders at the
front line stood the greatest chance of being killed and one of
their heads taken. Yet they might equally be the first to take the
head of an enemy. That head would be sent back to the Tenka-
dono to inspect and be declared the *ichiban kubi*, the first enemy
head to be taken in battle. Needless to say, such a feat would
be copiously recompensed after the battle.

Masanori's chances to be the first went up in smoke when,
shortly after eight o'clock, a small group of mounted warriors
carrying Matsudaira and Ii banners detached itself from the
troops in Munenori's rear and forced their way through the gap
between his ranks and those of the Tanaka and Tsutsui. They
were led by Ieyasu's fourth son, Matsudaira Tadayoshi, seconded
by Ii Naomasa. The sudden action caused consternation among
the commanders in the front line, especially among Fukushima
Masanori. For no sooner had the contingent rode out into no
man's land, than they swerved leftward, right into Masanori's
line of attack, from where they headed straight for the Ukita
and Shimazu banners in the enemy line.

Realizing the two commanders were stealing a march on him,
Masanori immediately ordered his musketeers to open fire on
the enemy. The fire was answered by a group of musketeers on

Munenori's left, causing the Ii horsemen to be caught in the crossfire. Within moments of this first exchange, a thin plume of smoke began to climb skyward from the foot of Mount Maru: Kuroda Nagamasa too had given orders to commence overall hostilities—the Battle of Sekigahara had begun in earnest.

Mayhem

Spotting the signal fires, all the commanders along the front line now ordered their musketeers to open fire. Thick plumes of smoke belched forth from the arrayed muzzles. It mingled with the misty morning air, and within moments a dense layer of smog covered the thin stretch of land between the two armies. Then, after several volleys, Munenori could hear the bellowing voice of Tsutsui Sadatsugu, ordering his musketeers to stand aside and let the phalanx of spearmen advance.

As he rushed forward through the acrid smog Munenori could make out little except the flashes of muskets being fired on the other side, shortly followed by a sound not unlike the clattering of hail as the molten lead wreaked havoc among his fellow warriors. By now his senses were being overloaded. Underfoot, the ground reverberated with the rumble of the advancing hordes, while his ears filled with the battle roar of men and the clatter of their armor. It felt as if he were being swept along on the crest of some giant wave that would soon engulf the enemy lines and drown him and his fellow warriors along with it. Within a few agonizing moments, they reached the enemy lines. There the mounted Ii and Matsudaira warriors had already picked their men, all, of course, commanders of their own rank.

From the corner of his eyes, Munenori spotted how one of them, Ii Naomasa, had wrestled to the ground a western chieftain and took his head. He didn't have the time to see him raise it aloft, for at that very instant he and his fellow warriors clashed with the Ukita forces, who had dug in the rear end of their *yari* to halt the advance.

Total mayhem now ensued around Munenori as the bulk of the two armies began to clash and warriors began to grapple with each other in man-to-man combat, like their ancestors had done for more than five centuries.

In the heat of battle, Munenori reaped the benefits of his father's patient training over two decades. All the precepts transferred from Aisu Ikō to Kamiizumi Nobutsuna, and from the latter to his father, now rushed to Munenori's aid as if some invisible hand had beckoned them. He no longer had to think to turn his body sideways to his opponent, to make a shield of his fists, to put his weight on his forward knee, to let the enemy strike first. All these vital techniques came to him naturally as he stood his ground and tackled one foe after the other.

Open Fire!

Western opposition remained fierce, especially from the Ukita and Konishi warriors, some twenty-thousand in all. They fought with such determination that by eleven o'clock the eastern forces were pushed back beyond the same positions from which they had advanced three hours before. Worried by the lack of progress, even Ieyasu became restless. Standing in his stirrups he looked on, nervously biting his hand. Then, unable to bear it any longer, he left his camp at the foot of Mount Momokubari to take up a position at the center of the plain, right behind his forces. But even by noon, there was still no way to tell which way the pendulum would swing.

Mitsunari, too, began to lose patience. He sent up smoke signals, urging those who hadn't yet joined him in battle to do so, especially Mōri Terumoto and Kobayakawa Hideaki. The former, still facing the Ikeda contingent from Mount Nangu, found himself cut off by his vassal Kikkawa Hiroie, who had been persuaded by Ieyasu to change sides in exchange for his lord's domains. Hideaki, who had taken up positions on Mount Matsuo, toward the south of the scene of battle, also stayed put. On the eve of battle, he had arranged with Mitsunari to join the fight on the latter's signal and attack Ieyasu's forces from the rear. Yet even when Mitsunari sent a messenger over to Mount Matsuo with an urgent request for assistance Hideaki failed to budge.

Ieyasu had also spotted the signal, and he had a good idea why Hideaki dithered. While in Edo he had had a letter from Hideaki in which the latter had apologized for attacking Fushimi castle, claiming that circumstances had forced him to participate in the siege. Seeking to capitalize on Hideaki's sense of guilt, Ieyasu too had sent missives to Mount Matsuo, but they had come back without any firm commitments—the young chieftain was obviously torn by conflicting emotions. He needed a good prodding, something to stir him into action, damn the outcome.

Turning to his gunners, Ieyasu shouted, 'Open fire on Hideaki's troops!'

The gunners hesitated. Why fire on an ally?

But again Ieyasu shouted his orders, 'Open fire, damn you!'

This time they did. And now Ieyasu's genius for reading men's minds revealed itself. As if roused from a slumber, the young Hideaki stood up in his stirrups, pointed his battle fan in the direction of the western forces and called out to his men, 'aim for the Otani ranks.'

The effect of Hideaki's defection was almost instantaneous. A loud cheer went up among the eastern warriors as they saw how Hideaki's six thousand warriors rushed down the slopes of Mount Matsuo and began to attack the Ōtani and Toda troops, who were wedged between the huge Ukita force and the foot of the mountain. Through superhuman effort the Ōtani and Toda men repelled the first attack, driving Hideaki's men back up the mountain's slopes, but then disaster struck as four other western commanders, who had taken up positions at the foot of the mountain, also changed sides and ordered their men to join those of Hideaki. Under these enormous pressures, the ranks of Ōtani and his fellow commanders collapsed one by one. Those who were still standing began to retreat northward, first into the ranks of the Ukita, then into those of the Konishi, and before long they too were overwhelmed.

There was no response from the other western warlords. The Mōri, the Natsuka, the Ankokuji, the Shimazu, all of them stood by as their allies were being butchered. Unwilling to lose his men in the rescue of others, Shimazu Toyohisa even ordered his men to erect a *yari fusuma*, a dense wall of lances, to keep the fleeing warriors from mingling with his own ranks and thereby weaken them. Even Mitsunari failed to come to their rescue. One final time he issued a command to his troops: to pack up and retreat west along the Hokkoku Kaidō.

It was two o'clock, the hour of the Goat. The fighting would go on till late in the afternoon, but Mitsunari's flight confirmed that the outcome of the battle had been decided.

CHAPTER 13

A strange calm descended over the country in the wake of the Battle of Sekigahara. Things seemed to go topsy-turvy as those who had turned on their allies were rewarded and those who had fought valiantly were hunted down to the corners of the realm. Four days after the dust had settled on the plains of the old Seki barrier, Takenaka Shigekado, a local chieftain who had joined the eastern forces at the last minute, apprehended Konishi Yukinaga as he was trying to cross the Ibuki Mountains into Ōmi. On November 6, Yukinaga was beheaded at the Rokujōgawara execution grounds.[1]

Yukinaga's head rolled together with that of a host of others, including that of Ishida Mitsunari, the mastermind behind the western campaign. Following his flight from the battlefield, the fugitive had made his way to Furuhashi, a small village along the Takatoki River. There he had taken a boat and, dressed in the guise of local fisherman, rowed upstream to find shelter among the snow-clad slopes of the Ibuki Mountains. When he was finally seized, he was found cowering in a cave, suffering from cold, hunger, and failing health. His fate and that of his allies had been sealed by a widely distributed flyer in which Ieyasu promised to reward all those who aided in their arrest and threatened to kill all those who abetted in their escape and shelter.

Ieyasu now set about to consolidate his position as Tenka-dono. In

1603, he moved his headquarters to Edo castle and founded the Edo Bakufu (1603–1867). Then, in the image of the great Minamoto Yoritomo, he had himself appointed Sei-I Tai Shōgun, the 'Barbarian Subduing Generalissimo.' At the same time, he abolished the go-tairō. But he stopped short of dealing with Hideyori, to whom many warlords still looked up as their true overlord. Instead, he sought to contain Hideyori and his allies.

Starting in 1601 with the construction of Zeze castle on the shore of Lake Biwa, over the following years, he steadily widened the ring of reinforced strongholds in the Home Province to include Himeji, Fushimi, Nijō, Hikone, Nagahama, and Nagoya. In the Kantō region, he set about on the large-scale reconstruction of Sunpu, Ueno, and his headquarters of Edo castle. When he had entered Edo in 1594 he had given little attention to his castle, preferring, instead, to look after the pay and housing for his men. Now he was the highest authority in the realm and Edo was its center—it had to be felt by all who came to visit, lord or commoner alike.

Reconstructions were conducted on a grand scale. At Edo castle alone a force of more than a hundred thousand men was put to work to dig wide moats, flatten hills, and heave into place the huge blocks of granite from which the walls and foundations were constructed. New western and northern wings were added, increasing the circumference of the main castle to a staggering ten miles.[2] The scale of the castle was of such grandeur that no one who entered one of its thirty-eight imposing gates could fail to be impressed with the wealth and power of the Sei-I Tai Shōgun.

Higakubo

Being a *hatamoto*, Munenori was entitled to build his own *yashiki* near Edo. He was assigned a large plot of land in Azabu, an old hamlet on Edo's southern outskirts. It was an auspicious place. Situated in a green and undulating landscape, it was surrounded by ancient shrines and temples. On the west, it ran up to the grounds of the Sakurada shrine, a temple founded by the great Minamoto Yoritomo. On the east, only a stone's throw away, stood the famous Zenpuku temple. Founded in 824, it was one of Edo's oldest temples. Beyond the temple, on the opposite side of the meandering Ko River, lay the Tōkaidō, the old highroad that connected Edo with Japan central cities, Nagoya, Kyoto, and Osaka.

As the new leader of the Yagyū clan, Munenori took to his new task with relish. He had always had an interest in architecture. On his travels, he had noticed subtle differences in the architecture of castles and temples from region to region. Being from Yamato, he was eager to build a dwelling that would remind him of home. Given the work at Ieyasu's castle, Edo craftsmen were hard to come by, and thus he hired a small army of craftsmen from his home province of Yamato: stonemasons, plasterers, sawyers, carpenters, and roofers. Many of them had worked on Nara's famous temples, some even on Hisahide's sumptuous Tamonyama castle.

They built him a modest *yashiki* in the beautiful symmetry of the *shoin zukuri* tradition. Fresh *tatami* from Nara were laid out in the auspicious *shūgijiki* format, in causing all corners to form three-pronged junctions. The plastered *shikkui* walls were framed by fragrant cedar pillars and lintels, while the *fusuma* sliding doors divided the many rooms were decorated with various Yamato landscapes. Being only recently reinstated, the clan's funds were limited. Yet through his lord, Munenori managed to hire Kanō Sansetsu, one of the great painters in the Kanō school of painting, who enlivened the *fusuma* that led on to the *yashiki*'s main reception room with beautiful monochrome landscapes.

The main building was flanked by several outbuildings, including a small *dōjō* with cedar floors sawn from trees that had grown in the Kasagi Highlands. These floors had a warm and absorbing quality that was easy on the joints and tendons, even after a full day of indoor practice. The *dōjō* was merely for private use, for the Shōgun had his own grand O-Keikoba within the walls of Edo castle.

Delighted with the pleasant way in which the sun even reached the lower lying parts of his estate, Munenori named his Edo abode the Higakubo, or Sunny Hollows. And while small compared to the grand *yashiki* of the Kuroda, the Uesugi and the Shimazu inside the castle's outer moats, for Munenori, who had grown up homeless and dependent on the generosity and hospitality of others, the Higakubo *yashiki* was as grand as Edo castle must have been to his lord and master, Tokugawa Ieyasu.

Marriage

Work on the Higakubo *yashiki* and its gardens took Munenori over two years to complete. But well before that, he began preparations for his wedding to the young woman he had met on his journey down from Oyama: Orin, the daughter of Matsushita Yukitsuna. Ever since he had set eyes on her, Munenori had seized every opportunity to visit Kuno castle and spend some time with Shigetsuna's captivating daughter. Now the time had come to make her his wife.

Though not a man of limited means, Munenori couldn't afford the kind of luxuries the more powerful feudal lords tended to lavish on their future spouses, whose dowries could contain up to four hundred items. There was simply no way he could raise that kind of money. It hadn't been long since his clan had still been relying on the hospitality of the Enjō temple. Having fought bravely in the front lines among the troops of Tsutsui Sadatsugu, Munenori's stipend had been raised to a thousand *koku*. And in the nationwide redistribution of lands that followed in the wake of Sekigahara, all the Yagyū domains confiscated in 1585 by Toyotomi Hidenaga were returned to Muneyoshi, who was raised to the rank of *hatamoto*. One year later the Yagyū domains were increased by another thousand *koku*, bringing the total amount of revenue that accrued to the clan to four thousand *koku*. Yet the upkeep of those domains was a costly affair, and though Munenori had accumulated some wealth since he had entered into Ieyasu's service, much of it he had spent on his new *yashiki*.

Still, he was determined to wed Orin in style.

Thus, late at night, as was still the tradition among the ancient Yamato clans, a ceremony was held at the Kasuga Taisha. All the beautiful lanterns for which the shrine was famed were lit and shrine maidens lined the beautifully lit forest path that ran from the Kōfuku-*ji* to the Kasuga Taisha. When still studying under Eishun at the Ichijō-*in*, he had often gone for walks here with his tutor. Now, with much pride, he accompanied his future wife up the same path as they slowly made their way to the shrine's inner court. There, in the presence of the Yagyū and Matsushita clans, the two solemnly had their nine sips of ceremonial *sake* from the flat lacquered *sake* cups—the *san-san kudo*: three sips by her, three sips by him, and another three by her.

They were a good match. She was of the same social strata as the Yagyū, and her father had been a man of great standing whose good name and reputation still reflected on all those associated with the Matsushita clan.[3] She was young, attractive, and accomplished in all the arts associated with a woman of her standing. Soon she bore him two sons, Jūbei and Matajūrō, both of whom went on to become great swordsmen in their own right and *hatamoto* to the house of Tokugawa.

Though, like men of his class, Munenori would take concubines who gave him more sons and daughters, his love for Orin proved genuine and lasting. There was an irresistible charm in her face, erotic even—the way her eyelids hid half of her large, deep dark pupils; the small dimples in her cheeks whenever she laughed. Every time he looked into her face, Munenori knew why he had recalled that old poem by the great Murasaki Shikubu—the same poem his mother would recite whenever she and his father talked about their early courtship, when Muneyoshi had still been a hostage at Tsutsui castle.

CHAPTER 14

Impressive though Edo castle was, in the Kinai region the largest castle was Osaka castle, and it was there of all places that Toyotomi Hideyori was allowed to reside and receive vassals loyal to the Toyotomi cause. To dedicate himself to this problem, Ieyasu had stepped down as Shōgun in favor of his son in 1605, only two years after he had assumed the title himself. Leaving Edo castle to Hidetada, he moved back to Sunpu castle, from where he reinforced his clan's strategic position against the western warlords with renewed vigor, partly by building and strengthening castles throughout the realm, partly by consolidating his clan's ties with allies through intermarriage.

He had already tried this strategy on the Toyotomi in 1603, when he wedded Hidetada's daughter, Senhime, off to Toyotomi Hideyori at the tender age of six. Yet despite an apparently happy marriage, it did not produce the political stability Ieyasu had envisioned. To Ieyasu's great chagrin, Hideyori remained under the influence of men with vehement anti-Tokugawa sentiments. Yet Ieyasu's greatest antagonist was a woman, Hideyori's mother, Yodogimi, who had moved in with her son and left no stone unturned to restore her crumbling family fortunes. Painfully aware of her clan's increasing isolation, it was especially Yodogimi who grew ever more intransigent, giving Ieyasu all the more reason to remove this obstacle to a Tokugawa hegemony.

For a decade Ieyasu kept his nerve. Then, in the summer of 1614, he found the pretext he had been looking for. It was while at Sunpu castle, that he learned that the House of Toyotomi intended to celebrate the reconstruction of the Hōkō temple in Kyoto with an inscription on the huge temple bell. The inscription on the temple bell read:

> *May the state be peaceful and prosperous;*
> *In the east, it greets the pale moon;*
> *In the west, it bids farewell to the setting sun.*

Likening the house of Ieyasu (which had always had its power base in the eastern provinces) to the moon—and a pale one, at that; and the house of Toyotomi (whose supporters resided chiefly in the western provinces) to the sun, went a step too far for the Tenka-dono. He immediately ordered all celebrations to be canceled, though he carefully refrained from moving against Hideyori. Instead, he patiently waited for the Toyotomi camp to make the first move.

By November the first signs that Ieyasu's plot was having effect were appearing. His spies inside Osaka castle informed him that the Toyotomi were stocking up on rations and ammunition. They even had the temerity to raid his private yashiki within the castle compound. Then word reached him that, on November 3, Hideyori had sent missives to befriended chieftains, calling on them to join him at Osaka castle— he was clearly preparing for a long, drawn-out siege. It would take a major effort to crush them; from his spies' detailed reports his advisors estimated that, backed by their allies, the Toyotomi would be able to muster as many as a hundred thousand warriors in all.

The time had come to act. On November 11, Ieyasu departed from Sunpu at the head of a huge army. On its way southward along the Tōkaidō, it was joined by the forces of allied chieftains, so that by the time Ieyasu entered Nijō castle in Kyoto, his army had reached a strength of well over a hundred thousand men.

Chapter 14

Mobilization

As a Tokugawa bannerman, Munenori was one of the first to be
mobilized. He was ordered to get ready to march shortly after
Ieyasu had departed from Sunpu. He and a number of other
shihan were selected to be part of Hidetada's private escort of
thirty-four mounted warriors. On November 24, after months
of careful preparation, they departed from Edo castle at the
head of some sixty thousand men.

Hidetada had a lot to make up for. Tough fourteen years had
passed, Munenori vividly remembered how incensed Ieyasu had
been when Hidetada failed to reach Sekigahara in time. In truth
Ieyasu's response had been lenient. He had refused to see his
son, but only for three days, causing some warlords to suspect
that the shrewd strategist had conspired with Hidetada to
withhold his backup on purpose, just in case his main army was
obliterated at Sekigahara. This time round Ieyasu had made sure
his son had a clear brief: to march down the Tōkaidō to Fushimi
castle and get them rested and ready for battle.

Riding alongside Hidetada, Munenori couldn't help but notice
how tense the young Shōgun was. It impressed on Munenori just
how great the contrast was between father and son: where the
old man issued orders calmly, the son barked them out, expecting
his commanders to obey without question; where the old man
took his time to rest, the son seemed unable to sleep, rising well
before dawn and demanding his men do the same. The Shōgunal
army was the best in the realm; the men were well fed and
trained, able to easily cover a distance of up to forty miles a day
under normal conditions. But winter had set in early this year,
and a thick pack of snow covered the road all the way down to
Nagoya. Soon the toll it took on the men began to tell; trudging
through the thick snow, one by one the troops began to fall

behind. By the time they reached Ejiri on the Bay of Suruga, the eighteenth station along the Tōkaidō, only some two-hundred-and-forty foot soldiers had kept up with his mounted escort. But Hidetada, eager not to be late this time, still pressed on. Forcing to keep up the grueling tempo, his troops covered the distance within a stunning seventeen days—by then, only his mounted warriors were fit enough for combat.

Thankfully, on its way south, Hidetada's contingent was joined by a large number of smaller ones, so that by the time he reached Fushimi castle, on December 10, their combined force had swelled to two-hundred thousand men. Yet even now, Hidetada didn't give his men the time to recover. He and his father had arranged to meet for a war council within three days at Chausuyama, a shallow hill just south of Osaka castle. By the time his father rode out from Nijō castle, on December 15, Hidetada and his troops had already reached Nara.

Home

Munenori was glad to be back in his home province. He had spent much of the last two decades in Edo, instructing the various members of the Tokugawa clan in the tenets of the Yagyū Shinkage school of swordsmanship. By now he had become a celebrity in Edo, known to every practitioner of swordsmanship at the capital's many *dōjō*, but his heart still lay in Yamato.

He looked forward to seeing Nara again and visit his brothers Kyūsai and Tokusai at Nara's Kōfuku monastery. His old tutor, Eishun, had long since passed away. Having completed his *Tamon-in nikki*, that great chronicle spanning six decades of Yamato history, he had passed away peacefully at the old age of seventy-eight. Munenori had attended the funeral. It had been held on the last day of January 1596, only weeks before he had moved to Edo in Ieyasu's service. All the Yamato dignitaries had been present, including the chief members of the Yagyū and Nakanobō clans. And it was with Hidemasa, the current head of the Nakanobō clan, that Munenori met on the eve of their departure for Osaka, for the Nakanobō too were to join Ieyasu in battle, as they had done at Sekigahara. Munenori had been surprised to find that Hidemasa and the rest of the Nakanobō clan were now living in Nara again, and no longer in Ueno.

'Yes,' Hidemasa said in answer to Munenori's query into the reason for his clan's return, 'we have moved back here to Nara, where I am now again the *machi bugyō*. You must know that we have left the service of Lord Tsutsui Sadatsugu.'

'How come?' Munenori queried.

'It is a long story,' Hidemasa said with a solemn expression. 'It all began when my father observed with growing anxiety how, in the wake of Sekigahara, our lord began to lead an increasingly dissolute life. As you well know, Lord Sadatsugu is a great leader on the field of battle. However, back home in Ueno, away from the rigor of the battlefield and surrounded by the temptations of court life, he found it hard to contain his passions...'

Hidemasa sighed; he obviously found it hard to talk about this. 'Being one of his chief counselors, my father noticed how his lordship increasingly neglected his duties, spending his time instead in the company of courtesans and the pursuit of other corrupting pleasures. At length, the situation became untenable—so untenable that, as one of his lordship's senior counselors, my father felt compelled to appeal to the Bakufu in Edo to intervene. This they did, stripping Lord Sadatsugu of his lands and exiling him to the northern province of Mutsu. And thus my father, may his spirit rest in peace, decided to move back to Nara, where he was appointed *machi bugyū*.

'"His spirit rest in peace?"' Munenori said in surprise. 'Has he passed away since?'

Hidemasa's face darkened as he continued. 'He was murdered. His appointment was a generous one, for the Bakufu granted our clan its own domain among the Kasagi Highlands. But only a year later he was assassinated while visiting Fushimi on an official errand. It turned out his assassin was one of Satatsugu's henchmen. It seems our former lord, whom we have served so faithfully, believed my father denounced him merely to further his own cause. Since then I have taken my father's position as head of the clan and as Nara's *machi bugyō*.'

Hidemasa's story put Munenori in a melancholy frame of mind. Already eight years had passed since his own father had died. Muneyoshi had been seventy-nine years old when, on May 25, 1606, he had passed away peacefully at the Momiji *yashiki*. After modest ceremony he had been buried at the Enjō temple. His had been a life of considerable achievements, but also great setbacks. He had lost his castle to Nobunaga, his lands to Hideyoshi. Especially the loss of his lands had hit the old man hard. Munenori had been at Nara at the time, studying under Eishun, but his oldest brother had told him how he had found him during the surveyor's visit, collapsed at the foot of Momiji bridge. When Munenori returned home, his father had seemed ten years older, a broken man. And still, he had gone on. Under his leadership, they had weathered a decade of exile. They had done so by immersing themselves deeply in their art. Those years of endurance in the face of hardship had instilled in Munenori a spiritual depth he hadn't known before. Yet it had been his father's lighting example, his unshaken belief in the Yagyū school of swordsmanship, that had inspired Munenori and his brothers to carry on despite the odds, and that eventually brought about their clan's miraculous recovery.

Looking back on those bleak times, Munenori was grateful his father had lived to see his *yashiki* restored, his lands returned. He also realized that the pending battle could either undo or galvanize all he had accomplished.

Chausuyama

The hill Ieyasu had chosen for his headquarters was named after a traditional Japanese tea mortar (*chausu*) because of its steep slopes.[1] Munenori wondered whether the Tenka-*dono*, who hailed from eastern Japan, would have chosen the site had he known its true significance, for the hill on which he had set up his headquarters had once been a burial mound. Shaped like a keyhole and encircled by a wide moat, it had once contained the tomb of one of Yamatō's ancient rulers. During the previous centuries of incessant war, it had gradually been fortified, functioning at times as an outer defense of Osaka castle. Equally thorough in all his preparations, Ieyasu had ordered his chief architect to erect elaborate headquarters. Building work was already underway, and a large team of carpenters and laborers were at work erecting a palisade around the mound and laying the foundations for a modest dwelling at its crest.

Attending the war council at the foot of the hill in a makeshift tent as one of Hidetada's guards, Munenori couldn't help but raise an eyebrow when he suggested to his father they should attack forthwith. 'The enemy won't come out to fight in the open. So let us take the fight to them!'

'No!' Ieyasu said, not raising his voice but with sufficient force to silence his son. 'You will never succeed that way! The castle's inner defenses are very strong and will be difficult to take, even if we carry the outer walls. We have to adopt a waiting strategy, hem them in by way of fortifications so as to cut off their communications.'

'But we are in far greater numbers! Let us storm—'

Ieyasu was no longer listening. Standing up from his camp stool, he exited the tent as he called out over his shoulder, 'Let Hidetada take up positions at Okayama and see to it all. I am going hawking in the Kinai district!'

Clearly, there was a gulf between the minds of Ieyasu and Hidetada. Munenori only hoped he could live up to his own father's expectations in the great battle to come.

CHAPTER 15

Not many warlords had responded to Hideyori's call to arms. To make matters worse, the few who had, were soon at loggerheads with Hideyori's counselors. The latter favored a defensive approach. They felt that the castle with its deep moats and high walls was their best defense. Ieyasu's troops, they believed, would never be able to take the fortress. It was winter. Sooner or later the cold and fatigue would get the better of the besieging troops and force Ieyasu to enter into negotiations— negotiations, so they believed, into which they would enter from a position of strength.

Their plan was heatedly contested by the warlords. All of them hated Ieyasu with a passion, a hatred only equaled by their respect for his military talent. Sanada Yukimura, who fourteen years before had helped his father repel Hidetada's forces from Ueda castle, argued they ought to take the offensive and deal Ieyasu's army a decisive blow at the Seta River. The others agreed. They knew from experience that such a victory would inevitably persuade less bold chieftains to join their ranks. Only if they were to fail to do so should they fall back on Osaka castle.

In the end, the counselors' strategy won through. One by one, albeit grudgingly, the warlords fell into line, entrenching themselves as best they could among vast defenses in two extending circles around the stronghold. To further enhance their position, they ordered their men to break the dams along the Kizu River and flood the surrounding area, but their plan was thwarted by a Tokugawa contingent under the command of Honda Tadamasa.

Meanwhile, inside the citadel, the Toyotomi commanders made the most of what they assumed would be their imminent moment of glory. Oda Yorigana, a cousin of the great Nobunaga, made the rounds of the guards on horseback. Unlike his great rival Ieyasu, who liked to dress plainly, he was clad in gilt-laced armor with autumn-tinted thread. His attendant was a young woman warrior, in scarlet armor, with scarlet scabbards, and a scarlet arrow catcher gracing her slender back.

On December 19, the Bakufu troops launched their first assault on the northwestern approach to the castle, where the Toyotomi had built a fortification manned by some eight hundred men. More clashes followed over the next weeks, this time north of the castle, where it relied on the natural defenses of the Kizu River and its tributaries; first at Shigino and Imafuku, then at the strategic positions of Bakurōbuchi, Noda, and Fukishima, where fighting was particularly fierce. By the end of the month, the defenders on the north-side of the castle had been forced to abandon their positions and retreat behind the castle's granite walls. Now the stronghold was totally surrounded by Ieyasu's troops—the siege of Osaka castle had begun in earnest.

Eve of Battle

Standing atop Okayama Hill, Munenori had a perfect view of the citadel of Osaka castle and was struck yet again—how vast it was, how massive, how it seemed to rise from the surrounding marches by sheer force of will. Just two miles away from him now, its high grey walls rose out of shimmering moats that spanned the better part of thirty yards. Reflected on their mirrored surface, the walls seemed twice as high. Above them towered the five-storied donjon, its blue tiles and gold-leafed sides glaring at him through the cold winter air. He had seen it many times now, but each time he set eyes on the fortress, he couldn't help but feel small, intimidated. He recalled how, almost twenty years before, he had accompanied Ieyasu as he was being led around the castle by a boastful Hideyoshi. Then it had all been new and overwhelming; now he knew what awaited them: he had seen the steel-plated gates, the narrow inroads flanked by thick walls, the vast storehouses with provisions to sustain a year's siege—taking the castle still seemed an impossible proposition.

From where he stood, he could clearly see how a huge contingent under the banner of Sanada Yukimura had entrenched themselves atop the Sanadamaru, an earthwork barbican along the one remaining elevation in the landscape, just across the castle's southern moat. Facing them were equally huge contingents under the command of warlords of great repute. Like Munenori himself, many of them had fought on Ieyasu's side in the great Battle of Sekigahara. Their different banners were positioned at equal intervals, all along the outer embankment of the castle's only southern moat. Stirred into life by a stiff northerly breeze, they seemed like a vast, motley flock of birds, their wings fluttering in nervous apprehension.

Due west from where Munenori stood lay Chausuyama, the hill where Hidetada and Ieyasu had held their first war council two weeks earlier. It was a clear winter's day and beyond Ieyasu's encampment, still farther toward the west, he could make out the strangely calming glimmer of the Inland Sea. It was a sight to behold. Taking in the vast troop placements on both sides, Munenori reckoned that by now some four hundred thousand warriors were facing each other across the small strip of no-man's-land along the castle's southern defenses.

221

Discipline

Hidetada was more restless than ever. It was understandable: Since his failure to join his father in battle at Sekigahara, he had been haunted by the desire to redeem himself. This time he wanted to be sure he would not miss out on the action. Already shortly after his departure from Edo, while staying at the post station of Kanagawa, he had dispatched a letter to Ieyasu's chief counselor Honda Masazumi, beseeching him not to open hostilities prior to his own arrival. Now, from his new command post, he issued one order after the other. One of them was to Munenori. He was to go over the Chausuyama and report on the latest enemy activities at the Sanadamaru.

Arriving at the foot of the Chausuyama, Munenori noticed how, in the two weeks since his last visit, the carpenters had finished their work. At its top stood Ieyasu's new headquarters; the rest of his staff had erected their tents at the foot of the mound. A small storeroom stood below the hill's southern slope, while a bathhouse flanked the hill's eastern slope.

Rounding the hill he ran into Honda Masazumi, who was standing at the center of a small group of guards. A brilliant negotiator capable of tact and brutality in equal measure, he had been put in charge of negotiations with the enemy. Munenori detested the sight of him, not just for his brutality and coarseness, but also because his face was that of the devil incarnate. The man was an inveterate lecher, and it had probably been a severe strain of syphilis that had caused the skin on his face to turn into a pitted surface, like poorly tanned leather, a hallmark that had earned him the fitting sobriquet of 'Codskin-*dono*' among the foreigners with whom he had to deal on a regular basis.

He was just about to practice the hard end of his usual carrot-and-stick act. The guards were holding down a Toyotomi messenger, his limbs sprawled out in the winter snow around him. Walking up to the man, Masazumi drew his *tantō* and knelt down beside him. Then, as if he was preparing a piece of venison for that evening's stew, he proceeded to cut off the man's fingers one by one. Rising stiffly with a grunt, he sent the man packing, shouting after him, 'Tell your friends there are just one two avenues open: surrender or perish!'

Spotting Munenori, Masazumi's attitude changed as if by magic. 'Yagyū-*dono*' he greeted, as he bowed and beckoned Munenori to follow him up into Ieyasu's headquarters. Entering the gate on the hill's eastern side, they passed a small guard house and ascended the narrow steps to the hill's crest. The headquarters atop the hill was, for a man of Ieyasu's standing, remarkably small but exquisitely crafted. Built in the *sukiya* tradition, no nails had been used; all the joints in the sturdy beams were traditional *sashimono*: mortise and tenon.

Taking off their boots, they entered without formalities. The structure's floor space measured twelve *tatami*, divided into three rooms, one of which looked out on a five-foot wide veranda with eaves. The interiors had been done in plain and sober materials, *shikkui* plaster walls and woven bamboo ceilings, but plenty light poured in through large windows at the rear-facing south, and the rooms were fragrant with the summer-like smell of fresh *tatami*. Munenori followed Masazumi as he walked straight through and stepped onto the narrow veranda.

They found Ieyasu, sitting on his small camp stool, which was covered with the thick coat of highland deer. He was in the company of several generals, with whom he was pouring over a battle map, all the while noisily slurping from a lacquered bowl of thin rice-gruel that steamed profusely in the crisp winter air.

Prompted by a curt nod from Masazumi, Munenori kneeled on one knee and proceeded to give a concise account of the recent enemy activities at the Sanadamaru.

Ieyasu grumbled but didn't look up from his map. 'And how is my son faring?'

Taken somewhat aback by the question, Munenori though of nothing better to say than to list the long string of ordinances Hidetada had issued: 'Contingents are forbidden to trespass on the paths of others or advance prematurely; their men are strictly forbidden to plunder civilians; they are required to pay for requisitions, and they are…eh…'

'Well man, spit it out!' Ieyasu demanded.

'They are "forbidden to grumble," Tenka-*donosama*.'

Ieyasu seemed bemused when he looked up from his map. Downing the last dregs of his bowl of rice-gruel, he turned to Masazumi and chuckled: 'Well, I suppose that is what you would expect of a new Shōgun, though I never issued such orders when I was young. Ha!'

Masazumi too seemed embarrassed, not clear what to do with the old man's words.

Then, as if finishing his train of thought, Ieyasu said, 'If the men follow such specific orders and fail, you can't reproach them; but if they fail to follow them to the letter and nevertheless succeed, you can't praise them either. So perhaps it's better to decide the details according to the circumstances.'

Sasayama

On January 3, in the dead cold of night, two of Maeda Toshitsune's elite spearhead contingent silently prepared for battle and stole into the cold night toward the enemy positions. Their plan was to launch a surprise attack at night on Sasayama, a shallow hill immediately in front of the Sanadamaru on which Yukimura had entrenched his frontline troops. Ordered by Ieyasu to dig trenches toward the enemy positions, Toshitsune's men had come under constant fire from Yukimura's musketeers, who, because of their higher position, could pick off their enemy with ease.

It was only a mile as the crow flies from Okayama to Sasayama, but it was a moonless night, and Munenori could make out nothing except the glowering campfires of Sanada's men. For several hours everything remained quiet. He almost began to believe the assault had been called off when, at the hour of the Ox, the nightly quiet was disturbed by the sound of musket fire and the muffled battle cry of the Maeda men. Munenori could make out the dim flashes at the foot of Sasayama. Then, just as suddenly as it had erupted, the clamor died down again, and the hill was swallowed up again by the black night as if nothing had happened.

Before long the eerie spell that had descended on the encampment was broken by the arrival of a messenger from the front line. It seemed that somehow the enemy troops had caught wind of their approach and had safely withdrawn to the safety of the Sanadamaru—not one enemy head had been taken.

The next day, disappointment among the Maeda warriors made way for enraged indignation when the enemy troops, who were now well within earshot, began to taunt them from the safety of their defenses. By noon the tale of their futile venture had been cast in song, yelled down at them gleefully from above with ever increasing mirth.

Cold and riled by their detractors, the Maeda men could contain themselves no longer and began to attack the barbican. They were met with a barrage of matchlock fire from atop, causing a great number of casualties among the hapless men, who were now forced to slowly struggle toward the top behind sandbags they had to push uphill in front of them. But they continued to push forward, even after Toshitsune repeatedly ordered his generals to withdraw.

Seeing their fellow men being butchered on the hill's slope, Ii Naotaka and Matsudaira Tadanao, both young and inexperienced, ordered their men to attack the two southern bridgeheads across the moats at Tanimachi and Hatchōme, immediately west from the Sanadamaru. But like Maeda's men, their men spent themselves on the enemy's impenetrable defenses whilst being showered with hails of arrows and bullets. By noon, more than five hundred Bakufu troops had fallen in vain.

Just then, as if on cue, a huge explosion from within the castle rocked the vast castle walls, causing parts of it to disintegrate and men atop to plummet to their deaths.[1] Spotting the huge billowing cloud that rose above the castle keep, and taking it as a sign they were being aided by inside allies, other commanders too now ordered their men to attack, so that before long fierce fighting broke out along the whole southern section of the castle's defenses.

Observing the scene, Hidetada beckoned to Munenori to follow him. Mounting their horses, they sped off toward Chausuyama, closely following the rear of the front line, their horses nervous from the occasional bullets whizzing past.

They found Ieyasu on his horse, some five hundred yards north of his headquarters. Leaning forward in his saddle, he was peering through something that looked like a brass pipe, but in sections that slid into each other. The outer shell was covered in leather, and delicately engraved silver mountings adorned both extremities. Its most remarkable feature was the smooth crystal bead mounted in its front end, which played tricks on the light as it reflected off its convex surface. It looked like a giant's eye. Munenori was fascinated by the device—he had never seen anything like it.

Equally intrigued, Hidetada nudged his horse closer to that of his father and inquired, 'Chichi-*sama*, what on earth is that you're holding?'

'It's a distant-looking mirror,' the old man muttered as he continued to peer through the strange device. 'It was given to me by the Englishman Anjin-*san*. It can see much farther than the human eye, taking details as far away as a league and presenting them as if they are within a few hundred yards.'

But Hidetada had already lost interest. Moving his horse forward he looked at the scene of battle in agony as if he was missing out on some grand feast. Turning back in his saddle, he pointed toward the scene of battle. 'They're being slaughtered in front of our eyes,' he almost cried. 'Now is the time to deal the decisive blow—to open the all-out attack and—'

Ieyasu didn't let his son finish. Lowering his instrument and resting it on the pommel of his saddle, he said, 'Be cautious not to despise your enemy! Think instead of how you can defeat them without fighting!'

Taking his looking glass, he caused it to contract with a sharp snap. Pointing it in his son's direction like a wand, he smiled mischievously as he said, 'At least this time round we might not have to fight, for luckily this here wasn't the only present the foreigners gave me.' Then, turning to his chief of staff, he bellowed, 'Bring on the cannon!'

Cannon

No sooner had the Tenka-*dono* given his order than several dozens of large caliber cannon were uncovered.[2] They had been sitting under makeshift tarpaulins made of large numbers of *mino*, the straw raincoats used by farmers, partly to keep the cannon dry, partly to hide them from the enemy. Now the heavy weapons were being hauled into place opposite the castle's main gate, from where they began to pound its impressive defenses.

'Aim for the upper donjon!' Ieyasu shouted as the foreign gunners trained their culverins on the towering structure. 'It is where that damn Yodogimi resides!'

After a few shots, the gunners found their range. The first, a thirteen-pound shell, crashed through the stuccoed wall, sending up clouds of chalk dust and causing part of the wall to break away and tumble down on the lower-lying roofs.

The shelling over the next few days was relentless. Special squads of gunners, trained by Dutch and English mercenaries, loaded and fired the huge weapons with such clockwork precision that at times their blasts seemed to extend into one protracted, deafening roar that shook one's inner cavities when one stood nearby. To Munenori, it was a totally new aspect of warfare. Under the constant grind of the weapons' heavy ammunition, some sections of the castle's mighty walls were already beginning to yield and disintegrate.

Pounded by Ieyasu's cannon throughout the first half of January, the besieged party made repeated attempts to halt hostilities and arrive at some truce. All of them were turned down by Ieyasu, even an attempt by the imperial court. Finally on January 17, after two weeks of shelling, Ieyasu relented, allowing his chief negotiator to receive the Toyotomi delegation at his encampment.

This time, it was the carrot-end of his stick that Masazumi dangled in front of his guests, though his words had this time been dictated by the Tenka-*dono*: 'Yodogimi will not have to serve as a hostage—those are to be provided by the Ōno and

Oda clans. Likewise, the Toyotomi will be allowed to keep their possessions, and the lives of all those who have fought on their side will be spared. However!' he continued with more relish, 'With the exception of the inner citadel, the castle's second and third tier must be demolished and its moats filled in.'

The following day, the nineteenth of January, in the nineteenth year of Keichō, the signed pledges having been exchanged, the guns finally fell silent.

CHAPTER 16

Under the terms of the peace settlement it had been agreed that both parties were to participate in the castle's partial dismantlement: the second tier and inner moats were to be demolished and filled in by the house of Toyotomi; the third tier and the outer moat by the house of Tokugawa. Not surprisingly, the latter were eager to see the work completed, especially given the half-hearted efforts of the former. And thus, while Ieyasu returned to Sunpu, Hidetada took control of the demolition. He mobilized part of the besieging army and press-ganged the local populace into a vast workforce that was put to work in filling in the moats. Spurred on relentlessly by Hidetada's construction magistrates the work proceeded at such a pace that, despite the freezing cold, the outer moats were filled by the beginning of February. Still not satisfied, Hidetada ordered his magistrates to also fill in the moat that surrounded the castle's second tier. The houses and yashiki that stood in the way were summarily torn down, without even consulting their owners. When challenged by the Toyotomi camp, he simply observed that they were making so little progress that he had decided to lend them a hand. By the time Hidetada set off for Fushimi, on February 16, the southern crescent of the outer two moats, from the eastern Morimura gate to the south-western Matsuyamachi gate, had been filled.

At Sunpu, meanwhile, Ieyasu prepared for future eventualities by sending out orders to the country's foundries in Sakai and Kunitomo to cast him more cannon. They had proven their destructive effectiveness in the winter campaign and he wanted as many of these new and powerful weapons as possible. By the end of January the foundry at Kunitomo alone had cast twenty-three cannon of varying calibre.

Ieyasu's main worry was the continued mobilization of Toyotomi warriors. He had called the amnesty into life so they might return to their respective domains. Yet the Toyotomi camp saw it as a license to keep them on. Worse still, they were even seeking to increase their number. Already in February, Kyoto's head of police reported that Toyotomi scouts were recruiting warriors throughout the Kinai region. Many of them were rōnin who had lost their masters in the winter campaign. Lured by the prospect of good wages and daily food, they returned to Osaka castle like bees to a beehive.

Bored and spoiling for another fight, the rōnin soon began to run amok in the streets of Osaka, threatening to set fire to Fushimi and Kyoto. Their actions were played down by the Toyotomi camp. Confirmation that this was more than a few rōnin running wild came when Kyoto's chief of police sent an urgent missive to Sunpu that the unrests had been carefully orchestrated by none other than Sanada Yukimura, the general who had given Ieyasu's men such a hard time during the winter campaign. More worrying still, within days of Hidetada's departure, the Toyotomi set about reconstructing stockades and digging out the moats that had just been filled—sooner or later, the fragile truce was bound to collapse.

And it was sooner rather than later that hostilities recommenced, though it was already summer, which allowed for a protracted siege. The defenders' tactics, too, had changed, though more by necessity than inclination: with much of the castle's moats filled, they could not rely on a defensive strategy; they had to take the initiative if they were to stand a chance of winning—they had to deal a decisive blow to Ieyasu's allies before he could come to their rescue.

On May 23, Ōno Harufusa led a force of three thousand men to attack what was left of Kōriyama castle. Having set fire to what was left of the castle and much of the town,[1] Harufusa next marched on Ieyasu's supply base of Sakai, indiscriminately setting fire to villages and farms along the way. Much of Sakai was sacked. But when he turned south toward Wakayama castle, seeking to repeat what he had done at Kōriyama, the tide turned against him. Its lord, Asano Nagaakira, was aware of Harufusa's approach, and he was an able warrior. Leading a force of five thousand men north along the coast, he intercepted Harufusa's troops on May 26 at Kashii, a small fishing village halfway Sakai and Wakayama. Harufusa was now forced back on the defensive. For several days he engaged his enemy while being forced back to Sakai. But when two of his commanders were killed, he ordered his troops back to Osaka.

Ieyasu and Hidetada, meanwhile, expecting an escalation, had stayed in the vicinity, the former at Nijō castle, the latter at Fushimi castle. Now, as word came in of Harufusa's rampage the geared-up Tokugawa war machine kicked back into action.

Mount Shigi

It was late in the afternoon of June 2, when Ieyasu set up camp at Hiraoka, some five miles due east from Osaka castle. Hidetada set up camp at Chizuka, a few hundred yards farther south. It was an auspicious place, chosen on the advice of his *shihan* Munenori, who was familiar with the region. They were camped at the western foot of Mount Shigi, a mountain steeped in history. It was said that long, long ago, Prince Shōtoku had gone up the mountain to pray for victory over the Mononobe while encamped near the mountain. Deep at night, at the hour of the Tiger, high up on the mountain, the prince had had an apparition in which he was visited by Bishamonten, the deity of war, who assured him he would prevail. The next day, the arrow of one of his archers struck the Mononobe leader in the heart.

For Munenori the mountain was more than just a repository of anecdotes. Once it had been widely known for its eponymous castle, a stronghold that had played such a pivotal role in the fortunes of the Yagyū clan. Already half a century had passed since his grandfather, Ieyoshi, had allied himself with its founder, the governor of Kawachi, in a last attempt to retain independence. The latter's death in the Battle at the Taihei temple had evaporated these hopes and forced the Yagyu to submit to the rule of the Tsutsui. It had been Muneyoshi's desire to regain his clan's freedom that led him to form his fateful alliance with the castle's last occupant, the treacherous Matsunaga Hisahide. Though not yet born at the time, Munenori vividly remembered his father's remorse on the few occasions he had talked about Hisahide's despotic rule, his depravity— the tragic end of the young lovers during the siege of Ido castle. Looking back, It seemed only fitting that when Hisahide blew himself up, Shigisan castle went up in flames too.

Shortly after they had set up camp, Munenori had decided to climb Mount Shigi. It was a brisk walk up the mountain's twelve-hundred-feet slope. His chest filled with emotions as he reached the mountain's crest. It was late in the afternoon and the mist that had plagued both armies during the day had miraculously lifted. Stretched out before him lay the fertile plains of the Yamato basin, the place where he had been born and where the long history of his clan had played itself out. Gazing eastward he could just make out Nara's massive Daibutsuden, less than ten miles as the crow flies, its structure still scarred by the ravages of war. Protruding from the ruins he could even make out the decapitated torso of the Great Buddha, a constant reminder of the immorality of Hisahide's tumultuous rule. There had been so many warlords like him, bent only on immediate effect and personal profit. Only few had the unifying wisdom of visionaries like Ieyasu. Could it be that Japan's long history of civil strife would come to an end in only a few days? Could it be that a country plagued for so long by the likes of Hisahide would finally be able to live in peace and prosper?

On his way down, Munenori descended the mountain's southern slope to visit the Chōgosonshi temple. His father had recounted how he had stayed there on his first *musha shugyō* and seen the scrolls with the *Shigisan engi*. Only recently, in 1592, Toyotomi Hideyori had dismantled the temple's main hall and moved it higher up the mountain. He had reconstructed it on the very foundation that had once carried Hisahide's notorious castle. Would Hideyori too find Bishamonten on his side in battle? He would soon find out. Given its history, it didn't seem an auspicious place to rebuild a temple. Around the temple's newly erected walls, one could still see the charred ruins of what had been a mighty castle only a few decades ago.

Ambush

Dusk was setting in when Munenori finally returned to the camp. Being part of Hidetada's guard, his tent stood immediately next to that of his lord. It was difficult to guard Hidetada: having missed out on most of the action thus far, he had been in a foul mood ever since they had left Fushimi. Walking into camp, Munenori found the young Shōgun pacing up and down in front of his tent and scolding his officers.

It was well after dark that Hidetada suddenly decided to visit his father and impress on him once more that he wanted to lead tomorrow's vanguard. He refused any elaborate escort, insisting curly that only Munenori join him. From Chizuka to Hiraoka was only a few miles, but Munenori was ill at ease. For a few hours the mist had dissolved, but now, as dusk set in, it rolled back in thick and fast from the shores of the nearby Inland Sea.

They had ridden only a few hundred yards north along the mountain's slope when out of the mist, a small band of warriors on foot, perhaps a dozen, suddenly emerged, rushing toward the two men on horseback. Without thinking twice Munenori spurred on his horse, driving straight into the group of heavily armed men. Ookage trampled one man underfoot, while Munenori made short shrift with two others, dismembering the hands of the second assailant and plunging his *katana*'s *kissaki* into the other's neck. Then he felt his horse give way under him. With no time to think he dismounted to pursue the rest, who were now fleeing toward a nearby stream. By the time he had caught up with the last bandit, they were both knee-deep in the cool mountain water. The man made one last attempt with his *yari*. But Munenori seized it and pulled it toward him, causing the man to topple headlong forward into the water before he felt Munenori's cold blade sever his spine.

Walking back to his horse and a startled Hidetada, Munenori's heart sank. Ookage hadn't risen; she was just lying there, panting for air. She had served him well. Fifteen years earlier, on the eve of the Battle at Sekigahara, still young and fiery, she had carried him at breakneck speed, all the way home from Ieyasu's war council at Oyama to his father at the Enjō temple. Now she was old—and she was dying. Munenori loved his horse, perhaps more than anything else, but he knew what he must do. Raising his *katana* high in the air he plunged the blade deep into the small of the animal's neck, just behind the jaw, severing both carotid arteries in a single thrust. One last time her eye flashed white at him, questioning. Then it lay still forever.

When the two men finally rendezvoused with Ieyasu at Hiraoka, the old man was sitting on a camp stool in front of his tent, wearing a white-lined garment, matched with a tea-colored *haori*. He was inspecting the head of Kimura Shigenari, an enemy commander who had been cut down from his horse earlier that day at Wakae. Munenori noticed how Shigenari's hair, shaved in a half circle from forehead to crown, was heavily scented. Breathing in through his nostrils, the Tenka-*dono* grew pensive, as if trying to recollect an old memory. Then, turning to Hidetada, he muttered: 'Shigenari-*dono* took this splendid precaution to teach young people like you whose head they have taken. Experienced warriors scent their hair so their heads may not end up among those of the common soldier. Now here was a true warrior in the old mold!'

Mounted Council

The next day, June 3, 1615, Hidetada and Munenori got up at two o'clock. Hidetada was dressed for battle: he was in full armor, detailed with black lacings, over which he wore a sleeveless *haori* of feathers, and on his head a hood-shaped helmet. He had dismissed his bannerman, having chosen to hold his own signal flag of white bear's fur. Getting on his chestnut horse, he beckoned Munenori to follow. They first rode out to Yao and Wakae. The previous day it had seen heavy fighting, and its marshes were still littered with the decapitated torsos of fallen foes. From there, they rode on to the banks of the Hirano River, a few hundred yards east of Okayama, to meet up with Ieyasu for a final council.

It was already ten when father and son met up with their commanders. All were now in full armor and couldn't be bothered to dismount. And thus, staying in their saddles, they discussed the latest enemy movements. Some five thousand men under the banner of Ōno Harufusa had positioned themselves just north of Okayama. But the largest troop placements were around Chausuyama. There, some fifteen thousand men had gathered under the banner of Sanada Yukimura.

'I am confident of victory,' Hidetada began. 'Though we have less troops at our disposal than during the winter campaign, we still outnumber the enemy. Some ninety chieftains have responded to my call to arms. Together they have brought to the field well over one hundred and fifty-thousand warriors—twice those of the enemy.'

'Yes,' his father chimed in, 'and the battlefield will be smaller, too. 'The enemy have dispersed themselves in a defensive belt stretching from Chausuyama to the Hirano River, so it's clear that all fighting today will be concentrated south of the castle, either at Okayama or Chausuyama. More likely halfway, at Tennōji, the high and arid plain just east of Chausuyama.'

'Let me be in the vanguard,' Hidetada again beseeched his father.

'No! You are to leave the bulk of your army along the Nara Kaidō, just behind Okayama, while I will leave mine just south of your's, along the Ishi River.'

Hidetada was stunned, his face flustered with frustration. 'The roads around Okayama are bad and difficult to pass. The enemy will never attack in that quarter!'

But Ieyasu insisted: 'You go to Okayama; I will go toward Chausuyama!'

Hidetata looked crestfallen; despite his magnificent outfit, he had something of the thwarted child about him.

Ieyasu's mood, too, had blackened. And he wasn't done yet: 'Your vanguard will be led by Toshitsune; The vanguard against Sanada Yukimura's force at Chausuyama will be given to Tadanao; my own vanguard will be led by young Tadatomo.'

By now all who were present were moving uncomfortably in their saddles, and it wasn't because of their cumbersome armor. Munenori, too, was puzzled. Had it just been to spite his son that Ieyasu had given such critical commands to men who had screwed up so badly during the winter campaign? Both his son-in-law, Maeda Toshitsune and his grandson, Matsudaira Tadanao, had made a poor performance to say the least, while the inexperienced Honda Tadatomo had heaped scorn on himself by withdrawing his troops in the heat of battle while in a drunken stupor. How on earth was it possible that at such a crucial moment Ieyasu should entrust the fate of the nation into the hands of such men?

Father

It was a glorious day and Munenori was in good spirits. For a change, he had been assigned as one of Ieyasu's guards, instead of his son. It was a joy to accompany the seasoned warrior, who invariably exhumed an air of authority—an unshakable sense of control that instilled respect in his warriors.

At noon, Ieyasu and Munenori climbed in their saddles and set off from Hirano, making their way south to join Ieyasu's own troops. It was a wonderful sight to see Maeda Toshitsune's troops moving into position on and around Okayama. Together with the left- and right-hand flanks of Ii and Honda men, they numbered close to thirty-thousand. Moving in unison on the command of their generals, they looked like a giant swarm of glimmering beetles, about to fall on some hapless prey.

Spurring their horses on, the two men soon reached the Nara
Kaidō, where some fifteen thousand men under the command
of Kuroda Nagamasa were fording the Ishi River. Looking east
along the winding road toward Nara, Munenori could clearly
make out the banner of Hidetada, who had grudgingly obeyed
his father's orders and taken command of a rear guard of another
fifteen thousand. Just behind him, where the road curved into
the mountains, he could see the banner of Hidetada's stepbrother
Yoshinao, who commanded an equally large rear guard.

It was already nearing noon when they reached Ieyasu's own
troops along the Ishi River, some fifteen thousand in all. It wasn't
the ideal setting for a pitched battle. Flat and marshy, the
landscape was carved up by a web of streams and rivulets, many
of them man-made to irrigate the checkered blanket of rice
paddies that ran straight up to the upper slopes of the distant
mountains. Movement in such terrain was cumbersome,
especially for large numbers of men, who had to fall in line to
negotiate the narrow dikes and roads that crisscrossed the land.
And thus they were forced to approach the castle along it's main
routes of access, the web of old highroads that emanated from
the castle in all directions.

Just west from them ran the Kōya Kaidō, the old inland route
to the ancient temple town of Mount Kōya. It was along this
road that the rest of Ieyasu's allies had taken up positions—not
so much positions: they were rather standing in line, waiting
for the signal to march on Tennōji. Matsudaira Tadanao's
vanguard had occupied the hamlet of Abeno, just a mile south
of Chausuyama. They were flanked on the east by two equally
large contingents, comprising the united force of some nine
allied chieftains. Flanking them on the west, along the Kishū
Kaidō toward Sakai, were the forces of Date Masamune and
Asano Nagaakira.

It was a magnificent site. All the way from Sakai to Fujidera Munenori could see banners of allied clans. It was hard to take in the numbers—he had never seen so many men in the field, not even at Sekigahara.

To Munenori's surprise Ieyasu suddenly began to laugh, though more to himself than to anyone around him. Clearly his mood had lifted. Was it because he was relieved of his sulking son? But no. Turning to Munenori he pointed toward Chausuyama. Less than two miles west from them, the old burial mound now blazed in the warm rays of a sun that had just risen above Mount Shigi. Atop the burial mound, fixed to the roof of Ieyasu's former headquarters, they could clearly make out the Sanada banner, the same banner that had fluttered so stubbornly over the Sanadamaru the previous winter.

'Ha! They've claimed my old headquarters.' Ieyasu laughed again, derisively this time. 'They have finally shown some initiative in this game called war. Yet it is *I* who still sets the rules!'

Crisis

By noon Ieyasu was peering hard through his looking glass again. He was tense now; as if he were looking for something specific. Following the trajectory of the old man's mysterious instrument, Munenori saw what held the old man's attention. Just between the Maeda and Matsudaira vanguards, he spotted Honda Tadatomo out in front, ostentatiously inspecting his troops with a small group of mounted warriors. They were dressed in bright-red laced armor, a crimson feather gracing Tadatomo's helmet.

Munenori couldn't help shaking his head in disbelief. Already part of a vanguard, Tadatomo was way out in front of the bulk of Ieyasu's army. What had gone into the young warrior's head to expose himself and his men like this? Was he drunk again, like the previous winter?

Just beyond Tadatomo, some five hundred yards across no man's land, were the enemy vanguard. Among them Munenori could clearly make out a large contingent of musketeers, Negoro sectarians, dressed in their typical black robes and white hoods—men who loved to kill, just out of religious zeal. They were under the banner of Watanabe Tadasu, Hideyori's personal fencing instructor, a man who had disgraced himself that winter by picking a fight with a fellow commander in the midst of the siege. It was an incendiary mixture: a bunch of fanatics led by an impulsive hothead.

And sure enough, as soon as the young Tadatomo blundered within range, smoke bellied forth from some three-hundred enemy muskets. For a brief moment Tadatomo was flustered. Then, as if welcoming the invitation, he ordered his men to fall on the enemy lines.

Only now did Ieyasu's wisdom in choosing his commanders dawn on Munenori: the wily old man had used Tadatomo as bait, drawing out the enemy from their entrenched positions, thus leveling the odds in his favor.

It worked. Four thousand *rōnin* who had been facing them impatiently for hours from Tennōji's southern gate, now stormed down from the elevation's slopes toward them. Hungry, revengeful, and with little left to lose, they were eager to draw blood. They were led by Mōri Katsunaga, who was barely able to split his forces into two so as to fall on Tadatomo's vanguard from the flanks. Seeing Tadatomo's distress, Ogasawara Hidemasa, a seasoned commander who had seen action at Sekigahara, sought to relieve the Honda men, but soon came face to face with another fierce enemy attack and was mortally wounded.

Now the battle began in earnest, as one contingent after the other joined in the fighting. Storming down from their high ground on Chausuyama, Sanada Yukimura's ten thousand well-trained warriors fell on Matsudaira Tadanao's ten thousand. For a brief moment they clashed. Then, as if repelled by each other's strength, they began to brush past each other, the Matsudaira force toward Tennōji, the Sanada force toward Tadatomo's struggling vanguard and Tadanao's exposed rear.

Then total mayhem ensued when Asano Nagaakira, marching forth from Sakai, mistakenly attacked Tadatomo's left flank, raising fears among the latter that he had changed sides. Cashing in on the confusion, the Sanada and Mōri forces pressed on hard, crushing the Honda vanguard, and penetrating deep into enemy lines. One more time Munenori was able to make out Tadatomo, firmly astride his saddle. Above the din he could clearly hear his resounding voice call out, 'Here I am, Honda Izumi no Kami Tadatomo!' as he pointed his lance toward the advancing wall of men. Then, driving his weapon home until it broke, the young commander was swallowed up by the angry hordes, his honor restored.

Moving uncomfortably in his saddle, Munenori looked on as the enemy *rōnin* drew near. They kept driving deep into their lines, each time drawing closer, hewing and stabbing their way toward Ieyasu's position. Munenori shuddered involuntarily. It was as if he could feel the heat of battle, about to engulf them like an evil wave in a raging storm.

Then, all of a sudden, as if they had reached the center of the storm, they were all alone: Ieyasu, his page Oguri Masatada, and Munenori. Time seemed to slow down as Munenori's martial instincts kicked into action under the looming threat. Nearer and nearer the enemy drew. At one stage all seemed lost when the Tokugawa banner fell to the ground. A few enemy *ashigaru* broke loose from the writhing mass, rushing toward them, but Munenori cut them down swiftly before they could do more damage.

For just the briefest of moments Ieyasu lost his composure. Drawing his horse to the side of the road he began to talk to himself. Munenori thought he heard him stammer the words '*seppuku yarō*,' but couldn't be sure. Then, just as suddenly, the old man recovered himself and regained his composure. Moving back a few hundred yards toward his staff, he ordered them to draw up reinforcements, arrange them in close ranks, and drown the enemy's attack in numbers. Then he turned to Munenori. 'Do you now go to my son, Hidetada-*dono*! I see his men have joined the fight. Be sure to keep him from harm too.'

Son

The scene that greeted Munenori at Okayama wasn't encouraging. Rounding the western slope of the ancient mound, he could see Maeda Toshitsune's vanguard, some eight hundred yards out toward the castle. They weren't doing well: they were pinned down, having come under intense fire from Ono Harunaga's musketeers.

From the slope's elevation he could now make out Toshitsune himself, valiantly standing his ground among the mayhem. Clearly eager to make up for his botched night attack the previous winter, he was issuing orders left and right, trying to keep his men in line, yet unable to prevent part of Harunaga's troops slipping through. By the time Munenori reached the front of the hill, some of them had even reached its foot, just below where Hidetada had taken up position to command the theatre of war southeast of the castle.

Then he heard a sound that disturbed him even more—a stirring of horses, muffled orders issued in fear. Looking toward the mound's eastern slope, his eyes now saw what his ears refused to believe: two of Hidetada's chief bannemen—Oi and Sakai—were turning their backs on the enemy and fleeing toward the Hirano River, some three *ri* behind the lines.

Riding into Hidetada's camp on the mound's crest, Munenori found the young Shōgun beside himself with fury. Unable to keep his generals in check behind him, and seeing his men being cut down in front of him, he made ready to join the action. He grabbed a *yari* from one of his lancers and ordered his guard to follow, when Munenori seized the bridle of Hidetada's horse and hung on tight.

Now Hidetada turned all his anger on Munenori. He was about to strike him with his *yari* when Honda Masanobu drew up beside him and took hold of the Shōgun's wrist. Then, pointing toward Chausuyama with his other hand he shouted above the roar, 'Look, *Dono-sama*! The enemy is already in retreat!'

It was true enough. After three fierce assaults on Ieyasu's center near Abeno, Yukimura's *rōnin* had spent themselves. Slowly but gradually they were beginning to give way under Ieyasu's overwhelming numbers, who kept pouring down on them from the castle's southern approaches.[2]

Again Masanobu spoke, this time in calmer tones. '*Dono-sama*! There is no need for men like you to risk their life in a battle they are already winning. Let me ride down and bring back order among the ranks.'

To Munenori's intense relief, the young man desisted—had the Shōgun struck him with his *yari*, he wouldn't have let go.

Then, just at this critical moment, two more Eastern generals came to the Shōgun's rescue: first Katō Yoshiaki; then Kuroda Nagamasa, the man so pivotal in the reversal of the Yagyū's for-

tunes. Leading their men down from Okayama to join the struggling Maeda vanguard, they soon tilted the balance of power
squarely in Hidetada's favor.

By three o'clock in the afternoon, though at the cost of huge
casualties on both sides, the Toyotomi forces were driven back
into the castle. A scramble now ensued among the eastern troops
to be the first to mount the walls of the exposed castle. Mizuno
Katsunari, leading an advance guard of lancers, was the first to
enter the Sakura Mon, ordering his bannerman to climb onto
the gate's roof and plant the banner over the imposing entrance.

That same night the castle tower went up in flames. The
embers were still smoldering, early next morning, when
Hideyori admitted defeat by committing ritual suicide. The
battle for Osaka castle was over: the house of Toyotomi had
been extinguished; the realm had been united under the house
of Tokugawa.

CHAPTER 17

Within a year of the fall of Osaka castle Ieyasu was dead. Early in March 1616, the great unifier fell ill having eaten tempura made of sea-bream. Growing weaker and weaker, he took to his bed. By the end of May he stopped eating, drinking only some hot water. Then, on the 1st of June, he passed away peacefully, having written his death poem:

Whether one passes on or remains behind—it is all the same.
That one can take no one with one is the only difference.

From that early morning in 1594, when Munenori and his father rode into Ieyasu's camp on the bank of the Kamo River at Takagamine, Ieyasu had been the Yagyū's benefactor. It was a sign of the man's greatness that their recovery had started with his defeat when he and Munenori had dueled. A lesser Daimyō would have resented having bitten the dust at the hands of a mere swordsman. Not so Ieyasu. His very defeat had made him recognize the superiority of Nobutsuna's mutōtori technique. Instead of angrily dismissing the swordsman, he had welcomed Munenori among his fencing instructors. From then on the Yagyū star had only risen, from the return of their former domains, through their role in the Battle of Sekigahara and Osaka campaigns, down to the establishment of their own yashiki on Edo's outskirts.

Ieyasu's generosity toward the Yagyū was continued by his descendants. By 1621 Munenori was official fencing instructor to Hidetada and his son Iemitsu. Born in 1604, the young man had just come of age and was rapidly being prepared to succeed his father. That moment came on August 23, 1623, when at a grand ceremony at the Emperor's palace in Kyoto, Iemitsu was formally appointed Shōgun. Hidetada went into retirement and took up residence in the western wing of Edo castle, but he continued to occasionally practice with Munenori.

Edo Life

As a *shihan* to the Tokugawa, Munenori spent a lot of his time in Edo. It was only two miles as the crow flies from the Higakubo *yashiki* to Edo castle. Most of his time he would spend at the O-Keikoba, the huge training hall on the castle grounds.

Edo had changed dramatically since Munenori and his father had moved there early in 1596. Then, it had been no more than a large fishing village on Edo bay with a small castle, and even the castle had been in bad repair. The place had had the feel of a colony, an outpost, especially to Munenori, who was used to the high culture of Nara and Kyoto. Only Edo's many old temples, scattered throughout the town and beyond, had given the place a vague resemblance to home. Now, Edo was rapidly turning into one of the country's largest cities. Indeed, it had grown at such a pace, and in such density, that many of the temples and shrines that had hitherto adorned the town's main roads, had to be moved farther afield, to places like Azabu, the area where Munenori had built his *yashiki*. In their place had come the grand residences of the country's many Daimyō, crowded around Edo castle, the queen bee of Edo's buzzing beehive.

Whenever he had the time, Munenori loved to walk around the city. Having spent much of his youth in seclusion, he still reveled in the sense of untrammeled freedom it gave him, as during the early nineties in Kyoto, when he had taken up studies at the Daitoku temple and explored the ancient capital with his friend Takuan. He loved to go up in the crowd and lose himself among the town's many diversions. He would make long excursions, all the way north to Kanda Hill to make offerings at the famous Kanda Myōjin, the shrine that still stood at the bridge of Kandabashi when he had first arrived. On his way back home, exiting the castle through the main Ōtemon gate, he would pass through Daimyō Koji, the district with its impressive Daimyō residences skirting the castle's eastern moat. From there it was only half a mile to the huge fish market of Nihonbashi, though the air was already full of its smell. He always wondered how the realm's most powerful lords were able to endure living in such stench. As for him, he preferred the rarified air of Azabu and its surroundings—its smell of pine reminded him of home.

Being from the interior, Munenori preferred meat over fish, a food for which he never really developed a serious taste, though he was mad about broiled eel—an invigorating dish on which he could spar a whole day. Meat in Edo was considered medicinal food, and in a town that boasted one of the county's largest fish markets, it was hard to come by. Only in Kōjimachi had he found a restaurant to his liking. Inside, heaped in piles for those who could afford the exorbitant prices, lay the carcasses of dear, antelope, boar, rabbit, otter, down to foxes, wolves, and bears. Then there were the Korean and Chinese shops. The pungent smells of the vapors that escaped through the split curtains over their entrances were intoxicating. So were the many geisha. Tripping through the cramped and crowded streets on their lacquered *geta*, they made their way to Edo's many *ageya*, spending the night entertaining guests with song, music, and dance.

Munenori too had developed a taste for the *ageya* and its diversions. Ever since he had arrived in Edo, he had frequented these dens of pleasure, at first sporadically, but then more frequently, until it had become a habit. His father had invariably reproached him, reminding him of his uncle Shigeyoshi, how his dissolute ways had been his undoing. If anything, the criticism had caused Munenori to indulge even more, though he had moderated his habit with his father's death more than a decade ago now. There had been an economic reason too: the way their womenfolk managed to hold off one's advances while extorting ever more presents was infuriating. Yet he had taken a liking for one woman in particular. Her name was O-Yuri. She wasn't the most ravishing in her trade, nor was she a high-class geisha. She was a *tsubone*, a low ranking geisha, but she had a quiet inner beauty that touched Munenori. It wasn't long after he had met her that he made her his concubine. She bore him two daughters and a son by the name of Samon. Though illegitimate, Samon grew into a capable young man and entered the service of Tokugawa Iemitsu, the next man in line to be Shōgun.

Wounded

Not all of Munenori's children were a source of pride. Especially Jūbei caused him grief. Born in 1607, Jūbei had been a troubled child from the start. Possessed of a dark and brooding disposition, he was given to sudden, inexplicable outburst of anger. As he grew older the outbursts became less frequent but deepened in intensity, especially when he took to drinking. As a father, Munenori couldn't help but feel his son's anger. It seemed as if all the hurt and frustration his ancestors had suffered had found their way into Jūbei's heart. Secretly, he also admired him: of all his sons, Jūbei was the one with the true warrior spirit. If only the lad had been born a few decades earlier; then he would have been able to prove his mettle on the field of battle, in man-to-man combat, and rid himself of his inner demons.

Only when he entered the *dōjō* was Jūbei able to forget himself and shake off the dark thoughts that crowded in on his mind. Yet even here his hotheadedness got him into trouble. Intent on winning each and every bout, he would resort to every trick in the trade to gain the upper hand over his opponent, often taking great risks in his defensive stance. He became so feared by his fellow practitioners, that those in his age group refused to join him in practice. At length, only Munenori and equally fearless fellow *shihan* like Ono Tadaaki were willing to take on the young man.

And it was during one such heated bout that Munenori inadvertently added to his son's woes. They had been going through the standard Yagyū Shinkage techniques for many hours at their private *dōjō* one day, when Munenori proposed to take a short break. Jūbei refused; he wanted to perfect his command of *ma-ai* in his execution of the main *tachi* techniques. *Ma-ai* referred to the relative distance between opponents, a most crucial aspect of any combat technique. In fencing, it was tied to a most delicate interplay of foot and handwork, requiring total concentration in the timing of one's attack. In this case, it required Munenori to stop his *katana* just above his son's forehead. It was something he had done so often that he could split a grain of rice stuck on a man's forehead if he wanted to. Yet it required equal control in Jūbei. Being forty years older, Munenori assumed it was just himself who was feeling the strain of a long day of practice. But when they went through the paces for a third time, Jūbei lost his footing and lunged forward, causing the tip of his father's *katana* to enter his right-hand eye. It didn't go in far, but the damage was done: from then on the young man could only see with one eye.

Jūbei didn't hold a grudge toward his father. He merely reproached himself for the lack of concentration that had cost him an eye, and he was soon back at practice. Nor was he ashamed of his missing eye. Instead, he seemed to revel in the way his eye-cap added to his rogue appearance. Among's Edo's samurai community his fierce reputation gave him almost unlimited credit—a credit on which he capitalized with increasingly outlandish escapades as he grew older.

House Arrest

Partly out of admiration, partly out of guilt over his son's handicap, Munenori found it hard to reproach his son for his misdemeanors—he remembered how hard his own father's words had stung him. Only once did Munenori lose his temper with Jūbei. It was in the summer of 1624, a few months after Jūbei had gone through his *genpuku* ceremony and received his adult name of Mitsuyoshi, that they had a fierce argument.

Munenori had just been visiting his brother Yoshikatsu at the Momiji *yashiki*. It had been to celebrate a special occasion, for Yoshikatsu's son, Toshiyoshi, had recently been promoted to the position of *shihan* to none other than Ieyasu's ninth son, Tokugawa Yoshinao, a man known for his passion for the martial arts. It was a great honor; next to Munenori, Toshiyoshi was the only member of the Yagyū clan to reach such a high position.

Munenori didn't begrudge Toshiyoshi's rise. He deserved it—and besides, it reflected well on the Yagyū clan. As the oldest son he was naturally destined to succeed his father, but due to Yoshikatsu's disability, he had been forced to assume a lot of responsibilities at a far younger age than Munenori had. And thus, during the Battle of Sekigahara, when Munenori had gone off to fight in the hope of restoring the clan's fortunes, Toshiyoshi had remained behind in Yagyū, looking after his crippled father and aging grandfather. Frustrated at being robbed of his opportunity to prove himself, the young Toshiyoshi developed had sought to make up for his lack of battle experience by pouring all his energy in his practice of fencing under the stern hand of his grandfather. In 1603, at the age of twenty-four, he had entered the service of Katō Kiyomasa, the Daimyō of the vast fiefdom of Kumamoto in the southern island of Kyushu. Twelve years later, he had moved to Owari to enter Yoshinao's service. There, building on what he had learned from his grandfather, Toshiyoshi went on to develop a school of swordsmanship known as the Owari Yagyū Shinkage-*ryū*.

Toshiyoshi had just published a tract called the *Jijūfujasho, The Indispensable Alpha and Omega of Fencing*. He had proudly presented his uncle with a copy, and though Munenori found the title somewhat overly ambitious, he was impressed with Toshiyoshi's learning. His classical training was conveyed by the tract's foreword, which spoke of that distant mythical era in Chinese history of the Three Sovereigns and the Five Rulers:

> Our style of *heihō* did not yet exist in the magnificent imperial reign of ancient times, when the Three Emperors set the world to their hand. The Five Rulers, too, adhered to the Way of Heaven, governing the whole nation through the

rule of law. At the time of the Three Sovereigns, commoners were likewise ruled according to the Way, when powerful Kings, using inappropriate means to a worthy end to guard against a world of decadence, subdued the country using retainers on stipends. And thus, there was both good and evil in the relationship between ruler and ruled, and from this sprang the malady of strife and the recourse to the art of *heihō*. And thus too it follows that, in the eye of the commoner, the Way of the noblemen and the Way of the Emperors is one and the same thing. For to study the ways of the commoner is to merely learn how to govern one's heart; to study the ways of our lords is to learn how to govern a province; and to study the ways of our emperor is to learn how to govern the realm.

The rest of the tract too had impressed Munenori. A detailed exposition of all the school's techniques and rules, it was firmly rooted in the Yagyū Shinkage-*ryū*, yet imbued with a fresh approach to the clan's long-cherished traditions.

All the greater, then, was Munenori's disappointment with his own son when, on his return to Edo, he learned Jūbei had again injured a fellow practitioner. This time he had fractured a man's skull with a *bokutō*, and though the man still lived, he was bound to spend the rest of his days a cripple.

Arriving at the Higakubo late that evening, he found his son in a stupor; he had spent the day drinking with friends, most of them *rōnin* visiting the capital to enroll in one of its many schools of art.

'How can you expect to serve a Shōgun,' he reproached his son, 'if you spend your career crippling his men?'

Jūbei glared at him with his one good eye, though Munenori wasn't sure what it said. Was it a trace of contempt that lurked in its black depths?

'What care I for a man bad at his craft? The man would never have stood his ground on the field of battle anyhow.'

Munenori winced. What did Jūbei know about the field of battle? Yet how could he reproach his son for being born too late?

'But why the need to consort with *rōnin*?' he tried again. 'You know it reflects poorly on our clan! Look at your cousin Toshiyoshi! He is already a *shihan* to one of the Tenka-*dono*'s sons. If you carry on like this, you'll never amount to anything!'

'What's wrong with being *rōnin*? Didn't they almost defeat Ieyasu at Osaka? And speaking of *rōnin*—wasn't my good cousin Toshiyoshi once a *rōnin* too? It doesn't seem to have hurt his career a bit.'

This time Munenori had no words to counter. Why was it that some sons were born to torment their fathers? And Jūbei was right about his cousin too. Less than a year Toshiyoshi had been in Katō Kiyomasa's service when peasant revolts had disturbed the peace in the Kumamoto domain. Being in charge of policing, Toshiyoshi had suppressed the revolts hard-handedly. In doing so he had gone directly against the advice of Kiyomasa's most senior counselor, Itō Mitsukane, who had long favored a conciliatory approach. The revolt was crushed, but in another heated argument with Mitsukane, Toshiyoshi drew his sword and struck him dead. Forced to resign his post, the young swordsman had spent the next twelve years in the pursuit of *musha shugyō*, traveling throughout the country in search of a new master. For a while he had lived at Tanabe castle in Maizuru, honing his skills under Kamiizumi's former disciple Hikida Bungorō Kagetomo. Then he had moved to Kumano,

becoming a *deshi* to the great master of the halberd, Bōan
Nyūdō. It had only been through the good offices of Naruse
Masanari, a senior Bakufu counselor, that Toshiyoshi eventually
got a second chance as Yoshinao's *shihan*.

Never again Munenori argued with his son, partly out of fear
for his son's ability to cut to the quick, partly out of fear that
the next time round it might end in more than just an argument.
Perhaps it was the only way: some things were just too painful
to confront. And besides, there was no curing rebels like Jūbei:
it was simply their nature to defy authority. Had Jūbei been
born fifty years earlier, he could have made it to chieftain; now,
he was doomed to a life of obscurity. It was probably because
of his refusal to accept the realities of life, too, that his adult
name never stuck, and that he continued to be known simply
as Jūbei, a man equal to 'Ten Imperial Guards.'

Munenori still hoped his son might stand a chance with the
future Shōgun, whose service he had entered as a page at the
age of thirteen. Extremely fond of the martial arts, Iemitsu
was one of Munenori's most diligent students. Like Munenori
he enjoyed getting out, and when young had regularly escaped
from Edo castle to mingle with the people he would be
governing. His behavior was frowned on by the court officials,
staid and surly men, who seemed to have long forgotten what
it is to be young. When Iemitsu did end up in a brawl with a
drunken rogue, it was rumored they had hired the man to
scare him into submission. After 1623, when he succeeded his
father as Shōgun, the responsibilities of office forced him to
desist from his secret excursions, but he still took every opportunity to travel and thereby escape the oppressive rigor of the
Bakufu court. He enjoyed the long rides on horseback, and
every now and then he would spur on his horse and leave his
retinue far behind.

From the first moment they met, Iemitsu had taken a liking to Jūbei—just three years his junior. Together, they would go and swim in the castle moat or play pranks on their overseers. If they were caught out, Jūbei would generously take the blame so that Iemitsu could magnanimously pardon him. It was just a game, yet even this small pleasure was taken away from the young Shōgun when, in 1626, following another prank, the court officials successfully conspired to have Jūbei put under house arrest. Wounding a swordsman in practice was one thing; corrupting the future Shōgun was something else. Jūbei was sent to Odawara, where he was placed under the strict tutelage of Abe Masatsugu, one of the heroes of the Siege of Osaka castle. When, four years later, Masatsugu was promoted to another fief, Jūbei was allowed to return to the Yagyū domain, yet he remained under house arrest.

The Purple Robe

There were other worries that kept Munenori awake at night during these years, even if they were years of peace. One of them concerned his old friend the monk Takuan. Ever since they had met on the grounds of the ancient Daitoku temple, they had stayed in touch. Yet they had busy lives and their encounters had been short and far between. Like Munenori, Takuan had made rapid promotion, albeit in the realm of the Buddhist church. From being a novice he had quickly climbed the ranks of the temple's elaborate hierarchy. The crowning moment came in 1609, when he became the Daitoku-*ji*'s head abbot. Munenori had been present when, at a grand ceremony at the imperial court, emperor Go-Yōzei presented Takuan with a beautiful robe made from silk of a deep purple hue, the color of the imperial court. Takuan had gracefully accepted, though not to enjoy the perks of high office. Within three days of his appointment, he hit the road. He had other plans. The temple, which dated back to the early fourteenth century, was in bad repair, and he wanted to put his influential position to good use. Though frail, he had spent the next decade traveling the length and breadth of the country, raising funds for its renovation. It was during this period that the two men were able to renew a friendship that had long remained dormant.

Munenori recalled one particular summer evening when Takuan had conducted a tea ceremony at his newly erected tea house on the Higakubo estate. It had been a particularly hot day, and the air was filled with the constant hum of locusts. Leaning back on his arm bench, Munenori had complained of the boredom of high office. As a warrior, he preferred the battlefield, movement, decisive action. He had just spent a gruelingly long day at court, having to wait for old and febrile men to decide on some trivial administrative matter concerning training schedules and the upkeep of the massive O-Keikoba: their self-important deliberations, their scheming prevarications, their half-hearted oscillations—they exasperated him no end. It felt as though the only relief from all the tedium were his furtive exploits among Edo's nightlife. It wasn't that he wanted the country to return to that terrible state of anarchy, when honest men like his father had ended up serving despicable men like Matsunaga Hisahide. Yet at times he yearned for the days of his youth, when Ookage had swiftly carried him from one corner of the realm to the other. How different it all had been when the great Ieyasu was still alive—the great Battle of Sekigahara, the winter and summer sieges of Osaka castle!

Listening to his friend's musings, Takuan had looked pensive. Silently he had poured hot water on the small heap of tea powder he had dropped into a carefully rinsed and beautifully sober tea bowl. Turning the bowl in his hands he had placed it on the *tatami* in front of his friend. Then he had straightened out a piece of paper, taken up his brush and written in bold strokes, *Not twice this day, inch, time, foot, gem.*

Munenori had looked bemused. 'What does it mean?'

As was his habit, Takuan had shut his eyes, their eyelids trembling as he became immersed in thought. Then he had slowly opened them, blinking, as if dazzled by the light. 'Every moment passes in an instant. What are human measurements like feet and inches against the eternity of time? Every moment in this short life of us is unique. It happens only once. One should cherish every minute as a priceless gem.'

It was these profound insights that made Takuan a favorite at the courts of Daimyō. They enjoyed the monk's sharp wit and put on grand tea ceremonies so they could indulge in exchanges of witty repartees. Aware of their financial clout, Takuan was happy to indulge them, yet the strain of travel and the late nights with men of far greater stamina proved too much. He fell into a deep depression. In the winter of 1620, he returned to his hometown of Izushi, in Tajima Province, where he built a hermitage on the grounds of the Izushi temple. There, in the cool, rarified air of Japan's west coast, he found the peace and quiet to work on his recovery, dedicating himself to an ascetic life of study, meditation and his favorite pastimes of poetry and making his delicious yellow daikon pickles.

Yet even from his small retreat, he continued to campaign on behalf of his Rinzai sect. One of his concerns was the Bakufu's growing interference in religious affairs, especially in the Daitoku temple's close relations with the imperial court. And it was here where he had landed himself in deep trouble. The sway of the great Buddhist sects in Kyoto had always been a threat to those in power. And like the great unifiers before them, the Bakufu wanted to curb the sect's influence once and for all. Already in 1615 it had promulgated a directive by which only the Bakufu in Edo could make ecclesiastical appointments. A string of additional regulations dictated when such appointments were made. Thus an abbot could only be ordained after he had diligently studied no less than seventeen hundred *kōan*. Consisting of an unsolvable riddle, they helped acolytes to abandon their reliance on reason and instead gain enlightenment through a sudden intuitive insight.

The next time the two friends met, it was Takuan's turn to express his frustration. 'I know *kōan* are an important instrument in a novice's training. I learned enough of them to last me a lifetime. Yet the study of words had its limitations. As in your art of swordsmanship, it is *bunbu-ryōdō*—the dual way of study and practice—that lead to the deeper insights in life. The study of words alone is fruitless.'

For a while the monk remained silent, but Munenori didn't speak: he knew his friend was merely collecting his thoughts.

'Were we, for instance, to discuss the nature of water and fire for a whole night, could either of us quench his thirst with one word, warm himself at a sentence even for a minute? To make the sole study of *kōan* a requirement for high office runs counter to all logic! Is it not possible to gain enlightenment having heard just one single *kōan*? Why then waste one's time in their study if one can help others to gain equal insight through diligent meditation?'

Having been appointed head abbot long before the Bakufu had issued its directive, Takuan naturally assumed he was beyond reproach. In 1628 he penned a stinging rebuke to the retired Shōgun Hidetada for his clampdown on the Buddhist sects and the Bakufu's interference in religious affairs. It didn't take the

Bakufu long to respond. Takuan was still living in Izushi when, in the autumn of the following year, he was summoned to Edo castle, where he was put on trial along with the abbots of three other temples. Munenori was present at the trial.

Takuan seemed undaunted. Sitting before the Shōgun's commission in his plain Buddhist garb, he spoke quietly, looking down at the exquisitely brocaded rims of the *tatami* on which he sat: 'I profoundly believe in the sanctity of the Buddhist church. Nor can anyone deny its ancient and holy ties with the imperial court.'

Munenori grew nervous: better not to press his case too hard before these men.

Raising his head and looking straight at the commission's head, Takuan continued, 'The Rinzai sect respects the authority of the Bakufu. It is a mighty institution. Yet do not the Shōgun's servants also pray to the gods? Indeed, does not the Shōgun himself confess his loyalty to His Highness the Emperor?'

Munenori's heart sank: he had warned his friend not to be his outspoken self. The best strategy was to show humility—if need be to grovel.

It didn't take the commissioner long to reach their verdict; within an hour they reemerged from their chambers. The sentencing was swift and unceremonious. Being again led into the commission's presence, all monks were sentenced to a life in exile. Takuan was sent northward, to the remote province of Dewa, to be placed under house arrest at Kaminoyama castle.

Munenori was somewhat reassured when not long afterward he received a long letter from Toki Yoriyuki, the master of Kaminoyama castle. Though a staunch Bakufu supporter, he was a devout practitioner of Takuan's Rinzai sect. He described how impressed he was with the monk's uncompromising dedication to truth, noting how the monk, who was already in his late fifties, 'lightly suffers physical hardship in the knowledge that his conscience is clear.' To accommodate the monk, he had ordered his carpenters to build a small thatched house inside the walls of his castle, where Takuan was visited by a steady stream of followers seeking his advice.

Being close to the center of power, Munenori was more aware than his friend of the scale of the clampdown. Following the trial, the Bakufu had stripped some seventy abbots of their imperially bestowed robes and ranks. There was little Munenori could do. Earlier that year he had been promoted to the position of Junior Fifth Rank, Lower Grade, receiving the honorary title Tajima no Kami. It was a great honor. Yet it didn't give him the kind of leverage at court to get his friend released. Indeed, he hardly ever saw the old Shōgun these days. When still young Hidetada had been an eager student, but now he was too old and frail to practice. And even when he did see him, there was no way he could go against a law that bore the official seals of both Ieyasu and Hidetada. Even the emperor was clearly unable to oppose the might of the Bakufu. Within weeks he abdicated in favor of his daughter, Okiko. He did so without any prior notice, an unmistakable snub toward the Bakufu.

It was clear: they would have to wait for the right moment to present itself.

The Contest

On March 14, 1632, the old Shōgun Hidetada passed away after a short illness. With both his father and grandfather gone, all authority now came to lie with Iemitsu. Unlike his father, Iemitsu was an outgoing and fun-loving man, who enjoyed fresh views, especially when they went against the staid opinions of his father's counselors. Within weeks of his ascension, he had most of them removed, replacing them with men from his own circle. One of them was Munenori, who was now appointed ō-metsuke, the Bakufu's senior censor.[1] From now on it was Munenori's task to report on the activities of the country's many Daimyō, many of whom still harbored grudges toward the Tokugawa. It was a task for which the Yagyū and their long *shinobi* traditions were cut out. Yet in order to carry out his new duties, Munenori had to be of equal stature as these powerful men. And thus the size of his domain was increased to ten thousand *koku*, making Munenori the first Daimyō of the Yagyū fiefdom. Never before had a mere swordsman made such stellar promotion.

Munenori knew why Iemitsu favored him: the new Shōgun was mad about all things martial. He recalled how, as a child, Iemitsu had loved to sit on his grandfather Ieyasu's lap as the latter told of his exploits: how he and Nobunaga had underestimated Takeda Shingen at Mikatagahara, crushed his son at Nagashino, outwitted Hideyoshi at Komaki, and how he had routed the western forces in glorious battle at Sekigahara and Osaka castle. Yet Iemitsu was the first Shōgun who had never seen action—it was a void he sought to fill through his indulgence in fencing as he grew older.

Iemitsu wasn't a bad martial student. He was diligent, almost fanatical about his practice. Yet from day one it was clear to Munenori that the boy would never be a serious swordsman. He just lacked the dexterity, the precision, the timing of an ace swordsman. Sometimes Munenori felt sorry for the youth and his innocent pursuit of a perfection he would never attain. And what was it all in aid of? The country was now at peace; the Shōgun would never know—nor need to know—what it was to grapple with a foe at close quarters. And what, indeed, was

Munenori's own role? Had he come all this way to teach a novice? Had he and his ancestors fought so hard, suffered so much, for him to spend the rest of his life in this gilded cage just to enjoy the perks of office, the nightly escapades, the occasional payments for favors?

With Iemitsu's ascension, the martial arts had at least gained a new champion. Within weeks of his inauguration, Iemitsu ordered Munenori to stage a fencing contest at the O-Keikoba. Munenori had told him of the great contests organized by Hōzōin In'ei at Nara's Hōzō monastery. This was to be a similarly huge event, and over the next seven months, Munenori busied himself to enlist the realm's greatest swordsmen. It would consist of eleven *omae shiai*, so called because they were to be held 'in the presence' of the Shōgun. All the major fencing schools would be represented: the Sekiguchi-*ryū*, the Asayama Ichiden-*ryū*, the Chūjō-*ryū*, the Shingyōtō-*ryū*, the Sekiguchi Shinshin-*ryū*, the Enmei-*ryū*, and of course Munenori's Yagyū Shinkage-*ryū*.

For Munenori the event was a welcome relief from the tedium of the last few years, and he went about his new task with an enthusiasm he hadn't felt for years. One of the first swordsmen he was able to enlist was Ōkubo Tadataka, the commander of the Shōgun's color guard. Tadataka was already a legend in his day and the epitome of *bunbu ryōdō*. He had just published his third volume of the *Mikawa monogatari*, a detailed history of the proud history of the Tokugawa and Ōkubo clans. He was also a philosopher and had often conversed with Munenori on a warrior's purpose in a time of peace. Though now an old man Tadataka was still a splendid fighter, with behind him some fifty years on the field of battle. Like Munenori, he had last seen action during the siege of Osaka castle, when he had commanded a garrison of lancers. Already then in his sixties, he had still emerged unscathed. There wasn't a trick in the book Tadataka didn't know, and where his physical strength had waned, his uncanny ability to sense an opponent's weak spot had only grown.

This became painfully clear when, in the fourth match of the day, Tadataka was pitted against the twenty-year-old Kagatsume Naozumi. Both men were in full armor. Emboldened by the age-gap, Naozumi was full of zest. Yet facing the old man, it seemed as if his energy dissipated on some invisible shield of energy. Repeatedly he tried for a crack in the old man's defense, only for his *katana* to be deflected by a light parry, his body thrown off-balance by a subtle move. Despite the young man's thick armor, Munenenori could sense how he got more unnerved with every charge, his timing less precise, his poise less confident. Then, just as he raised his *katana* aloft for another attack, Tadataka was upon him. With a minimum of movement, a minimum of force, yet as swift as lightning, he pierced Naozumi's *nodowa*, the crescent-shaped plate protecting his throat. As if a puppeteer had dropped his doll, the young man fell on his knees, clutching his throat with both hands in an effort to get air. He wasn't fatally wounded; just enough to drive home the old man's point: never ever neglect your defense.

Most important to Munenori was the presence of a practitioner of the Enmei-*ryū*, the art of fighting with two swords invented by the enigmatic Miyamoto Musashi. For some years now, Musashi had been living in Akashi, where his adopted son, Iori, was a senior retainer to Ogasawara Tadazane. The latter had just been promoted to the Kokura fief in Kyushu and it seemed Musashi had gone on another of his famed *musha shugyō*. Only recently, there had been an encounter with Munenori's nephew, Toshiyoshi, still chief fencing instructor to Ieyasu's ninth son Tokugawa Yoshinao. Mad about the martial arts, Yoshinao had invited Musashi to test his style of fencing against the Yagyū Shinkage-*ryū* at his *dōjō* on the grounds of Nagoya castle.

It hadn't gone well. Fearful of a loss of face, Yoshinao had barred Toshiyoshi from dueling with the swordsman himself. Instead, he had been forced to pit Musashi against his *deshi*, none of whom were acquainted with the Enmei-*ryū*. Two of them had bravely taken up the challenge. Yet no sooner had they opened the attack than Musashi drawn his two *katana*, trained their *kissaki* on their noses, and steadily forced them to retreat until they had traced the circumference of the huge *dōjō*.

Munenori had tried to get Musashi to take part in the contest, but Musashi had declined. It couldn't be out of cowardice; he had fought plenty of duels, winning all of them. He had fought hard at Osaka, too, and had been part of Mizuno Katsunari's advance guard of lancers, the first to enter the castle's southern gate. Yet Musashi's refusal to show up didn't really surprise Munenori. He remembered how, not long after the Edo Bakufu had been established, Hidetada had invited Musashi to demonstrate his Enmei-*ryū* at court.[2] Then, too, Musashi had declined. It was a moment Munenori recalled with some glee, for Musashi had told the Shōgun's messenger that, 'it seems futile to me to give a demonstration to someone who already esteems the Yagyū-*ryū* so highly.' Yet if this was so, why visit Tokugawa Yoshinao's court in Nagoya? Yoshinao was known for his support of Toshiyoshi's Owari style of the Yagyū Shinkage-*ryū*, which did not differ that much from Munenori's Edo style. Was Musashi happy with the status quo? There was no way to know. It was certainly a source of frustration. True: Musashi had merely dueled with one of his nephew's *deshi*. Yet he wanted to test his own style on Musashi's unique approach to the art of swordsmanship.

Munenori was delighted, therefore, when he managed to persuade Musashi's son to take part in the contest. It had required a lot of cajoling. Lord Tadazane had charged Iori with preparing his move to the Kokura fiefdom, a complicated affair, requiring months of careful preparation. Yet in spite of his busy schedule, the swordsman had graciously accepted.

Being Master of Ceremony, Munenori was barred from taking part. And thus he had pitted Iori against the thirty-three-year-old Araki Mataemon. A native of Iga province, Mataemon had been born in the village of Araki, some ten miles east of Munenori's hometown. Mataemon knew Musashi and his style of fencing. In 1613 his father had remarried, and he and his brother had been adopted by a retainer of Honda Tadamasa, the master of Himeji castle. It had been two years later that Mataemon had first seen Musashi, who had just taken part in the summer siege of Osaka castle. Extravert, boastful, and outlandishly dressed, the already famed swordsman had made a deep impression on the youth. He had been one of the first to enlist when shortly afterward Musashi had opened a *dōjō* with Lord Tadamasa's permission. For six years Mataemon had studied under Musashi. Then, at the age of twenty-two, he had returned to Araki to have his *genpuku* ceremony. Back in Iga, he had studied under a string of teachers from different schools, including the Shintō- and Chūjō-*ryū*. His father, too, was an avid swordsman. And it was through him that Mataemon was introduced to Yagyū Jūbei, spending the next years in Yagyū as his *deshi*. Mataemon had withstood Jūbei's withering training regime and gone on to become one of his best students. He had remained in Yagyū village until 1630, when he had come up to Edo to perfect his skills under Munenori. Now the moment had come for Mataemon to show his worth.

It was just a little past noon, in the day's fifth match, when Mataemon and Iori took their positions at the middle of the O-Keikoba. They had chosen not to wear full battle dress, but newly developed training gear, a padded upper garment and a mask with a mesh of iron bars. Munenori could feel the sweat rise in his palms as he looked over toward where Iemitsu was sitting. Dressed in full regalia he was a sight to behold. He was nervously fanning himself with his battle fan, even though it was already November. Obviously, he too was keen to find out which of the two would come out on top. For a moment the two men measured each other up, each calmly but deliberately training his *bokutō* on the other in the stance of their school. Then, in a flash, it was all over. Both had struck out simultaneously; both with a full blow to the forehead—an *uchiai*! Had they been fighting in earnest, both would have been dead.

Munenori wasn't unhappy with the outcome. The match hadn't proven which of the two schools was superior. Yet neither had it made one inferior to the other. Iemitsu, too, seemed relieved by the draw and generally delighted how the event was going. There were six more matches to go, and he wanted to evaluate them with each and every contestant afterward. It was late in the afternoon, therefore, before the great *taikō* drum at the head of the *dōjō* was sounded to mark the close of the event. Munenori realized now was the time to take up Takuan's cause. For more than three years he had bided his time. He knew it had chiefly been Takuan's rebuke of the former Shōgun that had landed him in trouble. The monk might have been banished to Dewa in Iemutsu's name, but it had been on Hidetada's orders. This was the moment to seek clemency for his friend.

'Does the Shōgun know that the monk Takuan has written with great insight on the art of swordsmanship?' Munenori tried.

For a moment the young Shōgun looked genuinely surprised. Then he began to laugh: 'Ha! Takuan! I know he is a friend of yours. Yes, why not: let's have an amnesty for all!'

Posterity

Munenori was now in his early sixties and his sons were rapidly reaching adulthood. Even Jūbei seemed to make an effort to grow up. In 1632, following Munenori's repeated petitions, the Shōgun had finally lifted his house arrest; he was now free to travel, though he was barred from ever again entering the Shōgun's service. It didn't seem to bother the young swordsman too much; he accepted the Bakufu's punishment with the same stoic resignation as the handicap inflicted by his father. He had put his years in exile to good use, honing his art, studying his grandfather's writings, expanding on them, and teaching an ever-widening circle of students from among the highest echelons of military society. Jūbei's sporadic drinking binges and accompanying bouts of bad temper still worried Munenori, yet he was also a highly talented swordsman who enjoyed the Shōgun's secret support.

Munenori's other two sons, Samon and Matajūrō, were rapidly coming of age. They had both been born in 1613 and though they had different mothers, they were inseparable. Samon, who was born a few months before Matajūrō, showed great promise. Five years earlier, he had had his first audience with the Shōgun and, like Jūbei before him, entered Iemitsu's service as a page. And while he wasn't his older brother's equal in physical strength and endurance, he was a capable swordsman, who made up for his physical shortcoming by a mind that seemed to have no limits in its scope for learning. Taking after his mother, he was the most obedient of the three, and when his oldest brother was placed under house arrest, it was Samon who took his place as Iemitsu's regular fencing partner.

Matajūrō, too, became a page to Iemitsu. Being the youngest, he was the opposite of his illegitimate brother. He frequently skipped fencing classes and seemed more interested in literature and the exciting performances staged at the Nakamuraza, the newly erected *kabuki* theatre near Kyobashi. This in itself was a worry to his father. One of the reasons behind the theatre's success was that women played the roles of both sexes in ribald pieces that left little to the imagination. He had been to a few himself and knew that performers could be bought for the night if one had the means. It had only been a few years since the theatre had been founded, but its actresses were so loose that it was commonly known as *yūjo kabuki*, or prostitution *kabuki*. The Bakufu condoned theatre as a means for the populace to blow of steam, as it did the many *ageya*. Yet in its regimented world view, everything had its place. So did paid-for sex, and its officials were already drafting laws to bar the actresses from performing, be it on the planks or under a futon.

It was to coax his sons away from the Nakamuraza and its temptations that Munenori arranged for Matajūrō and Samon to attend a *nō* performance by the famous Kita Shichidayū Chōnō.[3] In contrast to *kabuki*, the art of *nō* was actively endorsed by the Bakufu, and regular performances were held in the Shōgun's presence.

It wasn't long after, while taking a break from one of their sparring sessions at the Higakubo *yashiki*, that Matajūrō turned to his father and said, 'Father, I think I now understand something I hadn't before. Chōnō's stunning performance has caused me to look at our Yagyū Shinkage-*ryū* tradition with new eyes. For I now see the nobility in total commitment to an art, be it acting or fencing. I see how the long hours we spend in the *dōjō* are the only true way to attain the level of excellence that enable actors like Chōnō to move their audience to tears.'

Munenori smiled inwardly—luckily not all his sons were like Jūbei.

Legacy

As the new Daimyō of the Yagyū fief, Munenori had greater responsibilities than just raising his sons and managing his fief. Having known the depths to which a clan could sink, he was determined to lay the foundations for his clan to prosper long after he was gone. That foundation consisted of *bunbu ryōdō*, the 'Dual Way of the Martial and the Literary.' Martial excellence (*bu*) was the indispensable wheel that supported the cart on one side; equally indispensable was the wheel of learning (*bun*). Only when the two were practiced in tandem was a samurai able to yield his *katana* with wisdom and fight for a righteous cause. And for someone of Munenori's stature, it wasn't sufficient to merely study the works of great warriors; he had to write one.

Ever since his appointment as Ieyasu's *shihan*, the Yagyū Shinkage-*ryū* had gained in status. For the first few decades, Munenori had to compete hard with other schools, among them the Arima Shintō-*ryū*, the Okuyama Shinkage-*ryū*, and of course Ono Jirōemon Tadaaki's Ittō-*ryū*. Tadaaki had passed away in 1628, but his influence on the world of fencing was still being felt. Ever since Munenori had arrived in Edo, the man who had studied under the great Itō Ittōsai Kagehisa had beguiled the young Yamato swordsmen with his uncompromising dedication to excellence. It was, at the same time, his undoing: the man just couldn't obey orders, especially if he thought they weren't worth obeying.

Tadaaki had really got into trouble when, during Hidetada's siege of Ueda castle, and taunted by enemy soldiers, he had taken a number of men and launched a sortie. Had the siege been a success he might have been promoted. Of course it had been a disaster. And when Hidetada himself was punished by his father for his failure to arrive in time at Sekigahara, the swordsman was charged with insubordination. Tadaaki had been placed under house arrest, though, partly through Munenori's efforts, he was reinstated within a few years. Brawls with fellow swordsmen during the siege of Osaka castle—in which he broke both wrists of a fellow practitioner with a *bokutō* during practice—again landed him in trouble. Not willing to look soft, and aware of the man's great reputation, the Tokugawa had kept him on. Following Tadaaki's death, they had remained patrons of the Ittō-*ryū*, and Iemitsu continued to practice with Tadaaki's talented son, Tadatsune. Yet by then, the Yagyū Shinkage-*ryū* had well eclipsed Tadakaki's Ittō-*ryū*.

Another reason for the Ittō-*ryū*'s demise was the lack of written sources. Tadaaki just hadn't been the literary type. Yet he had been close friends with Obata Kagenori, whose *Kōyō gunkan* had been an overnight sensation. The work was largely based on the records of Kōsaka Masanobu, the lord of Kaizu castle and a close vassal of the great Warring States chieftain Takeda Shingen.[4] Published in 1616, the work comprised no less than twenty scrolls covering fifty-nine chapters. Never before in Japan's feudal history had a work gone into the art of warfare in such depth and with such breadth. It gave a complete breakdown of Shingen's huge army, down to kitchen staff and horse doctors. It exhaustively described its commanders' philosophy on the art of warfare, their tactics, their weaponry, their reliance on ability rather than brute force. It gave an in-depth history of Shingen's rapid rise to greatness, how he ousted his father, how he clashed repeatedly with Uesugi Kenshin, how he outwitted no lesser men than Nobunaga and Ieyasu. And, drawing from Masanobu's and Masamori's experience, it listed all of the clan's major battles and their outcomes.

The *Kōyō gunkan* not only immortalized the high years of the Takeda clan under Shingen, but also described in painful detail the clan's decline under his son, Katsuyori—the poor appoint-ments, the bad advice, the disastrous results. First the crushing defeat at Nagashino, and finally that dramatic scene in which Katsuyori and his men were cornered and outnumbered by the Oda-Tokugawa alliance:

> Soon the enemy banners came in sight. At this time Lord Katsuyori's consort, her assistant Ohara Tango no Kami, and his younger brother Shimōsa Kinmaru Sukerokurō were at his side. This Sukerokurō had formerly taken on the name of Kanemaru, but was, in fact, the older brother to Tsuchiya Masatsune. Including Lord Katsuyori and his son, Lord Nobukatsu, there were forty-three in all.
>
> Tsuchiya-*dono*, was on Katsuyori's left hand, shooting arrows from his longbow to fend off the enemy, who were advancing in such great numbers, he had to savor each and every arrow.
>
> Lord Katsuyori, taking a white towel and twisting it into a headband, took his *tachi* and struck out on all sides. Master Nobukatsu, who was on his right side, had now also dropped his cross-shaped *yari* and was fighting in hand to hand combat wielding his long sword.

At length, having exhausted all his arrows,
Tsuchiya-*dono* was about to draw his sword when
he was struck by six enemy *yari* at once. Rushing
to his side, Lord Katsuyori parried the *yari* and
singlehandedly struck down the six enemy
warriors. Yet three more warriors struck out with
their *yari*, one piercing his throat, the two others
his lower side, and pinning down Lord Katsuyori
to the ground, they took his lordship's head.

There was no reason to doubt the *Kōyō gunkan*'s general verac-
ity—Takeda Shingen had undoubtedly been one of the warring
states period's most formidable chieftains. It was true, too, that
the brilliant Tsuchiya Masatsune, leading only a handful of
warriors, had held out against an overwhelming Nobunaga
force. Even Ieyasu's men had been impressed with his valor; in
his *Mikawa monogatari*, Ōkubo Tadataka had described him as
'the man who kept a thousand enemy at bay single-handedly.'
Yet he had only been able to postpone Katsuyori's inevitable
demise. Munenori knew from old hands who had fought among
Ieyasu troops that Katsuyori's demise had been far less
glamorous. Intercepted at the foot of Mount Tenmoku by one
of Nobunaga's generals, he, his son, and his family had been
captured and forced to commit *seppuku*.

Munenori shuddered at the thought of some distant
chronicler ever describing the decline of his own clan, be it
heroic or otherwise. For not even the patronage of the house
of Tokugawa could ensure its longevity. The Yagyū Shinkage-
ryū might have become the undisputed fencing school of the
Tokugawa Bakufu, but just like them, the famed Yoshioka clan
too had once enjoyed the patronage of the Ashikaga Bakufu.
They, too, had had their family record, the *Yoshioka-den*. Yet

none of their practitioners had ever written a definitive treatise on the actual school itself. Instead, they had relied solely on the transmission from father to son. With the notorious defeat of the two Yoshioka brothers in their duels against Miyamoto Musashi, the clan had gone into decline, a decline hastened by the demise of the Ashikaga. Munenori was determined the Yagyū would not in time come to share their fate, and one of the ways to ensure their continuity was to write a definitive work on the Yagyū Shinkage-*ryū*. It not only had to define its techniques but also convey a sense of its continuity, the long path from Kamiizumi Nobutsuna's Shinkage-*ryū* down to his own clan's Yagyū Shinkage-*ryū*. Indeed, there were really two Yagyū schools now: his nephew Toshiyoshi's Owari school, and Munenori's Edo school.

For some time now he had been working on just such a work. Unlike his father's *Gyokuei shūi*, the ancient records of the Yagyū clan, it was a specific work on the techniques and the philosophy behind their school of swordsmanship. His great inspiration was Kamiizumi Nobutsuna. His father had often told him how, during his stay at the Yagyū castle, Nobutsuna had written the *Kage-ryū no mokuroku*, a copy of which was now kept in the family's private library at the Higakubo. Nobutsuna's desire to record for posterity all that the great Aisu Ikkō had taught him had impelled him to do so. Munenori had never met Nobutsuna, but he had often read his writings, and each reading had given him new insight, revealed another nuance.

Munenori had no trouble in describing the various fencing techniques. But there was one aspect he grappled with. It wasn't so much related to the techniques of a warrior but to the profession itself. In his conversations with Ōkubo Tadataka, he had often discussed the role of the warrior. They both realized that the end of hostilities had profound consequences for their role in society, but also believed that the ultimate aim of a loyal retainer was to achieve such peace through the dual Way of *bu* and *bun*, the martial and the civil. To discuss such matters was one thing; to get them onto paper was a different thing. He needed help in organizing his thoughts. He thought of Takuan, the man whose mind was as clear as Lake Tazawa, its thoughts as deep, the arguments it put forth as forceful as the thrust of a *katana*. Takuan, too, had a profound interest in the martial arts. When young, he had studied the Yagyū Shinkage-*ryū* under Munenori and had shown a remarkable ability. Now the time had come for Munenori to become his friend's pupil.

The Visit

It was a bright spring day in 1632, when Munenori drew up his horse at a large *yashiki* at the center of Komagome, like Azabu a small village on Edo's outskirts. Far more grand than Munenori's Higakubo, the *yashiki* overlooked the beautiful lake of Shinobazu, a few miles north of Edo castle. Unlike in Edo, where the constant threat of fire stilted vertical growth, this *yashiki* stood several stories tall. Built in the modern *irimoya* style, its heavy, curved eaves seemed to reach out in blessing over wide cedar verandas below, its tiles embossed with three hexagons, the family crest of the powerful Hori clan. Munenori had been here often. It was the second residence of Hori Naoyori, a Shōgunal counselor and a good friend of his.

Munenori loved to come here. Komagome was stunningly beautiful, as well as a place of prestige. Not far from his friend's *yashiki* stood the residence of Tōdō Taketora, one of Ieyasu's most trusted advisers. Ever since the capital had been moved to Edo, Komagome had been a favorite playground of influential

Daimyō. Not anymore. Now the hugely influential monk Tenkai held sway around Lake Shinobazu.

Tenkai, too, had made his career as an adviser to Ieyasu and his son, Hidetada. By now he was an old man. He had a martial temperament, and though he no longer practiced, he had fought in numerous battles and been with Ieyasu during the Battle of Sekigahara. His age and martial disposition spawned many rumors, some that he had started out as a *sōhei*. Munenori's favorite one claimed the old monk was none other than Akechi Mitsuhide, the retainer who had assassinated Oda Nobunaga. It was nonsense of course—were it true, Tenkai would have been more than a hundred years old. Yet it did speak of the respect he enjoyed among the warrior class.

It had been in reward for his services that, in 1622, Hidetada gave Tenkai the grounds around Lake Shinobazu, as well as fifty-thousand pieces of silver. Using the money Tenkai had built himself a residence set in a large court surrounded by high walls with a roofed entrance toward the lake. More buildings followed, including a five-storied stupa only just completed. Now Tenkai had hatched an even more ambitious plan. A former student of the Enryaku temple, he envisioned a temple complex on the scale of Mount Hiei. Magnificent structures were being erected along the three-mile stretch of flat land from his residence to the lakeshore, all aligned in a straight line from east to west like the old capital. The main building, a mirror image of the Enryaku temple's Konpon Chūdō, was to dwarf all around it. Most eye-catching, and already under construction, was its grand entrance, two towers connected by an arched and roofed bridge spanning some twenty yards across.

Naoyori received Munenori in good grace, but in a foul mood nevertheless. To accommodate Tenkai's desire for grandeur the Bakufu had impounded the very land it had granted Naoyori only a decade before. Nao*yari*'s beautiful *yashiki* would also have to move. Hundreds of carpenters and masons already filled the air with the sound of their work, the sawing, the knocking, the chiseling—it reverberated around the lakeshore in an endless clatter. Every now and then all was drowned out when the voices of a huge workforce of laborers rose in unison to heave into place some massive foundation stone or huge beam. Executed to the highest standards, it would take decades to complete.

Naoyori cast an angry eye at the buildings that arose on his grounds and grumbled, 'It feels as if the Bakufu takes with one hand what it gives with the other.'

Munenori commiserated. He knew what it felt like to lose one's home.

'Ah well...' Naoyori reflected as he patted the sun-burned wood of the gate he had just opened for his friend. 'At least I can hold on to my *yashiki* a few more years. Of course they've offered to pay for the move. Yet I doubt I'll ever again find such a beautiful spot.'

'Have you found a new location yet?' Munenori inquired.

Naoyori shook his head. Then he laughed: 'Who knows? I might come and join you at Azabu!'

Preceding him into the vestibule, Naoyori led his friend straight through to a guest room overlooking the lake and tapped on its *fusuma*, for Munenori had come to visit another guest: his old friend Takuan. Following his release, the monk had moved back to Edo. He had first taken up lodgings at the Kōtoku temple in Edo's Kanda district. But his arrival didn't go unnoticed. The purple robe incident had gained such notoriety that when he entered Edo, its citizens came out in droves to watch the dissident monk. Over the next weeks, a constant stream of well-wishers and acolytes visited him at the temple.

It was too much. He wanted to get away, escape the attention. And what better place to hide than at Naoyori's *yashiki*? In the shadow of Tenkai's grandiose temple complex, whose expanding grounds invariably swarmed with monks, the self-effacing Takuan could go about his business unnoticed.

Takuan's face beamed as he slid aside the *fusuma* and saw his friend. 'Tajima no Kami-*dono*! What a delight to see you again! Come in, and please excuse the mess!'

The room was cramped and stuffy; it smelled of learning, a strange mix of incense, Indian ink, and the exotic mix of herbs that kept scrolls free from harmful insects. Piles of books lined the walls, and yet more covered the small desk beneath the *shōji*. A wide format scroll filled the bit of wall space left: a calligraphy with just one bold character, *yume*: 'dream.'

Takuan looked at his friend as Munenori admired the work's craftsmanship, a smile flashing across his emaciated face. 'Most of my calligraphies I have given away, but not this one. It is strange for a monk, I know, to cling to worldly things, even writings,' he said apologetically, 'But this one I somehow can't let go of.'

Always a master of timing, Munenori carefully unwrapped the bundle of papers he had brought with him. It was his manuscript.

Ah! A dream of your own!' Takuan smiled as he respectfully took the manuscript from Munenori's hands.

Making room on his desk, the monk placed the manuscript carefully at its center. Then he turned toward a small cabinet along the wall. Pulling up his right-hand sleeve he reached into it, took out a scroll, and handed it to Munenori. Its title was written in longhand on a narrow strip of *washi* paper glued to its spine. It read: *Fudō chinmyō-roku*, the *Wondrous Record of Immovable Wisdom*.

'Please read this for me,' Takuan said, 'and I will read your work for you.'

The Letter

Munenori was pleased with himself. Along with Takuan, he had also presented the Shōgun with a copy of his work. Not that he thought that Iemitsu could in any way contribute. The young ruler had never seen war, never had a serious duel; and while he was a dedicated student, he was a mediocre talent at best. Shōgunal endorsement nevertheless could help him to promote his work among the Daimyō, and thus promote the spread of the Yagyū Shinkage-*ryū*. It was something he was good at: playing the Shōgun. Iemitsu was thirty years his junior. He had just lost his father and, except for Munenori, there were few men in his immediate circle in whom he put his trust. In many ways he looked up to Munenori like a father. Munenori didn't mind. It was the way in which he could bring his influence to bear.

Now the Shōgun had sent him a letter. Breaking the seal and opening it, Munenori opened it. Yet what he read made his heart miss a beat:

> Recently you gave me a copy of your manuscript, and I, in turn, gave you a written pledge of my commitment to the Yagyū art of *heihō*. Indeed, you told me you had taught me the extent of your teachings, and I, being satisfied with your conduct, raised you to the rank of Daimyō. Yet, even though you taught me, your heart wasn't in it, and thus, in one way, my mastery is not what it could have been. I would like you to put your heart into it for my sake, for there is no benefit in teaching someone in such a perfunctory manner. What is the use if I cannot make a *katana* follow my will? It is up to you, then, to decide whether I should make progress or not.

> If you are content to let things be as they are, even
> while you know so well how dedicated I am to the
> art of *heihō*, then it seems to me that our friendship
> has meant nothing.

Munenori felt ashamed. The letter confronted him with a
truth he had been loath to admit. Iemitsu might be his junior,
yet the wisdom of his words was that of a man his senior—not
just in rank. The Shōgun was right. It wasn't a man's talent that
counted; it was his commitment to perfection. Iemitsu might
not be a natural talent, but his dedication to the martial Way
was beyond question. Had it not been Munenori's own father's
same honest dedication to perfection that had eventually saved
the Yagyū? Had it not been the lesson his own son had gained
from seeing Chōnō perform *nō*?

Another thing now came to mind, a thought that caused him
to break out into a cold sweat for the first time in many years.
Except for his promise to read Munenori's manuscript, Takuan
had said little at their last meeting. Munenori hadn't yet read
Takuan's work, even though he was going to meet him again
soon. Something told him he should do it right now.

Walking to his library he picked up Takuan's *Fudō chinmyō-
roku*. Feverishly he began to scroll through his friend's work,
and what he read hit him with its forthright clarity:

> I want to confront you with something that has
> been troubling me for a long time. It might be
> foolish of me, but I think this is a good moment to
> write them down for you.
>
> A master without equal in past or present, you
> are now at the apex of rank, stipend, and worldly
> fame. Yet you must never forget this great privilege,

whether you walk or sleep, and wholeheartedly
devote yourself to repay this favor by exerting
yourself in your loyalty day and night. In doing so,
you must first set your heart straight, be moderate
in conduct, and never ever entertain thoughts that
go against your lord.

Munenori's hands trembled as they transported the text from
one to the other. Never before had he felt so nervous, not even
on the field of battle. Feverishly he read on, eager to fathom
the full depth of the monk's message:

If one cannot refrain from evil in the full knowledge
that it is evil, it is only so because one is fully aware
that one enjoys it. It is precisely because one is
lustful, arrogant, and bent on living as one pleases
that the presence of good men fails to rub off, that
their counsel is not heeded. And thus the idiot,
because of one single favor, is promoted. If, due to
such favors, good men are not hired, even though
they do exist, they might just as well be dead.

As yet, Takuan's tone was detached, his words chosen as if
he might be talking about no one in particular. But Munenori
knew full well what he was on about:

It seems that this is even the case when you select
your *deshi*. I find this utterly disgusting. All this is
because you do it in a single moment's whim, and
thus, falling prey to this affliction, fail to see how
you fall into evil. You may think that people do not
know, yet since you yourself know, it follows that

281

all the gods in heaven and all men on earth will know, as sure as day follows dawn. Is it not perilous to govern the realm in such manner? Just think how disloyal such a state of affairs would be!

A sinking feeling took hold of Munenori as he continued:

That being what it is, with respect to your son's dissolute life, it is immoral for a father to admonish his son if his own conduct is not beyond reproach. First you must set yourself straight; only then will his conduct naturally correct itself when you voice your opinion.

But it was the closing lines of his friend's work that hurt most:

That you enjoy wild dancing, take pride in your abilities in *nō*, and insinuate yourself among Daimyō to show off to them your dancing skills—this I truly see as an affliction. Worse still, I hear that you liken the Shōgun's recitals to *sarugaku*, while in his presence you only speak highly of those Daimyō who flatter you. All this you should consider carefully. Does not the Buddha teach us:

It is the mind that leads the mind astray.
Be mindful of the mind!

For a moment Munenori was overcome by rage. Had he not saved his friend? Where was Takuan's gratitude? Who did this purple-robed egg-head think he was? Then he saw his folly. It struck him, like a *koan*—the sound of one hand clapping. If the monk thought anything of himself it was that he was *mu*: nothing. Only a true friend would go so far out of his way, be so blunt in his words, to bring another friend to reason. Munenori had strayed—and not without warning. He groaned as he thought of his father, his strong hand on his head when a boy, his hard words when he grew up, his sorrowful reproaches when a man. The little relief he felt was that his father hadn't lived to see him become so complacent. Yet it wasn't too late to mend things…

Writing

Munenori's initial urge was to rewrite his manuscript from scratch—immediately: it was too full of pride, too full of himself. But Takuan was right. He needed to set himself straight first. And what better way to do so than to remove himself from the temptations of the capital? Asking leave for an indefinite time, he withdrew to his Higakubo *yashiki* to meditate and study. He had to find himself.

With every day his heart felt a bit lighter, his head clearer, his soul more cleansed. He went on long walks, not through Edo this time, but through the surrounding countryside. He was stunned to find how unfamiliar the area around Azabu still was to him. Setting off southward along the coast he would walk all the way to Kamakura at the foot of the Miura Peninsula to visit the Tsurugaoka Hachimangū, the shrine dedicated to the God of War. Or he would strike inland, following the magnificent Tama River, toward Hachiōji. Or farther inland still, up into the mountains, to the forested slopes of the Kantō Mountains. On such pilgrimages he could stay away for days, enjoying the refreshing hospitality of locals. As he shared their meager meals amidst their poor living conditions, he began to better understand his Buddhist friend. It also cast his mind back to his childhood days, when his family had lived on the handouts of the Enjō temple. He had been in the Shōgun's service for nigh-on forty years now. He had gained fame and fortune. Yet, through his own indulgence, he had lost touch with the things that truly mattered.

It was a miracle, really, looking back, that he and Takuan had remained friends. Munenori was beginning to see now how much they had grown in different directions. A born and bred warrior, he himself had been taught to concern himself with the material world; his senses trained to deal with an armed opponent, his faculties dedicated to swift action. Takuan, by contrast, had been taught to concern himself with the immaterial world; his senses trained to connect with his unarmed inner self, his faculties dedicated to patient meditation. Takuan's insight into his own soul had not detached him from the outside world; but Munenori's focus on the outside world had detached him from his inner self. Given his calling, Munenori would never be able to follow his friend's example. Yet in order to follow the Way, he had to stay in touch with his inner self.

Most cathartic to Munenori were the long hours he spent amid the quiet seclusion of his study, pouring over the works he admired, Obata Kagenori's *Kōyō gunkan*, Ōkubo Tadataka's *Mikawa monogatari*, Nobutsuna's *Kage-ryū no mokuroku*, and Takuan's *Fudō chinmyō-roku*. There was something in these works that connected them; they all shared a deep reverence for the ancient traditions, be they religious or martial. Reading their works Munenori always had to think of his father.

It was already winter, and the hushed landscape around the Higakubo lay covered in thick a blanket of snow, when the sixty-one-year-old warrior was finally ready to put brush to paper. It seemed to Munenori, as he took up his brush and wetted its

tip in the dark pool of Indian ink, that everything he had experienced throughout his long and eventful career now finally fell
into place. It felt as if history came rushing in on him, the
struggles of his ancestors, the long chain of events that had led
his clan to the present. Then he began to write, beginning with
his father, the man who had built everything, the man who had
lost everything, the man who had endured everything:

> My father pondered the art of swordsmanship every
> day, even when he slept or ate. Having thus gained
> new insights, he would daily discuss and explain
> the subtleties and profundities with me at his side,
> and whenever there was something I thought I
> understood, I tucked it away, deep in my mind...

OLD PROVINCES

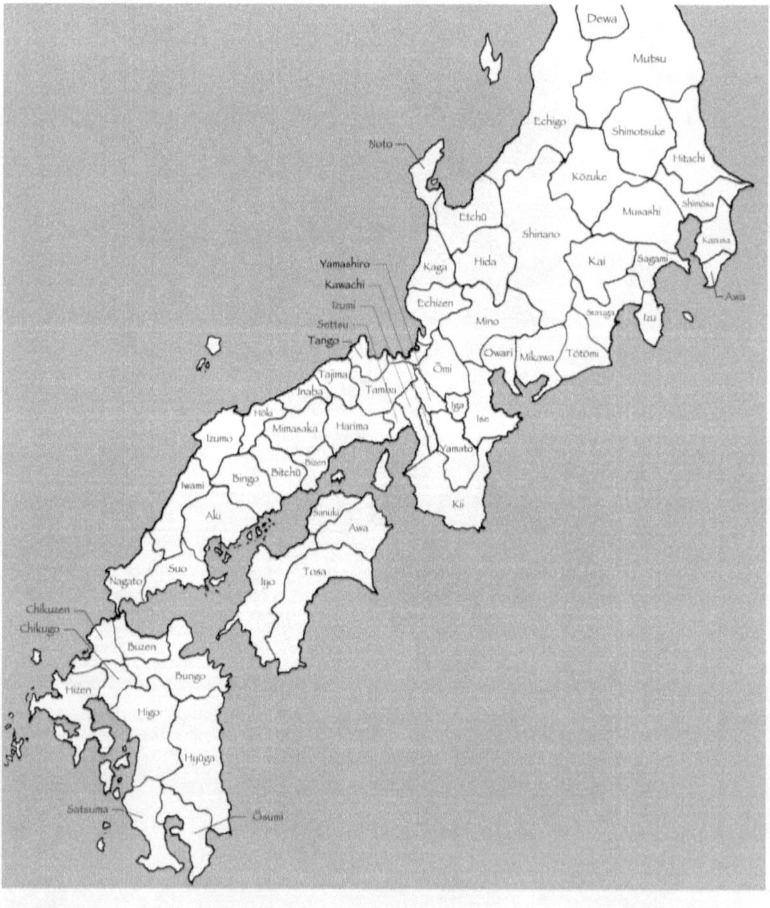

Old Provinces and Their Modern Equivalents

Aki:	Hiroshima	Kawachi:	Osaka
Awa:	Tokushima	Kazusa:	Chiba
Bingo:	Hiroshima	Kii:	Wakayama
Bitchū:	Okayama	Kōzuke:	Gunma
Bizen:	Okayama	Mikawa:	Aichi
Bungo:	Ōita	Mimasaka:	Okayama
Buzen:	Fukuoka	Mino:	Gifu
Chikugo:	Fukuoka	Musashi:	Saitama, Tokyo
Chikuzen:	Fukuoka	Mutsu:	Aomori
Dewa:	Yamagata, Akita	Nagato:	Yamaguchi
Echigo:	Niigata	Noto:	Ishikawa
Echizen:	Fukui	Ōmi:	Shiga
Etchū:	Fukuyama	Ōsumi:	Kagoshima
Harima:	Hyōgo	Owari:	Aichi
Hida:	Gifu	Sagami:	Kanagawa
Higo:	Kumamoto	Sanuki:	Kagawa
Hitachi:	Ibaraki	Satsuma:	Kagoshima
Hizen:	Nagasaki	Settsu:	Osaka
Hōki:	Tottori	Shimōsa:	Chiba
Hyūga:	Miyazaki	Shinano:	Nagano
Iga:	Mie	Suō:	Yamaguchi
Inaba:	Tottori	Suruga:	Shizuoka
Ise:	Mie	Tajima:	Hyōgo
Iwami:	Shimane	Tamba:	Kyoto
Iyo:	Ehime	Tango:	Kyoto
Izu:	Shizuoka	Tosa:	Kōchi
Izumi:	Osaka	Tōtōmi:	Shizuoka
Izumo:	Shimane	Wakasa:	Fukui
Kaga:	Ishikawa	Yamashiro:	Kyoto
Kai:	Yamanashi	Yamato:	Nara

CASTLES, TEMPLES, AND SHRINES

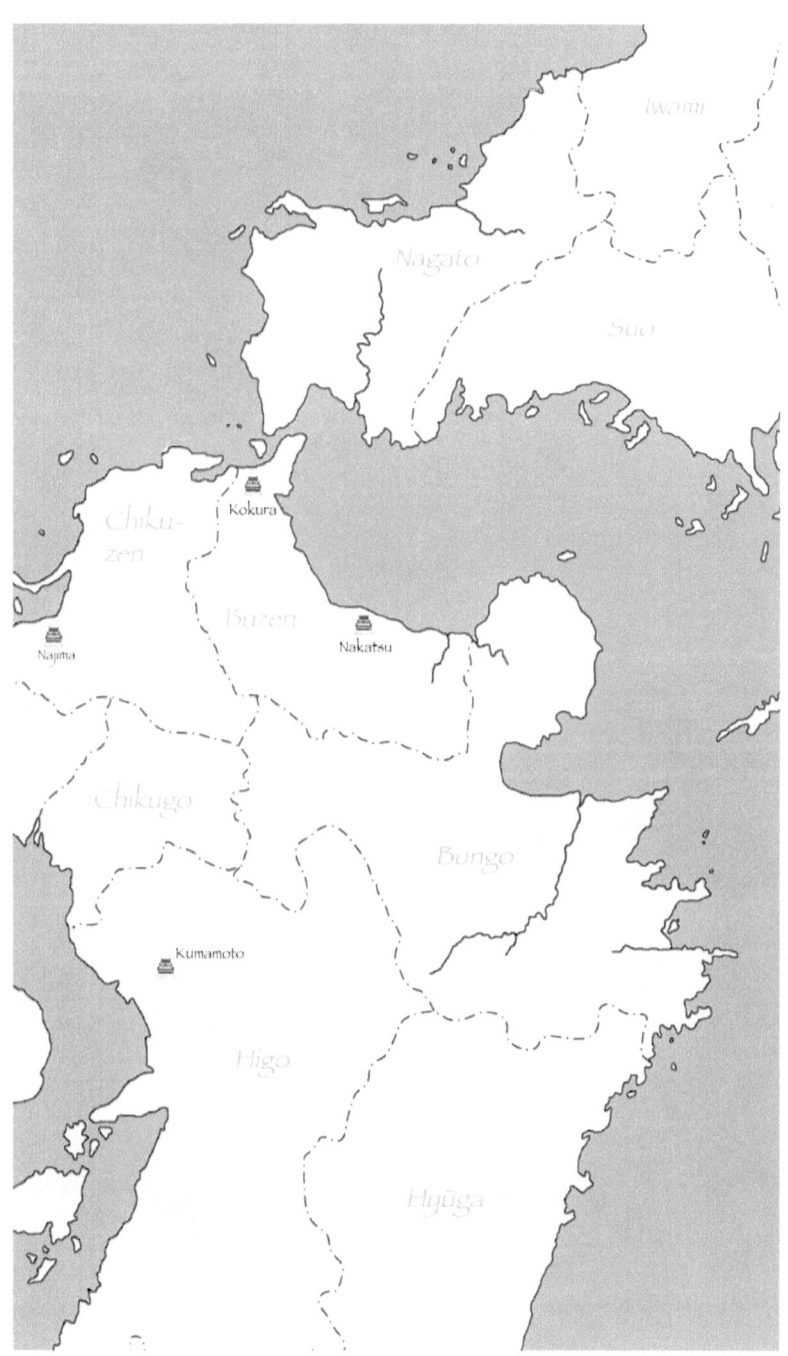

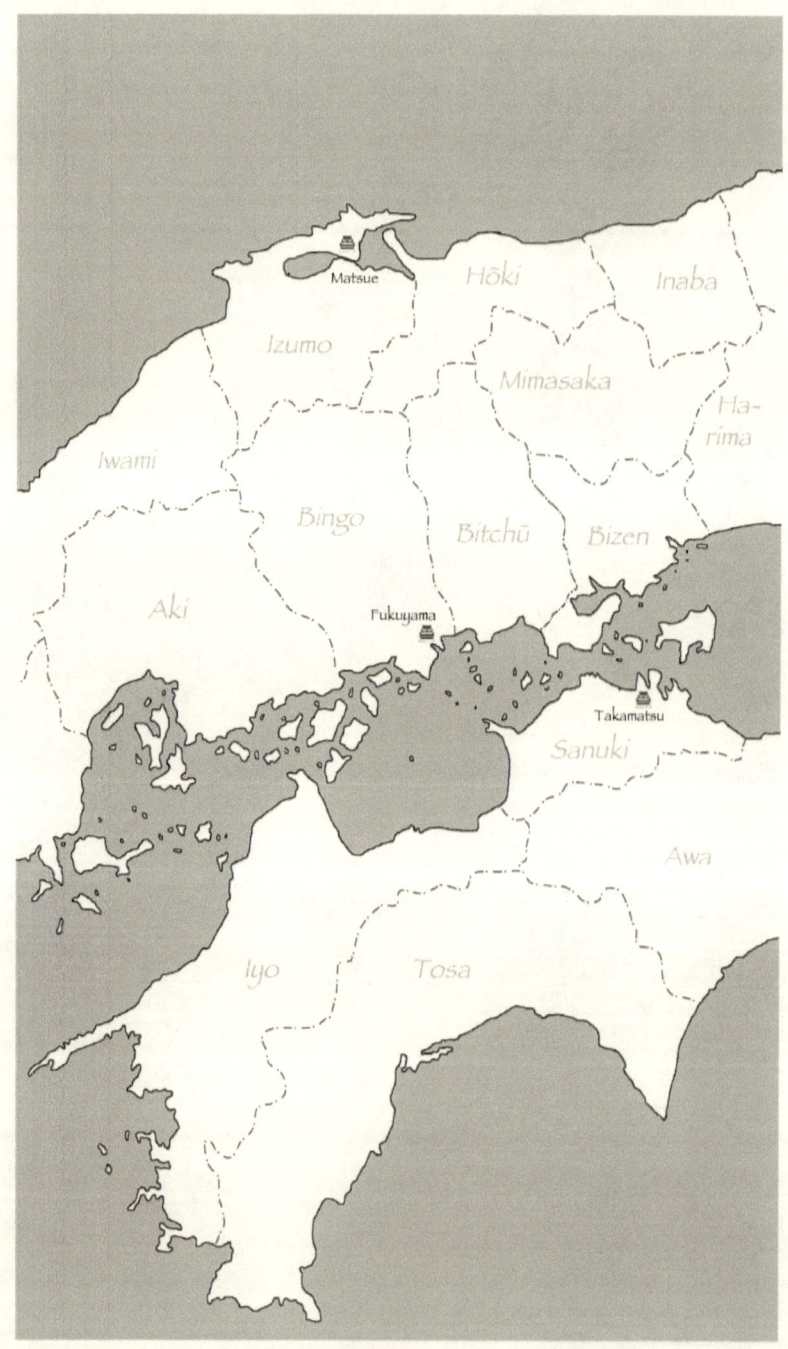

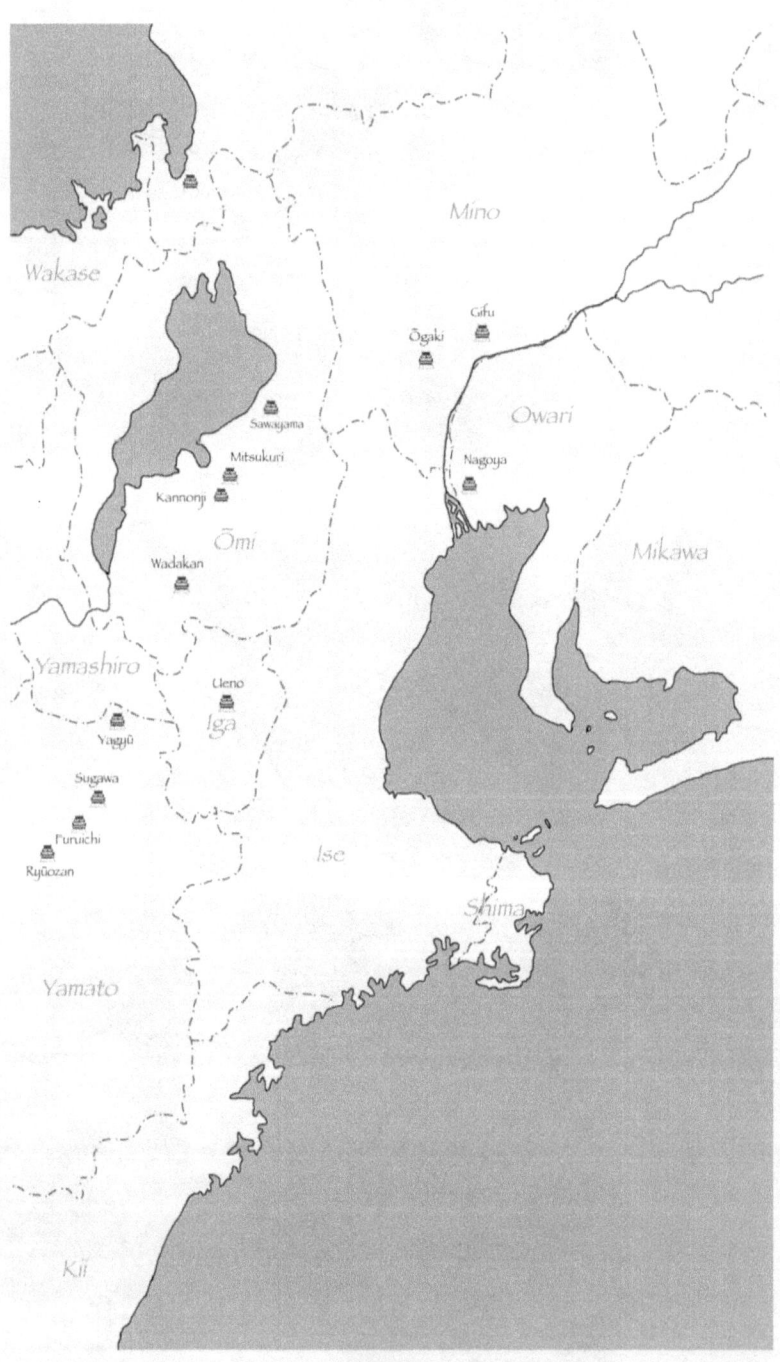

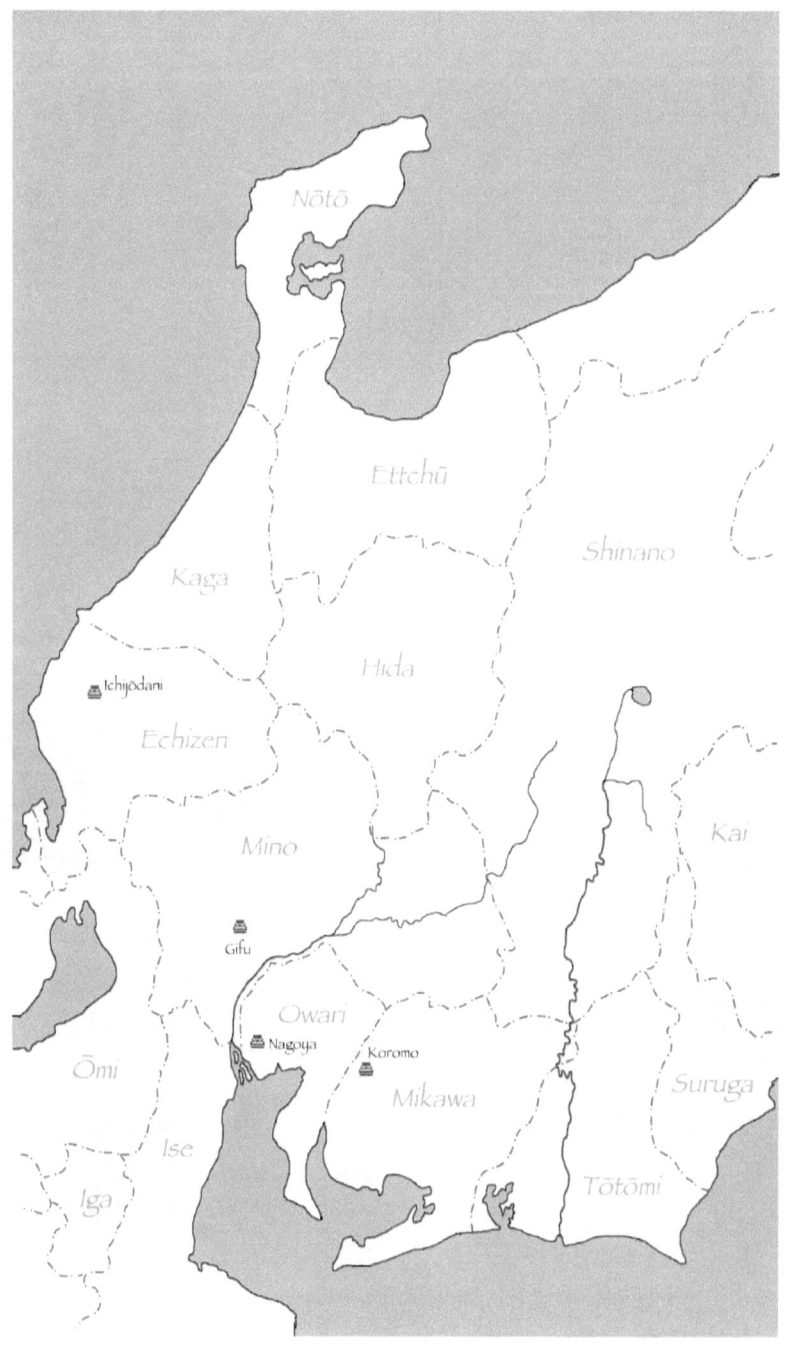

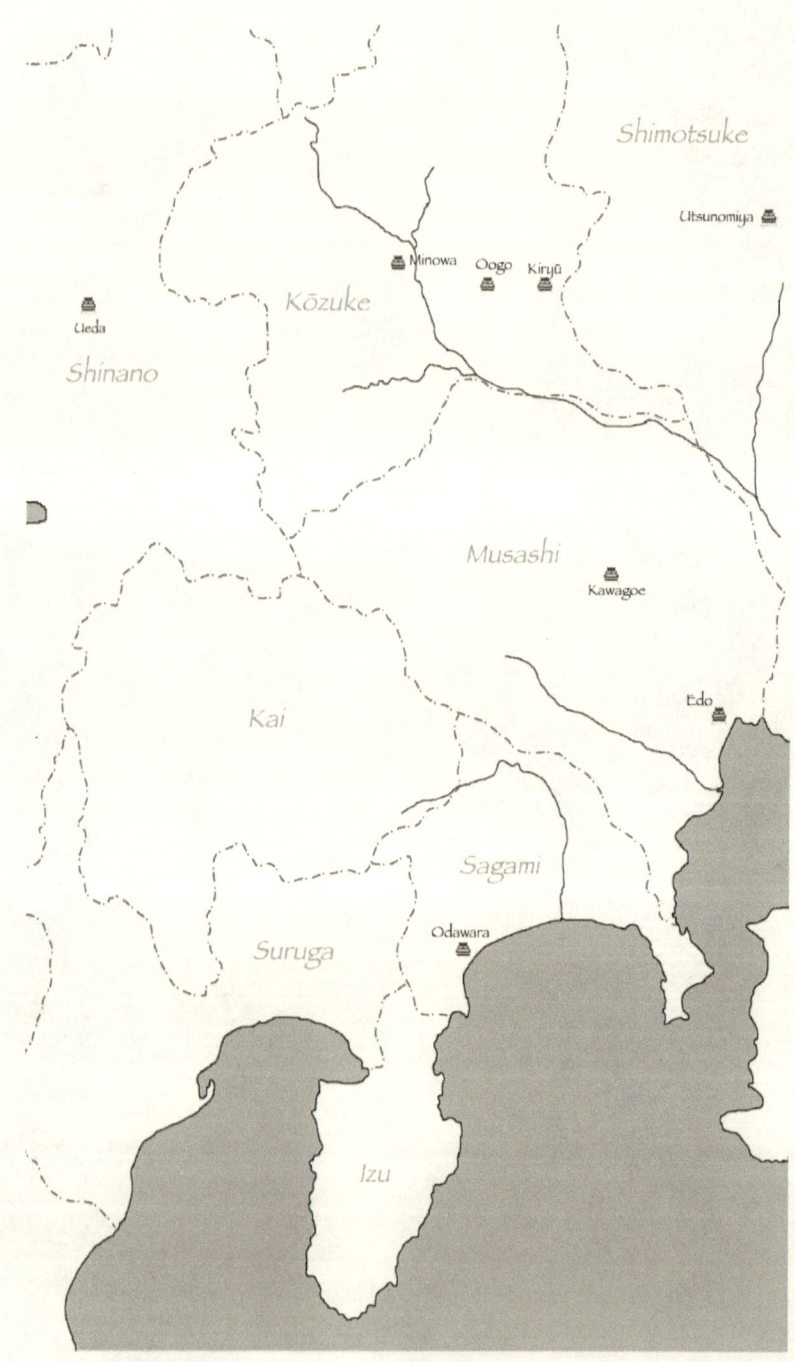

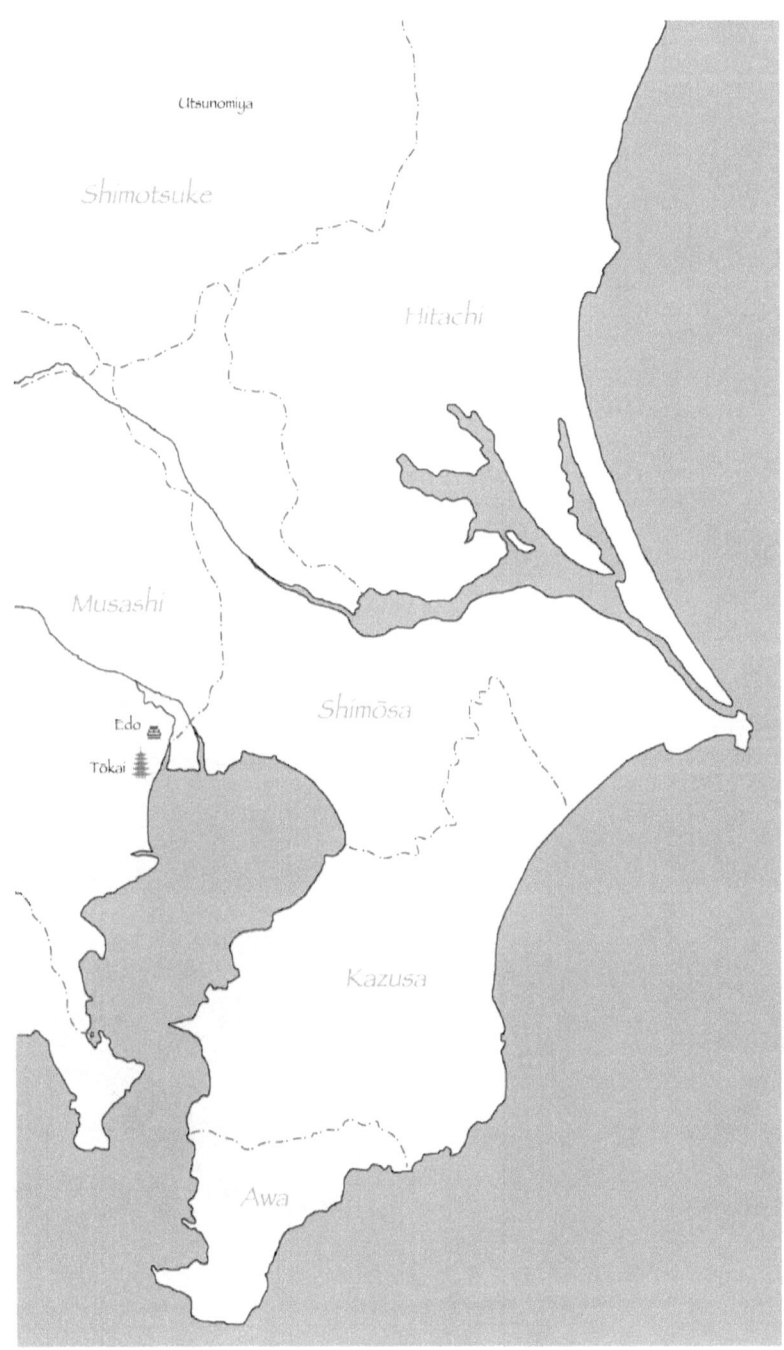

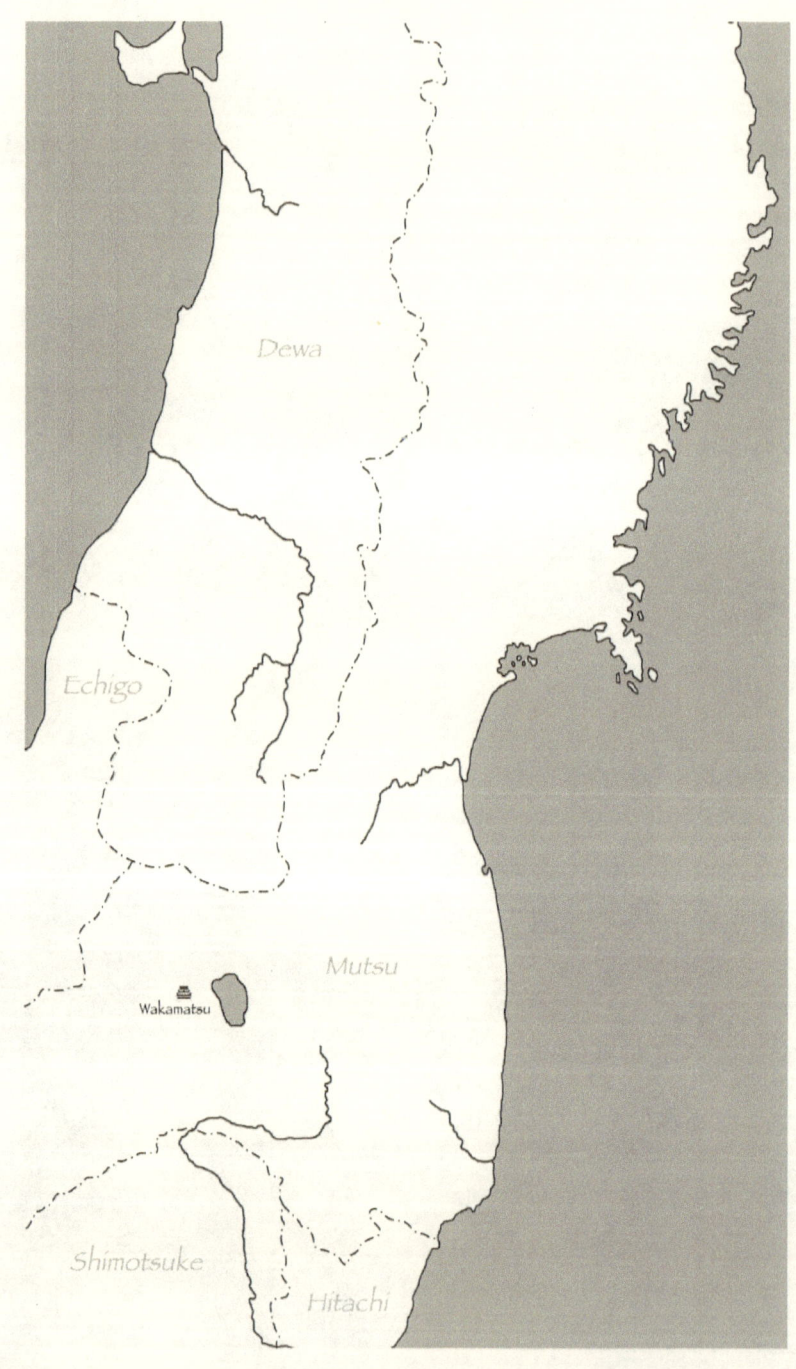

HISTORICAL PERIODS

Japan

Nara 710–94
Heian 794–1185
Kamakura 1185–1333
Muromachi 1333–1568
Momoyama 1568–1600
Tokugawa 1600–1868

China

Han 202 BC–AD 220
Three Kingdoms 221–65
Six Dynasties 265–581
Sui 581–618
Tang 618–906
Five Dynasties 907–60
Northern Song 960–1127
Southern Song 1127–1279

Yuan 1271–1368
Ming 1368–1644
Qing 1644–1911

Periods of Military Rule

Kamakura Bakufu 1185–1333
Muromachi Bakufu (Ashikaga Bakufu) 1333–1568
Edo Bakufu (Tokugawa Bakufu) 1603–1867

BATTLES AND SIEGES

Battles

Battle of Shizugatake 1583
Battle of Komakiyama 1584
Battle of Nagakute 1584
Battle of Sekigahara 1600
Battle of Dōmyōji 1615

Sieges

Siege of Kasagi-dera 1541
Siege of Furuuchi castle 1544
Siege of Odawara castle 1590
Siege of Gifu castle 1600
Siege of Ōgaki castle 1600
Siege of Osaka castle 1614–15

GLOSSARY

ashigaru:	Foot soldier.
biwa:	Japanese lute.
bokutō:	Wooden sword used for practice.
bu:	The martial arts.
bun:	The literary arts.
burei-uchi:	Killing someone for reasons of insolence.
bushi:	Warrior.
daimyō:	Fuedal lord.
denki:	Biography.
deshi:	Pupil or disciple of a master of an art or craft who has committed him- or herself to study the art or craft in question for a number of years.
dōjō:	Hall with a smooth wooden floor or covered with mats for the practice of martial arts.
eboshi:	Headgear traditionally worn by nobles in court dress, but also used in Shintō ceremonies.
fūdai daimyō:	Vassal *daimyō*.
genpuku:	Coming of age ceremony.
go:	Japanese chess.
haori:	Lightweight silk jacket originally meant to be worn by men as a component of the *hakama*.

hatamoto:	Direct retainer, or "bannerman," of the shogun.
heihō:	Art or method of warfare.
heihōsha:	Practitioner of the art of *heihō*.
kabuki:	Classical Japanese dance-drama known for its stylized drama and the elaborate make-up of its performers.
kaki:	Family records.
kamae:	defensive stance in which one awaits an attack in a defensive position, ready to parry and strike at any given moment.
kamon:	Family crest.
kanji:	Chinese ideograph.
karō:	Chief retainer of a *daimyō*.
katana:	Sword.
karusan hakama:	*Hakama* with trouser legs that are tapered toward the lower end so that they fit tight round the shins.
kissaki:	Tip of a sword.
koku:	Medieval unit of measurement, approximately 278 liters. Here it is used to express the annual rice yield of a plot of land, one *koku* being sufficient to feed a person for a year.
ma-ai:	Distance between two sparring partners or opponents in a duel.
metsuke:	Inspector.
miso:	Seasoning paste made of fermented soy beans.
mokuroku:	Written inventory of the techniques and tenets of a school of swordsmanship.
musha bugyō:	Magistrate of warriors.
musha shugyō:	Literally, "warrior training," the ascetic self-discipline going back to the ancient traditions of the so-called *yamabushi*, or mountain monks.
musha shugyōsha:	Practitioner of *musha shugyō*.
naginata:	Pole sword.

obi:	A belt worn under a samurai's *hakama* into which the sheaths of his two swords are inserted.
omae shiai:	Duel held in the presence of the Shōgun.
rōnin:	Masterless samurai.
ryūha:	Particular branch of a school of swordsmanship.
seppuku:	Ritual suicide.
shaku:	Measure of length, about one foot.
shiai:	Duel between two practitioners of a school of combat.
shihan:	Chief instructor.
shinai:	Weapon made of joined segments of bamboo and used in competitive practice.
shinken:	Real sword, as opposed to the wooden *bokutō*, or practice sword.
shōgun:	Hereditary military governor during Japan's feudal era.
sōhei:	Warrior monks of the great Buddhist temples.
sōjutsu:	Art of fighting with the *yari*.
tachi:	Longest of the pair of swords traditionally worn by samurai.
tantō:	Traditional Japanese dagger with a blade between 5.9 to 11.8 inches in length.
taryū shiai:	Literally, "contest of different schools," used to refer to a duel between practitioners of different schools of combat.
tatami:	Traditional Japanese floor mat made of woven soft rush straw and filled with rice straw.
teppō ashigaru:	*Ashigaru* (foot soldiers) armed with rifles (*teppō*).
uchiai:	Situation in a duel where both opponents execute the same—usually deadly—attack, leading to a draw in friendly duels.
wakizashi:	Literally, "side inserted sword," is an auxiliary sword with a blade between 12 and 24 inches in length used for fighting at close quarters.

wakō:	Japanese pirates during Japan's middle ages.
yamabushi:	Reclusive mountain monks of the Japanese Alps, who practiced austerities in the harsh environment of the mountains in order to attain superhuman powers.
yari:	Spear or lance.
yashiki:	Samurai mansion.
yukata:	A casual summer *kimono* with straight seams and wide sleeves made of cotton and usually unlined.
zōei bugyō:	Construction magistrate.

NOTES

Chapter 1

1   Visiting the Kasuga Taisha in 1561 the Jesuit missionary Gaspar
    Vilela described it as follows: 'This temple is very large and attracts
    many pilgrims of the Zen sect. When I visited it, I approached it
    along a path like a broad highway that had in the middle a row of
    stone columns about three hundred in number. Their use is in
    having lamps placed on top at night, which as I say, are lighted
    every evening and kept burning. They have been presented by
    several rulers and powerful people who have made endowments
    for lighting the lamps and keeping them burning perpetually.'

2   The great contest for supremacy between the Minamoto and
    Taira, the two most powerful clans of the time, is known as the
    Gempei War (1180–1185). In that war, the then leader of the
    Minamoto clan, Minamoto Yoritomo, emerged as the victor. He
    established his hegemony over most of Japan and made
    Kamakura the seat of feudal government. This institute of feudal
    government was referred to as the Bakufu, or 'tent government,'
    a Chinese term in origin, which had applied to the headquarters
    of the commander of the imperial guard. This was somewhat of

a misnomer, but not without purpose, for to give legitimacy to his dictatorship, Yoritomo was careful not to tarnish the authority of the emperor. The latter retained his throne and his symbolic position as the head of state in Kyoto, while Yoritomo had himself appointed Commander of the Right Division of the (Imperial) Guard. Thus, Yoritomo had become the de facto military ruler, controlling the eastern provinces from his power base in Kamakura. This was confirmed in 1192, the emperor appointed him Sei-I Tai-Shōgun, the 'Barbarian subduing Generalissimo' for life. After his death, in 1199, the balance of power gradually shifted to the Hōjō, a family of powerful regents of Taira origin, but they, too, maintained the Bakufu as their military instrument of dispersing power.

3   According to folklore, the Kasagi temple was founded in 682, when prince Otomo, the son of Emperor Tenchi (626–672), was trapped on Mount Kasagi while hunting deer. Praying to the mountain's spirits, he promised he would carve an image of the bodhisattva Maitreya into the mountain's surface if he were saved. During the following century, the mountain became the spiritual retreat of Rōben, the founder of the Tendai monastery. The temple reached the peak of its popularity towards the end of the twelfth century, when influential religious leaders contributed a number of buildings, including an octagonal Hall of Wisdom, and a three-storied pagoda.

4   At this time the longbow was still the chief weapon of many a warrior, but already the longsword or *tachi* as it was still called in Nagayoshi's day, had come to play a prominent role on Japanese battlefields. The earliest of Japanese historical records, the *Kojiki* (620 AD) and the *Nihon shoki* (720 AD) carry many references to the tachi, especially its role as a source of mythical power. By the middle of the twelfth century it had, next to the longbow and lance, become a standard weapon in the arsenal of the medieval warrior. Thus, in the *Heike monogatari*, the protagonists rely heavily

on the *katana* in hand-to-hand combat. At this stage the warrior, who spent much time on horseback, wore his katana with the sharp, convex side facing downward, the sheath suspended from a belt over his armor from two short braided ropes.

Chapter 2

1   Though it was built mainly of locally felled timber Chihaya castle proved more resilient than its predecessors. Situated high on Mount Kongō it had moveable bridges and was surrounded by high walls of mud. Outside its defenses, huge logs of wood and boulders were locked into strategic positions from where they could be cast down the steep mountain slopes to halt an approaching army.

2   The Ōnin Rebellion (1467–77), so named after the era with which it coincided, ended just as unexpectedly as it had started when, upon the sudden deaths of their leaders, the two armies evaporated with the same ease as they had materialized. When the troops finally poured away along the capital's approaches, all that remained of the once glorious capital was a sprawling ruin of charred remains. In the first few months of fighting flames had consumed thousands of buildings. By the time the conflict had ended, only a few of the capital's major structures were left standing. Even the streets had vanished, leaving only trenches as deep as ten feet and as wide as twenty.

3   The *shūriken* is a small, sharpened, hand-held blade thrown from a short distance. The *makibishi*, also caltrop in English, is a multi-thronged spiked object thrown on the ground to hamper the advance of enemy footmen or horses.

4   Muneyoshi's was one of four types of armor worn by medieval Japanese warriors: the *ō-yoroi*, the *dōmaru*, the *hara-maki*, and the *hara-ate*. The *ō-yoroi*, or 'large suit of armor' that came into use

during the Heian Period (794–1185), consisted of six main components (*roku-gu*), from top to bottom: the *kabuto*, or helmet; the *menpo*, or mask; the *kote*, or sleeves; the *dō*, or cuirass, the *haidate*, or cuisses; and the *suneate*, or greaves. Except for the *dō*, which was usually made of a solid plate of iron, the sleeves and other armor were made of small scales of hard leather or metal laced into plates by means of cord and then lacquered or covered with leather. Time-consuming and expensive to make, it was worn chiefly by the upper class of warriors, though it was still chiefly designed with mounted archers in mind.

Cumbersome and difficult to wear, the box-shaped *ō-yoroi* gradually made way for the *dōmaru*, or 'around the body,' or 'body wrap.' The whole harness, including the breastplate, was made of small scales of hard leather or metal laced into plates by means of cord and lacquered. To reduce the weight metal scales were only applied to those areas that protected the body's vital parts. Eight flexible skirt plates (*kusazuri*), as opposed to the *ō-yoroi's* four, protected the lower body, while each shoulder was protected by a broad plate (*sode*), and the throat by a curved plate (*nodowa*).

The *haramaki*, or 'belly wrap,' was essentially a stripped-down version of the *dōmaru*. Designed for *ashigaru*, it was originally made of the same materials as the *ō-yoroi*, but lacked a helmet (*kabuto*) and plates to protect the arms and legs. Over time the *haramaki* was gradually adopted by mounted warriors, causing it to evolve into a full-blown suit of armor alongside, yet with distinct features from the *dōmaru*.

The *hara-ate*, finally, was the lightest version of medieval armor and also the simplest. The suit's upper section now only protected the chest and abdomen. Unlike the *dōmaru*, it typically only had three skirt plates that protected the thighs.

5   Masamune is now recognized as one of Japan's greatest swordsmiths. Active between 1288 and 1328, Masamune, who lived

in Sagami, made *tachi* and *tantō* in the Sōshū tradition, though he is believed to have learned his craft from craftsmen from Bizen and Yamashiro, traditional centers of sword making.

6   *Takagi-nō* performances are still held annually at the Kōfuku temple on the eleventh and twelfth of May.

7   The practice of *musha shugyō* went all the way back to the ancient practices of the *yamabushi*, the enigmatic mountain monks of the inhospitable Japanese Alps. Those who chose this type of errantry committed themselves to an austere life of celibacy and self-denial. In this, it very much resembled the aesthetic monastic practice of *shugyō*, the aim of which was to deepen spiritual awareness through self-reflection and study and to root out worldly weaknesses. Yet while the true aim of the *musha shugyōsha* was to conquer the enemy within, the hardened warrior used the opportunities of a life on the road to test their prowess in duels with proponents of another school of fencing. The outcome of these so-called *taryū shiai* were often deadly. The weaker parties who survived such contests often chose to submit themselves to their superiors and follow them on their travels in the hope of ultimately emulating and perhaps surpassing their teachers. It wasn't uncommon to encounter on the road between one village and another, master swordsmen followed by a group of acolytes.

8   Writing home in one of his epistles in 1565, the Portuguese Jesuit missionary Luís de Almeida believed 'there can scarcely be a more beautiful sight in the world than this fortress seen from the outside, for it is a sheer joy to look on it. I went inside to see its palatial buildings, and to describe them I would need reams of paper, since it does not appear to be the work of human hands. For not only are they all constructed of cedar wood, whose delicious odor delights the senses of all those who enter, but all the verandas are built of single beams about seven feet long. The walls are all decorated with paintings of ancient stories

on a background of gold leaf. The pillars are sheathed with lead for about a span at the top and bottom respectively, and gilded and carved in such a way that everything looks as if it was covered with gold. In the center of the pillars are large and beautiful bosses decorated in the same manner. The ceiling of these buildings looks like a single piece of wood, since no join is visible even if you look very closely. I cannot write of the other decorations, for words fail me.'

Chapter 3

1 Like the monasteries of the other great Buddhist sects, the Hōzō monastery had its own specific schools of *sōjutsu*. To enhance and widen their skills, In'ei regularly organized contests, so-called *shiai*, in which *sōhei* would be pitted against each other in friendly duels. These contests were intended not only for sōhei of temples like the Hōzō-in and Kōfuku-ji, but were attended by monks from other branches of the Hossō sect, some as far afield as Kyūshū. Over the years these gatherings grew into massive events that could last for several days and draw hundreds of warrior monks from all over Japan. Nor were these contests dedicated solely to the art of spear fighting. In his eagerness to acquaint himself with new schools of martial arts, In'ei would often invite renowned martial experts from outside the Buddhist clergy to participate in contests between different schools of martial arts, the so-called *taryū shiai*.

2 The Aisu clan hailed from the province of Ise. They were a clan of *wakō*, pirates, who enjoyed the protection of Japan's western warlords and made a living by preying on the ships that carried silk and silver between Japan and China. Ikō, too, had led such a life and had visited China on his many voyages. His experiences deeply influenced his style of fencing, a style he gave the name

Kage no Ryū, the Shadow school of fencing. At the age of thirty-six, he suddenly turned over a new leaf. He began an itinerant life, spending many years on the road in *musha shugyō* honing his character and teaching his followers in the Shadow school of fencing, and how to disarm one's opponent without the use of one's *katana*, a technique he branded *mutōtori*.

3   Built at the turn of the fifteenth century by Narimasa's grandfather, Nagano Narihisa, Minowa castle was one of the most formidable strongholds in the Kantō region. It had three castle towers, and its manifold ramparts and defensive structures covered a total area of close to a hundred acres. It had withstood repeated attacks by hostile warlords and was considered an unbreachable fortress by those who had had the dubious privilege of testing its strength. Its foundations rested on the granite-like volcanic rock of Mount Haruna. Barring an all-out siege, its elevated situation, with hidden mountain paths leading north- and westward, enabled the uninterrupted supply of victuals and reinforcements, even during sustained attacks.

4   Though it is certain that Nobutsuna stayed at Yagyū castle during the fifteen sixties, there is some controversy about the exact year in which he arrived, since the records do not specifically state when exactly he and Muneyoshi first met. The most commonly held view among Japanese historians is that their encounter at the Hōzō monastery took place in the summer of 1563. This view is largely predicated on a comparison between various records, among them the *Minowa gunki*, the *Minowa-ki*, the *Kōyō gunkan*, as well as the Yagyū clan records. Another possible date is the year 1567, although this poses the problem that this year is predated by the *inkajō* Nobutsuna presented to Muneyoshi, which is dated April 1, 8th year of Eiroku (April 30, 1565).

5   A herbal medic by trade, Yamashina Tokitsugu was a towering intellectual, at home in a broad, eclectic range of subjects ranging from music to poetry, backgammon, and football. He was also

fascinated by the martial arts and had helped many an adept to establish themselves in the capital. He was incredibly well connected, a regular visitor at the imperial and shōgunal courts, and seemed to have the miraculous ability to simultaneously befriend warlords who thirsted for each other's blood.

Chapter 4

1   The Rokusai Nenbutsu was a Buddhist dance first performed by the Buddhist saint, Kūya (903–72), an itinerant priest of the Pure Land Sect. Originally intended to spread Buddhist salvation among the people by practicing chanting through song and dance, the custom spread throughout Japan and made into a religious festival, held on fixed days of the month. The dance is still performed at many temples during Obon (Festival of the Dead) as a form of prayer for ancestral spirits.

Chapter 5

1   Eishun, whose full name was Chōjutsubō Eishun, had gotten his first name of 'Prodigy' for a reason; the man was a walking encyclopedia of historical facts, especially those pertaining to the Yamato region.

2   The Daibutsuden, or Hall of the Great Buddha, was one of the treasures of the Tōdai monastery and, at that time, Japan's tallest building. Built around the middle of the eighth century, it was considered a national treasure, and every year thousands of pilgrims traveled from every corner of Japan to admire and venerate the forty-eight-foot-high bronze Buddha it housed. In the year following the great battle one of Junkei's uncles had the head of the Great Buddha repaired, but due to a shortage of funds

the head wasn't recast but repaired using copper plate. It took until 1684 before serious reconstruction of the Buddha and the hall was started under the head priest Kōkei (1648–1705). Finally, on April 30, 1709, the restored Buddha and structure in which it was housed were consecrated with a huge ceremony.

3   An upstart warlord from the province of Owari, Nobunaga's star had begun to rise in 1560 when, at the Battle of Okehazama, he defeated Imagawa Yoshimoto, the warlord of Suruga province. Nobunaga had pounced on Imagawa as the latter was passing through Owari province at the head of some twenty-thousand men. It had been a splendid and unlikely victory, for Nobunaga had achieved it with no more than three thousand men. It had also been a victory with far-reaching political implications. Imagawa had been on his way to the capital in a serious bid to seize the reins of power for himself.

Chapter 6

1   The Miyoshi were eventually driven all the way back to the island of Shikoku, retracing the very route they had followed in their rise to power. Embarking from Sakai they crossed the Inland Sea toward their last remaining stronghold, Shōzui castle, on the eastern tip of Shikoku Island. It had been from there that, half a century before, their ancestors embarked for Sakai and subdued the Kinai region with Hisahide's help.

Chapter 7

1   The Battle of Nagashino (1575) represented a watershed in Japanese military history. Up until then, most battles had been fought in the traditional way: huge forces would be arrayed in

several smaller units, usually those of a single clan and under the command of its chieftain. The battle would usually commence with an exchange of arrows, fired from intermediate range. When one side launched an attack, it would do so in several waves. At length the armies would clash in a pitched battle; soldiers would pick their man and engage in man-to-man combat.

Nobunaga, by now, had come to embrace a totally new way of warfare. His control over the capital and proximity to the port of Sakai had brought him into close contact with the Portuguese, who had arrived in Japan during the middle of the sixteenth century. They had introduced many Western inventions, including the musket, and Nobunaga had been one of the first warlords to fully recognize its potential on the field of battle. It was still a crude weapon, effective at no more than a hundred meters, muzzle-loaded, and fired by a spark from a tinder, but nevertheless superior to the ancient bow and arrow. To counter the musket's slow firing power, Nobunaga had divided his musketeers into three sections that fired in rotation. This required great discipline, and he had spent a lot of time and effort to make the unruly *ashigaru* grow used to this regimented way of fighting. To counter his enemy's cavalry charges, he erected wooden palisades, too high for the horses to leap over then, and arranged in zigzag patterns to trap and disperse their ranks.

All these innovations proved to be hugely effective. Brought up short against the high palisades the mounted warriors of his opponent, Takeda Katsuyori, were shot down like lame ducks, defenseless as they were against the reach of the deadly muskets. Katsuyori managed to get away alive, but of the fifteen thousand men who had ridden into battle under his command two-thirds left their life at Nagashino. Many of his top commanders, too, had lost their lives, among them Naitō Masatoyo, who had been appointed as the new lord of Minowa castle by Katsuyori's father a decade before.

2   Kenshin, too, had long had his sights on the capital, but thus far his arch-rival, Takeda Shingen, had kept him pinned down in the north. With Shingen's death, in the spring of 1573, that barrier had been removed. Early in 1576, Kenshin began to approach powerful chieftains from the Home Provinces in the hope of forming an alliance against Nobunaga, and Hisahide had been the first to respond.

Uesugi Kenshin is perhaps best known for his lifelong rivalry with another great warlord of the Warring States period, Takeda Shingen. Theirs was a curious meeting of minds, for while they only ever met in battle, they invariably relished the prospect of testing each other's mettle. They did so repeatedly from 1553 onward, when their forces met at Kawanakajima, a wide, triangular plain at the confluence of the Chikuma and Sai Rivers, just south of Nagano.

It is believed that the two rivals battled each other at Kawanakajima as many as five times. The fiercest encounter was fought on September 10, 1561, when a total of some forty thousand men locked in combat on the plains of Kawanakajima. The outcome of the battle was undecided and made neither of the two warlords any the wiser. Nor were any of the other four encounters at Kawanakajima to have any lasting effect on the balance of power in the region or the country as a whole, fought as they were on the periphery of the medieval centers of power. The last encounter at Kawanakajima came in 1564 when, after a standoff that lasted close to two months and that saw only some desultory volleys, both forces began to break camp and to withdraw from the battlefield.

3   To rebuild Shigisan castle, Hisahide had hired the best military architects. They had done a good job. The castle was almost impenetrable. Its donjon, consisting of four stories, was protected by three tiers. Lower down the mountain, natural shelves in the mountain's slope had been used to create

additional tiers, each manned with well-trained garrisons. In effect the stronghold consisted of increasingly impenetrable tiers, gradually stacked towards the mountain's crest, their roads of access riddled with traps, and mountain paths leading into carefully designed ambushes. Only Himeji castle, the headquarters of Nobunaga's brilliant general, Toyotomi Hideyoshi, was said to have more traps and dead alleys, yet even that magnificent stronghold did not enjoy the natural defenses Mount Shigi offered.

4   Of all the sects that populated Japan's medieval landscape the Ikkō was perhaps the most fanatical and dangerous sect to threaten the authority of centralized power. Compared to sects such as the Tendai of Mount Hiei and the Hossō of the Kōfuku temple, the Ikkō were relative newcomers. It had its power base in the distant province of Kaga on the Japan Sea. Its headquarters, however, were situated in Osaka, where, through the offices of the merchants of the nearby seaside port of Sakai, the contributions of the Kaga sectarians poured in steadily. Largely on the strength of these funds, the Ikkō had erected a vast complex of temples and fortifications at a place called Ishiyama, a group of islands at the confluence of the Yodo, Neya, and Hirano Rivers. Like the monasteries on Mount Hiei and in Nara, the defenses of the Ishiyama Hongan temple, as the complex was called, were manned by vast garrisons of *sōhei*. Like the Ikkō sectarians, its *sōhei* were a new brand of warrior, armed with the type of muskets introduced into Japan by the Portuguese a few decades earlier. The monastery even had a foundry that churned out these new and powerful tools of warfare in great quantities.

5   Nobunaga's decree was a drastic measure brought forth by an age of dramatic events. In the greater scheme of things, it was an act that immediately bore fruit. Already by 1581, when most of the castles in Yamato had been laid in ruins, Eishun recorded

315

in his *Tamon'in nikki* the effect of Nobunaga's policies, when he
observed that 'not a single battle has upset the tranquillity that
has descended on the region following the fall of the Ishiyama
Hongan temple.'

Chapter 8

1   Sadatsugu was the oldest son of Tsutsui Junkoku, one of Junkei's
uncles, who had helped him to recapture Tōchi castle. After
that, he had continued to support Junkei in his rise to power.
He had done so from behind the scenes: where Junkei had
pursued his enemies, Junkoku had forged ties with potential
allies. Junkoku's conciliatory stance had brought about a rapprochement between the Tsutsui and many of the local chieftains
from whom they had been alienated over the previous
decades—a rapprochement on which Sadatsugu intended to
capitalize on his succession.

2   The greatest threat to Hideyoshi's authority came from the east,
in particular from the Kantō plain, where the Hōjō were still
in control. The Hōjō were a formidable enemy, and neither
Uesugi Kenshin nor Takeda Shingen had managed to subdue
their stronghold of Odawara. Hideyoshi had made several
peaceful overtures to their leader, Hōjō Ujimasa, but all he
received in reply were words of defiance. Yet if he was to realize
his goal of a unified Japan he had to bring the Hōjō to heel.
There was also a powerful economic incentive to do so. The
Kantō was one of Japan's most fertile regions, and the territories
of the Hōjō alone had a total annual rice yield of more than
three million *koku*.

Hideyoshi's plan to bring the country's eastern regions under
his control reached fruition in the winter of 1589, when he convened a council at the newly completed Osaka castle, and

declared that the time had come for Ujimasa's head 'to be removed.' He mobilized all the provinces under his control. Together they mustered more than two hundred thousand troops. The campaign began early in April 1590, and ended on August 4 of the same year, when Ujimasa surrendered, and he and his brother Ujiteru were forced to commit suicide.

For more than a century the Hōjō had dominated the political landscape in the Kantō. They had started out as a small clan of warriors in the service of the Ashikaga, with no more to their name than a few hectares of land on the Isu Peninsula. At the height of their power they had ruled supreme over the provinces of Musashi, Izu, Sagami, Kōzuke, Shimotsuke, Shimōsa, and Kazusa.

Chapter 9

1   The term *shuriken*, or 'observing the moves,' should not be confused with the so-called 'hand hidden blade,' which is written with different Chinese characters. The latter were small, sharpened blades, thrown by hand from a short distance. *Shuriken* came in a variety of shapes, such as steel spikes (*bōshuriken*), or flat pieces of steel with a varying number of pointed blades (*hira shuriken*). Though the throwing of these weapons, or *shurikenjutsu*, became an art in its own right, the *shuriken* was essentially a supplementary weapon in a warrior's arsenal, intended to wound and unsettle an opponent before one came to blows.

2   Reaching old age, Kamiizumi Nobutsuna had first settled in Aizu Wakamatsu as the chief fencing instructor to Uesugi Kagekatsu. After that he had moved closer to home, entering the service of Yūki Harutomo, the master of Yūki castle. Finally, he returned to his native village of Kamiizumi, where he had died in 1577 at the age of sixty-nine.

3   Takuan was born in the village of Izushi, in Tajinoma province. His father had been a senior retainer in the service of a local warlord who had been killed when Oda Nobunaga had invaded Tajinoma in 1580. The now lordless retainer had entrusted his son to the local Sukyō temple, where Sōchū had been the abbot at the time. Sōchū had quickly taken a liking to the talented young acolyte and began to prepare him for high office within the temple's Rinzai sect. He had brought Takuan along when, in the spring of 1594, he himself was appointed head abbot of the Daitoku temple in Kyoto. Thus, in the same year Munenori and his father rode into Ieyasu's camp at Takagamine, Takuan and his mentor arrived in the capital to take up residence in the Daitoku temple, bringing him into contact with the young warrior from Yamato.

Chapter 10

1   The Plains of Musashi were one of the scenic beauty spots of old Japan. Already in 1290 the court lady Gofukakusa Nijō (1258–1306) recorded in her diary how struck she was by the beauty of the plains, through which she passed as she returned from a pilgrimage to the Zenkō temple in Nagano in the autumn. Its vast, undulating fields of pampas grasses, she recorded, 'grow so tall that even a man on horseback disappears from view,' and after three days of traveling she had lost all sense of where she was. See Fukuda Hideichi, Towazugatari, 325–26; and Brazell, Karen, *The Confessions of Lady Nijō*, 195–96.

2   In sharp relief with the mood of invincibility that accompanied the first invasion, a feeling of doom soon dominated the new mission. The mood already took hold of the warriors during the passage, a passage fraught with so many difficulties that close to half a year passed before the last warrior set foot on the opposite

shore. There the defeatist spirit deepened as winter set in and rations dwindled. Instead of thrusting northward, toward the capital of Seoul, the invasion force ensconced itself in strongholds built by remnant forces at Ulsan, Chinju, and Sunch'on, all situated along the southern coast, where ships could supply them with victuals and other provisions. Not just makeshift fortifications, but huge castles built to the exacting standards of Japanese craftsmanship, with massive stone walls and deep moats, their construction proved labor-intensive and time-consuming.

3   It had been only a year since that the sixteen-year-old Hideaki had become master of Najima castle, just north of Hakata, after his adoptive father, Kobayakawa Takakage, suddenly passed away. The latter had built the castle a decade earlier when it served as Hideyoshi's first foothold during his campaign to subdue the island. In return for Takakage's services, Hideyoshi had given him control over the provinces of Chikuzen, Chikugo, as well as parts of Hizen.

Chapter 11

1   In 1593 Hideyoshi's mistress Yodogimi had borne him a second son, whom he named Hideyori. To the Taikō Hideyori's arrival was a relief. His first son, Tsurumatsu, had died in infancy two years before. That premature death and his own advancement in age had led him to appoint his nephew Hidetsugu (a Myoshi by descent) as his rightful heir. Bestowing on him the title of *kanpaku*, he installed Hidetsugu in the Jurakudai, the official residence of men appointed to this high post.

    The new *kanpaku* took his task seriously and it was not long before his policies began to clash with those of his adoptive father. The latter had initially accepted these frictions as part of the process of succession, but with the birth of his natural son, they became an irritant. His growing dislike of Hidetsugu was fanned by his almost obsessive love for his natural son, and within a year of Hideyori's birth, he began to conspire against his appointed heir. Rumors began to make their way around the capital; rumors that the kanpaku was leading a dissolute life, that he enjoyed killing, that he was given to liquor and lechery, and, most outrageously, that he was plotting to capture Osaka castle by corrupting its guards. In a world in which most news was communicated by word of mouth, the rumors soon became fact, and before long the dutiful Hidetsugu, whose chief pastime was collecting old writings, was publicly branded as the *sasshō kanpaku*, the 'murderous regent.'

Hideyoshi's punishment was as swift as it was brutal. In the summer of 1595, he banished Hidetsugu to the Kōyasan monastery among the Kii Mountains in the northern part of the province of Kii. Shortly afterward he sent his adoptive son a messenger with an order to commit ritual suicide.

Hidetsugu's removal, however, was not enough. Jealous of everything that might threaten his natural son, the despot proceeded to persecute all the members of Hidetsugu's household, from his three infant children to his concubines and the many other women in his retinue. All were dragged through the long and dusty streets of the capital, down to the execution grounds at Sanjōgawara, the river bed of the Kamo River at the height of the capital's third main road, where travelers from the Tōkaidō entered the city. There, in front of a gibbet adorned with Hidetsugu's head, they were stabbed to death one by one until the ground was sodden with their spilled blood.

Following this act of barbarity, Hideyoshi ordered that all physical reminders of his adoptive son be destroyed. The order was carried out to the last letter and over the following weeks all the buildings where the hapless kanpaku had dwelled, including the Jurakudai, were torn down, never to rise again.

Chapter 12

1   The name Sekigahara, or the 'Plains of the barrier,' hailed back
    to the old Fuwa barrier. That barrier had been erected at the end
    of the seventh century when, in the wake of the Jinshin Rebellion,
    Emperor Tenmu ordered the erection of barriers along the
    Hokurikudō, the Tōkaidō, and the Nakasendō, the three main
    highroads connecting the capital to the rest of the country. Though
    the Fuwa barrier itself didn't last, throughout Japanese history
    the passage it had guarded had proven the place of the greatest
    strategic significance of the three. It had been along here that, in
    the wake of the Heiji Rebellion, Minamoto Yoshitomo and his
    sons had sought to escape the wrath of Taira Kiyomori by scaling
    the southern slopes of Mount Ibuki in the midst of winter. And
    it had been here, too, that Oda Nobunaga, having first subdued
    Gifu castle, had defeated the Miyoshi and Kitabatake forces,
    opening up the way to the capital and the Home Provinces.

2   Hidetada was driven by the desire to make his mark even before
    the major battle. The man he had singled out for conquest was
    Sanada Masayuki. Fifteen years earlier, in the summer of 1585,
    Ieyasu himself had attacked the castle with a force of seven
    thousand men, but after a siege of more than three months, he
    had withdrawn his troops without capturing a single stone.
    Hidetada was equally unsuccessful, and his failure to join his
    father in battle greatly damaged his reputation as a soldier and
    brought shame on the house of Tokugawa.

Chapter 13

1   The Rokujōgawara was the embankment of the Kamo River
    where it crossed the capital's sixth main road. The blood-stained
    grounds had been the capital's place of execution since 1156,

when Taira Kiyomori put to death all the members of his clan who had participated in the Hōgen Rebellion.

2   The construction of Edo castle put a huge burden on the country's *daimyō*, for it was they who had to provide the materials and manpower. Given the size of his domain, a *daimyō* like Orin's brother, Matsushita Shigetsuna, had to ship some eighteen hundred of the huge granite stones to be used in the fourteen hundred feet of stone ramparts, an order that required a fleet of more than four hundred ships to deliver. In addition, he had to send men. Thus, for the operation in which Kanda Hill was flattened and reused to fill the surrounding swamps, he would have had to provide some one-hundred-and-sixty men.

3   Orin's brother, Matsushita Shigetsuna, was also a great warrior. Like Munenori, he had taken part in the great unifying battle of Sekigahara. His stipend, too, had been raised in its wake. But when, in the summer of 1603, Shiegetsuna started on a large-scale project to strengthen the walls of Kuno castle, the action of the Bakufu was swift and unforgiving. Robbing him of his possessions, they demoted him in rank and ordered him to move to the small fief of Obari in the northern province of Hitachi. It was a serious blow to the fortunes of the Matsushita. For ten years they struggled like the Yagyū had struggled, until another great battle in which both men would again see action restored the fortunes of the Matsushita clan.

Chapter 14

1   Situated southwest of Shitennoji, Chausuyama appears to be one of many keyhole-shaped tombs, or *kofun*, found all over Japan, mostly were erected between the 3rd and early 7th century AD. Though the mound is similar to that of the Otsukayama *kofun* and the Okachiyama *kofun* of Sakai City,

according to the results of archaeological research in 1986, no *fuki-ishi* (stone shingles) or *haniwa* (clay figures)—the typical artifacts found at such tombs—have thus far been found.

Chausuyama seems to have been a popular name for any protrusion in the landscape, for even today there are some four dozen places throughout Japan that go by the same name. Interestingly, Oda Nobunaga's headquarters during the Battle of Nagashino—in which Ieyasu took part—was also situated on a hill called Chausuyama.

Chapter 15

1   The sound was mistakenly interpreted as a signal by Nanjō Mototada, a western warlord who was in cahoots with one of Ieyasu's generals. In fact, already the day before, Mototada had been exposed and forced to commit suicide. The explosion instead had been caused when one of the castle's powder magazines had accidentally detonated.

2   In the months preceding the siege Ieyasu had called upon the Dutch and English merchants in Nagasaki. Eager to continue their lucrative trade with the newly installed Bakufu both had readily complied, the Dutch by furnishing him with twelve cannon, the English with another five. These were heavy caliber bronze cannon that could propel rounds of up to forty pounds each. In addition, he had to his disposal some three hundred domestically wrought iron cannon, with a caliber of ten pounds each.

Chapter 16

1   The ruins of Kōriyama castle still belonged to the Tsutsui clan. On Tsutsui Sadatsugu's exile, Ieyasu had appointed his cousin,

Sadayoshi, to a reduced fief of ten thousand koku. Yet without either experience or a decent castle, Sadayoshi instantly panicked when his commanders presented him with inflated enemy numbers. Overnight, he abandoned his castle and fled into the mountains, bringing to a final end the long and eventful reign of the Tsutsui in Yamato province.

2 It was on their way to Tennōji that one of Matsudaira Tadanao's warriors, Nishio Munetsugu, passed through the grounds of the Yasui shrine, when he spotted a wounded Sanada Yukimura, resting on the shrine's steps. Up to three times Yukimura had penetrated as far as Ieyasu's camp, until he had run out of men and energy on Ieyasu's reinforcements. Seeing the Tokugawa warrior, he murmured, 'I am Sanada Yukimura, an adversary no doubt quite worthy of you, but I am too exhausted to fight any longer.' Then he removed his helmet and nodded to the warrior with an air of resignation as the latter raised his *katana* and cut of his head.

Chapter 17

1 There was a small corps of sensors, divided into one senior censor, or *ō-metsuke*, and ten regular censors, or *mestuke*. Both were charged with investigating instances of corruption, disaffection, or poor administration throughout the realm. They had proven the chief causes of disturbances that continued to threaten central rule. Both classes of *metsuke* were involved in similar activities, yet where the *metsuke* scrutinized the activities of the general populace, the *ō-metsuke* limited themselves to investigating the activities of *daimyō* and their counselors. They also resorted under different authorities. Whereas the *ō-metsuke* reported to the Shōgun's chief counselors, the so-called *rōjū*, the general metsuke reported to the *wakadoshiyori*, who ranked just below the *rōjū*.

2   In 1632, Musashi's school of swordsmanship was still known as the Enmei-ryū, the 'School of the Circle of Light.' It was after Musashi moved to Kokura that he renamed it the Niten Ichi-ryū, the 'School of the Two Heavens United,' the two united heavens signifying the superlative strength of the long and short *katana* when used together in combat.

3   Kita Shichidayū Chōnō was the founder of the Kita school of Nō. The son of an Osaka eye doctor, he had begun his career at the age of seven, when he gave a stunning performance before Toyotomi Hideyoshi. With the latter's patronage, he had rapidly risen to fame, becoming a frequent guest performer to famous *daimyō* clans, including the Kuroda in Fukuoka and the Hosokawa in Kumamoto. Yet the same allegiance that led to his fame became his downfall when, in 1614, he decided to join Hideyoshi's son in the defense of Osaka castle. Reduced to a *rōnin*, he had earned his living teaching dancing to Kyoto's geisha, until, in 1619, he was invited by Shōgun Hidetada to come and perform at Edo castle.

4   It was said that Masanobu had recorded his lord's achievements and his highly successful art of warcraft as an admonition to Shingen's less capable son, Katsuyori, who had dismissed the loyal vassal by way of punishment. Following his death, Masanobu's records had fallen into the hands of his garrison commander, Obata Masamori. Himself a practitioner of Shingen's Kōshū-ryū, Masamori sought to expand on Masanobu's work, but never really found the time to complete the massive task: he died in a snail fever endemic that hit his region during the eighties and died after a short sickbed. On his deathbed he had handed his work to his son, Kagenori, urging him to complete his work. For more than two decades Kagenori had worked feverishly to fulfill to his father's dying wish.

BIBLIOGRAPHY

Works in English

Adolphson, Mikael S. *The Gates of Power*. Honolulu, 2000.

—. *The Teeth and Claws of the Buddha*. Honolulu, 2007.

Bryant, Anthony. *Sekigahara 160: The Final Struggle for Power*. Oxford, 1995.

Carroll, John. *Lightning in the Void*. New York, 2006.

Cleary, Thomas. *Code of the Samurai*. Tokyo, 1999.

De Lange, William. *Famous Japanese Swordsmen*, Vols. 1–3. Warren, 2008.

Dening, Walter. *Japan in Days of Yore*. London, 1976.

Friday, Karl F. *Hired Swords*. 1992.

—. *Legacies of the Sword*. 1997.

Hiroaki Satō. *Legends of the Samurai*. New York, 1995.

Jansen, Marius. *Warrior Rule in Japan*. Cambridge, 2008.

Turnbull, S.R. *The Samurai*. New York, 1977.

Sansom, George. *A History of Japan*. Vols 1–3. Tokyo, 1963.

Sato Hiroaki. *Legends of the Samurai*. New York, 1995.

—. *The Sword and the Mind*. New York, 1985.

Stone, Justin F. *Bushido*. New York, 2001.

Sugawara Makoto. *Lives of Master Swordsmen*. Tokyo, 1982.

Turnbull. S.R. *The Samurai*. New York, 1977.

—. *War in Japan 1467–1615*. Oxford, 2002.

—. *Warriors of Medieval Japan*. New York, 2005.

—. *Warriors of Japan*. Honolulu, 1994.

Varley, Paul. *Warriors of Japan*. Honolulu, 1994.

Wilson, William Scott. *Ideals of the Samurai*. Burbank, 1982.

—. *The Lone Samurai*. Tokyo, 2004.

Works in Japanese

Akabane Tatsuo. *Musashi to Yagyū Shinkage-ryū*. Tokyo, 2012

Aramaki Nitōsai. *Nitōryū no nairaikata*. Tokyo, 1994.

Domoto Akihiko. *Kendō kojutsu-shi*. Tokyo, 1988.

Ezaki Junpei. *Nihon kengō retsuden*. Tokyo, 1970.

—. *Yagyū Munenori*. Tokyo, 1971.

Fukuda Akira. *Chūsei katarimono bungei*. Tokyo, 1981.

Fukuda Hideichi. *Towazugatari*, Tokyo, 1978.

Funabashi Takeshi. *Nagoya no Miyamoto Musashi*. Tokyo, 2004

Futaki Kenichi. *Gassen no butaiura*. Tokyo, 1976.

—. *Sekigahara gassen*. Tokyo, 1982.

Hasegawa Shin. *Nihon adauchi isō*. Tokyo, 1974.

Hayashiya Tatsusaburō. *Chūsei geinoshi no kenkyū*. Tokyo, 1960.

Hinatsu Shigetaka. *Honchō bugei shoden*. Tokyo, 2003.

Hioki Shōichi. *Nihon sōhei kenkyū*. Tokyo, 1972.

Hirai Takao. *Fukuyama kaiso Mizuno Katsunari*. Tokyo, 1992.

Hirotani Yūtarō. *Nihon kendō shiryō*. Tokyo, 1943.

Imamura Yoshio. *Shiryō Yagyū Shinkageryū*. Vols. 1–2. Tokyo, 1995.

—. *Yamato Yagyū ichizoku*. Tokyo, 1974.

Imano Nobuo. *Edo no tabi*. Tokyo, 1986.

Ishioka Hisao. *Hyōhōsha no seikatsu*. Tokyo, 1988.

Kaionji Chōgorō. *Bushō retsuden*. Vols. 1–6. Tokyo, 1964.

Kasaya Kazuhiko. *Sekigahara gassen*. Tokyo, 2008

—. *Sekigahara gassen to Ōsaka no jin*. Tokyo, 2007.

Katsube Mitake. *Bushidō*. Tokyo, 1971.

Kaku Kōzō. *Kyokui Ichiryū*. Tokyo, 2009.

Kitagawa Hiroshi. *Gunkimono no keifu*. Kyoto, 1985.

Kitajima Matsumoto. *Edo jidai*. Tokyo, 1958.

Kogure Masao. *Nitō-ryū no kensei Miyamoto Musashi*. tokyo, 1983

Kojima Hidehiro. *Kengō densetsu*. Tokyo, 1997.

——. *Sugao no kengōtachi*. Tokyo, 1998.

Kondō Heijō. *Shiseki shūran*. volume 24. Tokyo, 1967.

Kosuge Ren. *Bisan hōkan*. Tokyo, 1897.

Kurobe Tooru. *Akashijō wo meguru rekishi no tabi*. Tokyo, 2000

Kuroda Yoshitaka. *Akashi han ryakushi*. Tokyo, 1981.

——. *Shiwa Akashi-jō*. Tokyo, 1975.

Kuwata Tadachika. *Chosaku-shū*. Vols. 1–10. Tokyo, 1980.

——. *Nihon no kengō*. Vols. 1–5. Tokyo, 1984.

Maeda Hideki. *Ken to shisō*. Tokyto, 2009.

Maki Hidehiko. *Kengō zenshi*. Tokyo, 2003.

Matsumura Hiroshi. *Rekishi monogatari*. Tokyo, 1979.

Miki Seiichirō. *Teppo to sono jisai*. Tokyo, 1981.

Nagatanigawa Hiroshi. *Sengokudaimyō Amago no Kenkyū*. Tokyo, 2005.

Nagazumi Yasuaki. *Gunki monogatari no sekai*. Tokyo, 1978.

Nakajima Michiko. *Yagyū Sekishūsai Muneyoshi*. Tokyo, 2003.

Nakamura Akira. *Shinkage-ryū Kamiizumi Nobutsuna*. Tokyo, 2004.

Nakamura Kichiji. *Buke no rekishi*. Tokyo, 1967.

Nakayama Hakudō. *Kendō kōwa*. Tokyo, 1937.

Nakazato Kaizan. *Nihon bujutsu shinmyō ki*. Tokyo, 1985.

Nanjō Norio. *Nihon no meijō, kojō jiten*. Tokyo, 1999.

Naoki Sukeyama. *Nihon kengō retsuden*. Tokyo, 1983.

Naramoto Tatsuya. *Bushidō no keifu*. Tokyo, 1973.

Nishigaya Yasuhiro. *Kumamotojō*. Tokyo, 2009.

——. *Sengoku daimyō jōkaku jiten*. Tokyo, 1999.

Nitobe Inazo. *Bushidō*. Tokyo, 1938.

Okubō Hikozaemon. *Mikawa Monogatari*. Tokyo, 1980.

Ōmori Nobumasa. *Bujutsu densho no kenkyū*. Tokyo, 1991.

Omori Sōgen. *Sho to Zen*. Tokyo, 1973.

——. *Zen no kōsō*. Tokyo, 1979.

Owada Tetsuo. *Sengoku bushō*. Tokyo, 1981.

——. *Toyotomi Hideyoshi*. Tokyo, 1985.

Ozawa Chikamitsu. *Ken shin itchi*. Tokyo, 1978.

Saitō Shigeyoshi. *Ganryūshima*. Tokyo, 1930.

Sakai Tadakutsu. *Sekigahara kassen shimatsu ki*. Tokyo, 1991.

Sasamori Junzo. *Ittō-ryū goku-i*. Tokyo, 1986.

Satome Mitsugu. *Jitsuroku Miyamoto Musashi*. Tokyo, 1989.

Shiba Ryōtarō. *Nihon kenkyaku den*. Tokyo, 1982.

——. *Sekigahara*. 1992.

Shimura Kunihiro. *Shimabara gassenki*. Tokyo, 1989.

Shudō Yoshiki. *Keichō nikki*. Tokyo, 1980.

So Dōshin. *Shorinji kenpō*. Tokyo, 1963.

Sugai Yasuo. *Issatsu de yomu kengō Miyamoto Musashi*. Tokyo, 2002.

Sugimoto Keizaburō. *Gunki monogatari no sekai*. Tokyo, 1985.

Sukeyama Naoki. *Nihon kengō retsuden*. Tokyo, 1983.

Takahashi tomio. *Bushidō no rekishi*. Vols. 1–3. Tokyo, 1986.

Takano Samirō. *Kendō*. Tokyo, 1915.

Takayanagi Kaneyoshi. *Edo no kakyū bushi*. Tokyo, 1980.

Tanizawa Eiichi. *Gorin no sho no yomikata*. Tokyo, 1982.

Terada Toru. *Dō no shisō*. Tokyo, 1978.

Tokunaga Shiichirō. *Yagyū Munenori*. Tokyo, 1978.

Tokutomi Sōho. *Kinsei Nihon kokumin-shi*. Tokyo 1982.

Tominaga Kengō. *Nihon kassen zenshū*. Vols. 1–6. Tokyo, 1990.

Tsuge Hisayoshi. *Jissen Gorin no sho*. Tokyo, 1994.

Uozumi Takashi. *Sengoku bushi no kokoroe*. Tokyo, 2001

Watatani Kiyoshi. *Nihon kengō no hyakusen*. Tokyo, 1971.

——. *Bugei Ryuha Daijiten*. Tokyo, 2003.

Watanabe Ichirō. *Budō no meichō*. Tokyo, 1979.

Yamada Jirokichi. *Nihon kendō-shi*. Tokyo, 1960.

Yamane Yukie. *Tottori-han kendōshi*. Tokyo, 1982.

Yamazaki Masakazu. *Muromachi ki*. Tokyo, 1974.

Yasuda Motohisa. *Bushi sekai no jōmaku*. Tokyo, 1973.

Yasuda Takashi. *Kata no Nihon bunka*. Tokyo, 1984.

Yokoi Kiyoshi. *Chūsei wo ikita hitobito*. Kyoto, 1981.
Yokoyama Masakatsu. *Amagoshi ichimon no ruutsu*. Tokyo 1985.
Yoshida Seiken. *Nitō-ryū o kataru*. Tokyo, 1941.
Yoshida Yutaka. *Budō hiden sho*. Tokyo, 1973.

INDEX

Miyamoto Musashi: A Life in Arms

This it the first biography on Miyamoto Musashi to draw at great length from the the many available medieval text on the swordsman whilst relying on the most recent Japanese historical research. Many of the convenient myths that have arisen around the man Musahsi are debunked, while the more controversial and at times embarrassing aspects of the swordsman's life that have remained shrouded in mystery are uncovered—his troubled relationship with his father, his whereabouts during the battles of Sekigahara and the siege of Osaka castle, and the birth and death of his only child, an event that deeply influenced his art.

The complex yet deeply human portrait that arises is a far cry from the polished and sanitized portrayal of an invincible war-machine in which the swordsman is reduced to a two-dimensional and hollow caricature, It was, after all, Musashi's personal traits that shaped his remarkable path through life—his precocious youth, his reckless abandon in the face of danger, his sensitive intelligence in the field of art and architecture, his generosity toward his peers and pupils, and his stubbornness in old age.

335

The Real Musashi: The *Bushūdenraiki* (Origins of a Legend I)

Miyamoto Musashi (c. 1584-1645) is the most revered and celebrated swordsman in Japanese history. Unfortunately, our modern portrait of this folk hero is derived mainly from popular books, comics, and film, with little heed paid to the early *denki*, chronicles that faithfully recorded what was passed down by those who knew Musashi.

The *Bushū denraiki* is the earliest denki on Musashi still in existence. Completed in 1727 by Tachibana Minehide, the fifth generation master of Musashi's Niten Ichi school of swordsmanship, it is one of the most reliable record of Musashi's life and exploits outside those from the hand of the master swordsman himself.

Now, after almost three centuries, Minehide's insight into this enigmatic and solitary swordsman are available to the English reader. His text throws a new and refreshing light on many aspects of especially Musashi's early life—his troubled relations with his father, his first battle experience during Japan's period of unification, the sad death of his illegitimate child, and of course his legendary duel on Ganryū island.

The Real Musashi: The *Bukōden* (Origins of a Legend II)

Next to the *Bushū denraiki*, the *Bukōden* is one of the earliest records on Musashi still in existence. It was completed in 1755 by Toyoda Masanaga, senior retainer to the Nagaoka, a clan closely involved in the events of Musashi's later life. Masanaga's work ranks with the Bushū denraiki as the most reliable records of Musashi's life and exploits outside those from the hand of the master swordsman himself. Now, for the first time in two-and-a-half centuries, Masanaga's insight into this enigmatic and solitary swordsman is also available to the English reader.

Like the *Bushū denraiki* the *Bukoden* gives its own riveting account of Musashi's encounter with Sasaki Kojirō on Ganryu island, as well as his famed duels with the members of the Yoshioka clan. At the same time it throws a new and refreshing light on many aspects of Musashi's later life—his adoption of Iori, his return to Kyushu in 1634, and of course the gestation of his great work on the philosophy and art of Japanese swordsmanship, the *Gorin no sho*. For those interested in the sword culture of Japan, this true story of its most iconic figure is essential reading.

The Real Musashi: A Miscellany (Origins of a Legend III)

The *Bushū denraiki* and the *Bukōden* are not the only historical records on Miyamoto Musashi. Diligent research by Japanese scholars on the wave of a 'Musashi revival' has unearthed a plethora of hitherto neglected sources.

This work contains translations from the *Tomari jinja munefuda*, the *Hayashi razan bunshū*, the *Kaijō monogatari*, the *Numata kaki*, the *Yoshioka-den*, the *Hōkōsho*, the *Bushō kanjōki*, the *Kōkai fuhansho*, the *Watanabe kōan taikiwa*, the *Honchō bugei shoden*, the *Dōbō goen*, the *Korō usawa*, the *Kōkō zatsuroku*, the *Harima kagami*, the *Seiryūwa*, the *Saiyū zakki*, the *Gekken sōdan*, the *Sōkyūsama o-degatari*, the *Mukashibanashi* the *Tōsakushi*, and the *Mimasa ryakushi*.

Now the insight these works offer into this enigmatic and solitary swordsman is available to the English reader. It throws a new and refreshing light on many aspects of Musashi's life—his duels with the members of the Yoshioka clan, the events leading up to his duel with Sasaki Kojirō, his heroic role in the siege of Osaka castle, his contribution to the reconstruction of Akashi castle, and his remarkable artistic talents.

FAMOUS SAMURAI

The Two Courts Period	The Warring States Period	The Period of Unification
The tale of Nenami Jion, the fugitive warrior monk (*sōhei*) who founded the Nen-ryū, the first school of Japanese fencing. And the tale of his friend Chūjō Nagahide, the scion of an old family of courtiers, who went on to found the Chūjō-ryū, the school that became the formative influence on the great fencing masters of the Toda-ryū.	The tale of Iizasa Ienao, raised in the fencing traditions of the ancient Katori and Kashima shrines, and founder of the legendary Shintō-ryū. And the tale of Kamiizumi Nobutsuna, master of Japan's old pirate (*wakō*) fencing traditions, founder of the Shinkage-ryū, and patron-teacher to the members of the famous Yagyū clan.	The tale of Ono Tadaaki, a *rōnin* from the turbulent Kantō who inherited the old traditions of the Toda and Ittō-ryū and made it to shogunal fencing instructor. And the tale of Yagyū Munenori, the warrior of the Yagyū Shinkage-ryū who restored his clan's dwindling fortunes through his valiant role in the epic Battle of Sekigahara.

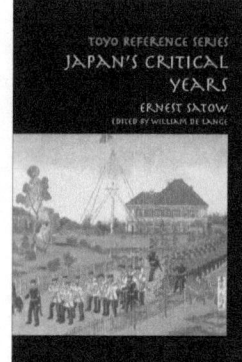

Samurai Battles: The Long Road to Unification

In this latest, richly illustrated work William de Lange returns to what he does best: highly anecdotal accounts from one of the most exiting episodes in Japanese history: the Warring States period.

TOYO PRess: Explore Dream Discover

Editorial supervision: Letitia van der Merwe. Book and cover
design: Chōkei Studios. Printing and binding: IngramSpark.
The typeface used is Perpetua.